THE GILA

THE GILA
River of the Southwest

by

Edwin Corle

Illustrated by

Ross Santee

UNIVERSITY OF NEBRASKA PRESS   Lincoln

To

JEAN ARMSTRONG CORLE

What is history but a fable agreed upon?

NAPOLEON BONAPARTE

Foreword

"The important thing about a river," wrote Captain Richard Bissell, an Ohio River pilot, "is that it is made of water, has fish in it, and steamboats, rowboats, or floating logs on its surface."

The Gila has been a changeable river throughout its lifetime of many millions of years, of which only the past twenty-five thousand years can be called history visible to man. It has never known a steamboat, very few rowboats, some floating logs, and only a fair assortment of fish. At one time it resembled the modern Everglades and at another time the Mississippi. In 1950 fully half its length, the lower river, was as dry as dust. Where it "flows" into the Colorado there hasn't been a drop of water come downstream in over four years. From its ice caves and raging mountain torrents, through its tortuous canyons and dam-impounded waters, across its broad desert valley to its parched, sandy and sunbaked confluence with the Colorado, this six-hundred-mile river of unpredictable liquid content has a history as long, as dramatic, and as significant as any in America.

The Colorado, entirely west of the Great Divide, might be called the river of the West; and the Rio Grande, entirely east of the divide, might be designated the international river. But the Gila is literally the river of the American Southwest. There is no other stream that even resembles it.

E. C.

Contents

PART 1

Theater of Operations

. . . to 1540

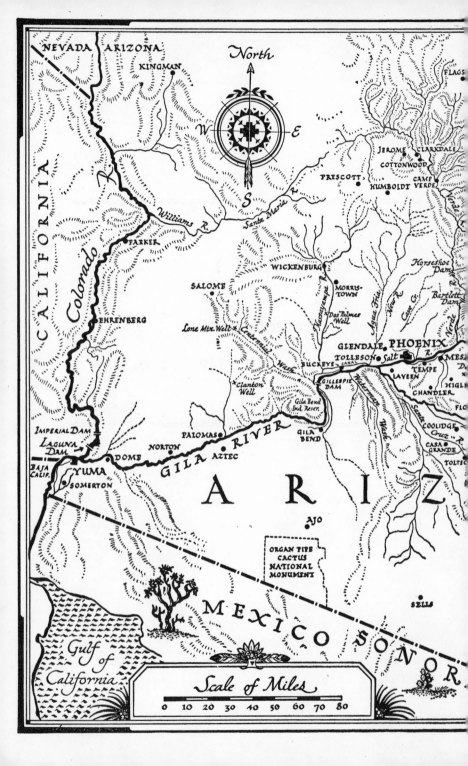

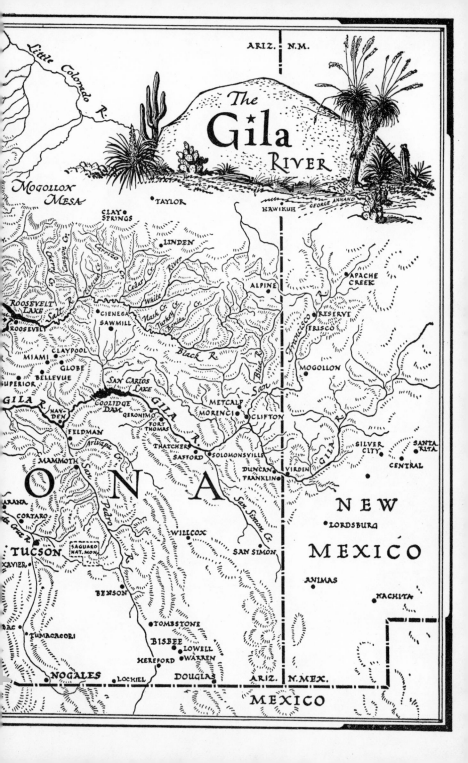

1

DEATH OF A DINOSAUR

THE DINOSAUR was sick and tired. He was one hundred and fifty-nine years old; he weighed twenty-eight tons; he was forty-two feet long; and he had a brain no bigger than a walnut. He was a stupid, sluggish, harmless beast, and in his dying days he wished only for one thing—to return to the scene of his youth, the place of miasmal swamps through which cut the great river. There he loved to wade and wallow and splash and gorge himself on the lush plants that grew along the banks, plants later called cycads by a species that was not yet on earth, a species that would never come face to face with a dinosaur because approximately sixty million years separated the last of the great dinosauria from the first of little *Homo sapiens.*

The great river was not very deep, perhaps forty or fifty feet at midchannel, although it was about two miles wide, and the dinosaur could walk on the soft muddy bottom and enjoy the warm water as it flowed gently over and around his bulky body; and he could always stick his long neck and proportionate pee-wee head upward above the surface until he resembled the fabulous sea serpent.

To call him a dinosaur is far too general. The reptile was a diplodocus, not the largest of dinosauria, nor the meanest, nor the

smallest, but simply an average dinosaur of the Jurassic period of
the Mesozoic era of geological history. To any diplodocus or other
plant-eating dinosaurs, the river was a haven from their natural
enemies, their terrifying flesh-eating cousins who preyed upon such
peaceful individuals as the vegetarians. And all of this was in an
area now known as Arizona, but which had no name at all among
dinosauria a hundred and fifty million years ago.

Through this antediluvian forest walked the diplodocus. And
not far behind him was the terror of his life, the smaller, aggres-
sive, belligerent, flesh-eating cousin called the allosaurus. In the
dinosaurian family tree there are two distinct divisions: sauropods,
who were generally very large by Jurassic times and usually walked
on all fours, had long necks, ate only plants, and loved to wallow
in marshes, swamps, or rivers; and then there were the theropods,
who were usually smaller, walked on two legs only and used the
diminutive front legs for attack, had short necks and sharp teeth,
ate only other reptiles, eggs, or insects, and had no interest whatever in wallowing in marshes, swamps, or rivers. A diplodocus of
twenty-eight tons was fair game for an allosaurus of twelve tons,
and the poor diplodocus's only defense was to flee.

A sick and tired diplodocus of advanced age could not flee.
So he sought the great river, where, if he got out far enough, the
dreadful and deadly and smaller allosaurus could not follow without the risk of being drowned. The Jurassic forests were composed
of a dense tangle of evergreens, mostly conifers with some gink-
goes and an ever-burgeoning mass of palms. Flowering plants and
hardwood trees did not exist, but there were ferns and rushes and
mushroomlike fungus that made up the thick undergrowth.

Through such a Jurassic jungle the diplodocus made his
weary way, his twenty-eight tons cutting a swath through the
lush undergrowth much as a man might walk through a field of
waist-high grass. For all of his weight he could not brush aside

the larger conifers, some of which ranged in trunk thickness from ten to twenty feet and towered upward to seventy-five or a hundred feet. These were the trees of North America that have long since disappeared under layers of geological sediment except for a rare exception where time and erosion have again revealed them in Arizona's Petrified Forest.

Following a path of least resistance through the trees, the diplodocus left a plain trail of crushed roots, broken boughs, and trampled herbaceous ferns and rushes. He made not the slightest effort to conceal his tracks, for he did not have that amount of intelligence. The ground under his five-toed feet was soft and then marshy and finally swampy. The diplodocus pushed clumsily on and at last the swamp ended and he emerged out of the forest at the edge of the great river. There was no bank for him to scramble down, for the swampy ground blended with the warm river until it was hard to say where one ended and the other began. The diplodocus waded out into the stream, but before he could reach the main channel, his weary and exhausted body collapsed and he lay partly on one side, enjoying the warmth of the water while his ridiculously small head remained above the surface and his dull eyes stared unseeingly out across the river.

Following along his trail, a mile or so behind, came the smaller and vicious allosaurus whose one-track mind was bent on one increasing purpose, to kill and eat the diplodocus who was not far ahead. The allosaurus ran rapidly on his two huge hind legs. His smaller forelegs were almost like arms and he had digits that could grasp and tear flesh. He had a long pointed tail, a thick neck, and a huge horrible head. His mouth was about two and a half feet long from the front teeth to the rear molars, and all the teeth were sharp incisors. In all, he was a dreadful-looking creature, bent on his kill.

The allosaurus had no difficulty whatever in following the

trail cut through the forest for him by the aged diplodocus. It was merely a matter of time until he dined. On he ran, far more nimble for all his twelve tons than his heavier quarry, and at last he reached the damp ground, then the marshy ground, and finally the swamp.

Ahead of him was the river, and apparently mired and bogged on one side in the shallow water lay the exhausted diplodocus.

The carnivore leaped upon his victim, his huge jaws seizing the diplodocus by the back of his long neck and the digital members of his forearms tearing hunks and gobs of flesh from the backbone. The dying diplodocus refused to submit to the inevitable. He put up his penultimate effort, as instinctive as his lifelong habits of eating and copulating, an automatic expression of the individual urge for self-preservation. He staggered and stumbled through the water, trying to reach the main channel of the river, where, if he could but shake off his terrible assailant, the aggressor might drown and the would-be victim might yet survive.

While riding on the back of the diplodocus, the gnashing, tearing allosaurus was carried farther out into the stream. Striving and concentrating on the killing of his victim with an energy as ferocious as that of the diplodocus in fighting for his life, the two creatures fought a duel to the death. The diplodocus made his final effort. He lashed his tremendous tail—over eighteen feet long—and all but knocked the allosaurus from his back by the weighty blow. But the carnivore attacked again and virtually severed the diplodocus's head from his body with the tremendous bite of his mighty jaws. The dying diplodocus sank into forty feet of river, and the smaller allosaurus sank with him. The diplodocus died of his wounds and the allosaurus died of drowning. Call it Jurassic justice or x equals o.

At one period of time, deep under the sediment of the river, there rested the bones of many dinosauria. But millions of the fossils have been washed to eternity by a series of geological denudations, commonly called erosion, with the result that traces of the Jurassic period in present-day Arizona are rare, although dinosaur tracks in limestone may be seen near Tuba city. A hundred and fifty million years after the Jurassic period, man called the stream (not even recognizable from its Jurassic characteristics) the Gila. A hundred and fifty million years from now the river will probably still be there. But the dinosaurs . . . and man?

2

ROLL, GILA, ROLL

The word should be pronounced "hee-la" with the accent on the "hee." It is a Spanish-spelled version of an American Indian word and to the Yuma Indians who so named the river the word meant salty water.

What the Yumas actually called the stream was Hah-quah-sa-eel with the accent on the final syllable. This can be translated as Running Water Which Is Salty. Apparently this is as far back as the name can be traced. With the arrival of the Spanish in 1539 the mouthful of Indian syllables was far too long. The predominating syllable was "eel." Dropping the first three syllables the Spanish tongue gave the final one an aspiration and tacked on a slurred "a". The result was "hee-la," spelled in Spanish, of course, Gila.

Some people call it Jee-la; some Guy-la; some Ee-la. And apart from these variations it has had a number of names through recorded history—the River of the Name of Jesus, the Hila, the Helay, the Xila, the Totonteac, the River of the Apostles, the River of Despair, the River of the Sun, the Fresh Water Abomination, the Blue, the Blaufuss, and the Poison. None has persisted except the Gila. But all its names are arbitrary, for this stream has been flowing in various degrees of swiftness or sluggishness for many millions of years and man, who named it, has been on earth only one million years.

Geology has proved that two hundred million years ago a shallow sea covered a large part of what is now called California. Where the lower Colorado River now flows was seacoast. Had the city of Yuma, Arizona, existed it would conceivably have been a seaport; and the river called the Gila unquestionably flowed westerly from the higher lands of eastern Arizona into this ancient sea.

Fifty million years went by and the contour of the earth changed. A portion of the land that was to become California and all of the Pacific Northwest rose above sea level, slowly pushed up by internal forces from deep within the earth. And a huge sea poured in from the north, inundating areas that would someday be called Alberta, Montana, Idaho, Wyoming, and Utah. This Jurassic sea spread south until its lower shores touched the Gila watershed, and the river flowed into the southern tip of this primeval ocean. In the history of the earth, this was the age of the reptiles. The whole Gila watershed was one huge, lush, tropical, miasmic swamp and the river flowed sluggishly through it down to the sea. In the thick vegetation lived the dinosaurs—diplodocus and allosaurus, and the various cousins of their genus—and the giant reptiles continued to flourish for another fifty million years throughout the Cretaceous period of geological history. During this time, over the river and over the changing seas, flew the huge pterosaurs, or flying reptiles, precursors of the first birds, vicious predatory creatures with a wingspread of as much as twenty feet. This Cretaceous period came to an end approximately sixty million years ago. To geologists this is a major milestone along the road of time, and the end of the Cretaceous period marked the end of the reign of reptiles on earth, and the end of the series of periods called Triassic, Jurassic, and Cretaceous, a group known collectively as the Mesozoic era, or approximately one hundred and thirty-five million years of the earth's history.

Geologically speaking, "modern times" began some sixty million years ago with the end of the Mesozoic and the beginning of the Cenozoic era. And in the first period of the Cenozoic—called the Early Tertiary—another form of life on earth began to develop even as the reptiles began to decline. These were the mammals. And they were to inherit the earth.

It was about this time (still sixty million years ago) that the geography of North America, as we know it today, began to take form. Most of Arizona ceased to be a tropical swamp and in western North America two great chains of mountains began to emerge and rise—the Rockies and the Sierra Nevadas.

As the chain of Rocky Mountains rose innumerable side streams flowed into the upper Gila; and the main stream itself, instead of originating in a swampy morass, began its flow to the west from the miniature glaciers and ice caves of what are today the Mogollon Mountains of New Mexico. Fed by numerous small creeks of melted snow, the main stream rushed rapidly down the mountainside and became a raging torrent long before it reached what had once been the broad swamp but was now the arid basin of south central Arizona.

All over the American West the face of the land was assuming new characteristics. Gone were the lush marshes, and in their place evolved mountain ranges, and valleys so deep that they are identified as canyons. The great Sierra Nevada range, rising in California, cut off the Pacific winds and the Pacific rainstorms. The Gila Valley, for all the affirmative flow of the main stream itself, became drier and drier, until land that was not immediately adjacent to the Gila and its tributaries became desert.

But the river rolled on, a mighty stream, fifty million years ago—forty—thirty—twenty—ten—and finally one million years ago roaring down its mountain canyons and fanning out onto Arizona's desert plain, flowing westerly and approaching sea level until it joined the Colorado only a short distance above the Gulf of California. At one time it was several miles wide as it flowed gently across western Arizona, greatly contrasting in character along its lower portion to the surging, roaring, canyon-locked mountain torrent that it was in its upper portion.

Today, from its beginnings high up in the ice caves of the Mogollon Mountains to its confluence with the Colorado, the Gila is over six hundred miles long—or longer than the Delaware and the Hudson combined. And its watershed comprises an area somewhat larger than the entire states of Kentucky and West Virginia, but somewhat the same shape if the city of Paducah, Kentucky, could be projected onto Yuma, Arizona.

Early in the Cenozoic era mammals became dominant. No longer was the Gila watershed ruled by reptiles; and although at first the mammals were small creatures, all the modern groups were represented. Fossils of some of these animals have been found in the Gila region, notably the skeletal remains of camels, peccaries, deer, three genera of Eocene horses, and a part of the skull of a mastodon. And forty-nine million years after the dawn of the Cenozoic era a new type of mammal appeared. After another million years of evolution he has called himself Man.

Thus it is plain that the American Southwest in general and the Gila Valley in particular have consistently supported life. Geologist James G. Bennett has found artifacts near the town of Willcox that are at least 10,000 years old and could reasonably be placed at 15,000. Dr. Bennett believes that man has lived in this area for a longer time than in most places on earth.

How man got to the Gila Valley can be little more than an anthropological guess. The generally accepted theory seems to be that he came from somewhere else, notably Asia, and crossed the land bridge that existed many thousands of years ago between Siberia and Alaska. Various migrating waves are supposed to have peopled the three Americas—North, Central, and South—from the Arctic Circle to Tierra del Fuego. This may well be so, and until a better theory can be advanced it will stand. But primitive man appeared at many places on the earth's surface: Java, China, England, Germany, France—and in 1931 a skeleton was found in Minnesota of a woman who had obviously been drowned in a lake that had ceased to exist 22,000 years ago. Thus it is reasonably certain that following the last glacial period, or about 25,000 years ago, men of some sort lived in North America. The so-called "Folsom" man of northeastern New Mexico lived approximately 15,000 years ago. This date coincides with the estimate of James G. Bennett regarding artifacts found in the Gila watershed. Conservatively, then, man was on the Gila 15,000 years ago, probably more, and possibly as many as 25,000.

The land from 15,000 years ago on down to modern times looked very much as it does today. It was either mountains or desert, save for an intermediate area of grassland between the two extremes. In the upper region of the Gila watershed the mountains reached elevations of nine and ten thousand feet, with large stands of pine, spruce, and birch; and the mouth of the Gila was virtually at sea level with a desert flora of greasewood, cholla cactus, and the giant saguaro.

As century after century went around the clock, the Gila

continued to roar down from its mountain canyons and fan out and roll gently across the great desert plain, keeping a generally westerly course except for a great bend to the south (Gila Bend today) until it merged with the even greater Colorado River and the waters of both streams, less than a hundred miles below this confluence, became lost in the Gulf of California.

3

LONG BEFORE COLUMBUS

ALMOST ONE hundred years before Henry Hudson sailed along the Jersey coast and discovered both the Hudson and the Delaware River, the first of the Europeans were in Arizona. The year was 1539, only forty-seven years after Columbus had arrived in what was euphemistically called the New World.

But long before Columbus there were thousands of residents in the valleys and canyons and mountains of the American Southwest, and many of these lived in the valley of the Gila River and up and down its numerous tributaries.

These pre-Columbian people are divided by archaeology into three major groups. Two of these are definite cultures, overlapping somewhat in time and in geography. These are represented by two basic terms: first, the *Anasazi* (a present-day Navajo Indian word used to define the people who lived in the ruins of the plateau country of Arizona and New Mexico), which includes all the arbitrarily set-up cultures of the Basketmaker-Pueblo system;

and second, the *Hohokam* (a present-day Pima Indian word meaning the ancient ones who inhabited the desert region), which includes six progressive stages of the aboriginal culture of the lower Gila Valley. The third grand division is called the *Mogollon* (the name of a large mountain range in southwestern New Mexico), and it is still a debatable issue as to whether this could properly be called a subpattern resulting from early merging of Anasazi and Hohokam peoples, or whether, in the light of further research, it will be found to contain sufficient individuality to stand on its own as the third basic southwestern culture. This last is such a reasonable probability that for practical purposes it is convenient to accept such an ultimate conclusion.

In the Gila watershed all three cultures are represented.

Perhaps their greatest achievement was the invention of the atlatl, or spear thrower. This was a primitive means of hurling a spear or javelin with great speed and force over a considerable distance. It brought down animals, and was as important in its time to the people of the Gila Valley as was the invention of firearms to the people of Europe.

Most of the people were Hohokam (pronounced ho-ho-kam, with a slight accent on the last syllable); quite a number were Mogollon (pronounced mo-go-yone, with a definite accent on the last syllable); and the minority were Anasazi (pronounced ah-nah-sah-zee, with the accent about equal on all four syllables. But it must be remembered at all times that these terms are merely functional, and that they form the most practical of general classifications up to date.

Since these people have lived in the Gila watershed for something like twenty-five thousand years, and since the white race has been on the Gila only a little more than four hundred years, it is reasonable to discover as much as we can about the aboriginal inhabitants before abandoning them to pre-Columbian obscurity.

In the earliest days lived the primitive cave dwellers, or the hunters; and eventually they evolved into the farmers; and finally into the potters. As far as is known, no pottery decorated with painted designs antedates A.D. 300 although it is not at all impossible that a crude pottery may have been made as early as A.D. 1.

Slowly a centralization of social groups began to occur—earlier in some instances and later in others—but by A.D. 800 tribes and clans began to form small community groups, for both agricultural and defensive purposes, and the pueblo type of civilization resulted. These were not the city-states that we associate with modern pueblos, such as Walpi or Tesuque or Taos, but were their precursors and were often begun as cliff dwellings. Examples in the Gila watershed can be seen today at Montezuma Castle National Monument and Tuzigoot National Monument, both sites on a tributary called the Verde, which joins the Salt River, which, in turn, flows into the Gila.

Montezuma Castle is a five-story cliff dwelling within a natural cave. The name is unfortunate, since it has nothing whatever to do with the Emperor Montezuma and was in no sense a castle. It had twenty-five or more rooms built of adobe, tapering upward to the fifth floor, which had but two rooms. It is believed to have been constructed about the year 1200, or perhaps half a century earlier.

Tuzigoot also was occupied about the year 1200. It consisted of three large pueblos upon which restoration work has been done. It must have housed at least three hundred people.

A third example of Pueblo culture of the Anasazi classification is Tonto National Monument at the junction of Tonto Creek and the Salt River. This consists of two pueblos, one of two stories and twenty-nine rooms, and the second of three stories and about seventy-five rooms. It was apparently a combination of resi-

dence, granary, and fortress, and was occupied early in the fourteenth century.

The Mogollon culture is found in the upper reaches of the
Gila, high in the mountains of the same name in New Mexico,
and is also evident in the Mimbres Valley, which is just beyond
the Gila watershed. Silver City, New Mexico, will make an identifying landmark for the Mimbres area. Primitive hunting and agriculture supported the Mogollon people. Dwellings were first
crude pit houses and brush shelters, and then developed into the
pueblo-type house about A.D. 1000. The finest example is to be
seen at the Gila Cliff Dwelling National Monument. There are
nine caves in this group, and among the "treasures" unearthed by
the excavators are corncobs, black and white pottery, turquoise
beads, and the mummified body of an infant.

These people evolved similarly to the Anasazi culture from
atlatl to bow and arrow, made pottery, and buried their dead or
occasionally cremated them. Much work is being done on the
Mogollon culture, and until more details are known it is unwise
to draw too hasty conclusions. The upper reaches of the Gila offer
some of the most inaccessible country in the United States, and
it may be a number of years before a proper evaluation of the
Mogollon people can be completed. For the sake of a visual comparison, this wilderness is larger than the entire state of Massachusetts, and you could toss in Rhode Island. Some fascinating excavations and some significant conclusions lie in the near future.

This leaves the Hohokam for third consideration among the
cultures of the Gila watershed. Generally speaking, these were
the desert people of the lower Gila. Their general area in the
Southwest covers a region about the size of the state of Tennessee,
or all of central and southern Arizona. To facilitate study, the
culture has been broken down into six arbitrary divisions: Pioneer

to A.D. 500: Colonial to 900: Sedentary to 1100: Classic to 1350: Recent to 1700: and Modern to 1900.

The public is often amazed at the extent and range of this culture, for the word "Hohokam," after all, is little known. In 1950 it may safely be said that 99 99/100 per cent of the radio, television, motion picture, and newspaper audience never heard of the word. Yet in the year 900 this race had 167 settlements—towns or communities of some sort—in the Gila watershed. And these 167 are not all, but are only those which had been discovered up to 1946 and upon which some archaeological work had been done. Countless others have been lost forever because of the leveling and grading by the Indian Service of Indian reservation lands. Well-meaning Washington has done this in order to make available to the contemporary Pima Indians soil for the growing of cotton. Economy has a priority over archaeology.

And it was these same Hohokam people, along with some of the Anasazi, somewhere close to the year 1350, in the midst of six adjacent villages, who constructed what is sometimes called America's first skyscraper, the "Great House" named by the Spaniards Casa Grande. There is nothing like it anywhere else in the Southwest, or in the entire United States.

We know why they built it. We know quite a bit about the life that went on there along the banks of the Gila. We know that the Great House was an abandoned ruin when the first white man set foot on Arizona soil in 1539.

But what we don't know for a certainty is—why did they abandon it? And these people who obviously knew something of masonry, irrigation, agriculture, architecture, astronomy, and had a calendar—where are the Hohokam today?

4

THE TOURIST was furious.

"I demand my money back!" he shouted.

And the National Park Service ranger, who had long since learned to become used to any and all types of the traveling public, cheerfully refunded to the man the sum of twenty-five cents.

The tourist left the administration building and slammed the door. He walked to his car, which he had left parked in the bright Arizona sunlight, and drove away, still in high dudgeon and muttering to himself. He would never return to Casa Grande National Monument again, and he'd certainly warn all his friends that the thing was nothing but a government racket.

In any democracy everyone has the right to express his opinion about the government. And when Casa Grande first became a government project there were indubitably some citizens who were in protest, vociferous or otherwise. These citizens were rather small brown-skinned men and women; the government was that of the Hohokam people and it was certainly a democracy; and the date of the project was approximately 1350, or about a hundred and fifty years before Columbus discovered America.

To some extent the indignant and irate tourist had a case. He had indeed paid twenty-five cents to see nothing more than the ruin of an old building made of caliche (mud to him) which was in such a state of decrepitude that the government had been forced to erect a huge protective shed over it or it would soon

19

have been washed by water and wind erosion to oblivion. But what the angry tourist did not see was the story and the significance beyond the immediate ruin itself. He was looking for a Pompeii or a Palenque. He wanted his quarter's worth. He didn't know that he was standing in the heart of a metropolis as great in its own way as Pompeii or Palenque, and that it was his own limitation for not realizing that such was the truth. It takes a willing and lively imagination to reconstruct from the scene at Casa Grande today any interpretation or visual dramatization of what life must have looked like there when Babylon fell, when Christ was born, when the battle of Hastings was fought, and when the first Crusade was launched. For just as surely as those events are history, so the Gila River, at those same times, was rolling across the Arizona desert and was supporting a race of people who can be described in no other way than civilized.

A glance at a map of the Gila watershed will show that the high country, for the most part, lies to the north of the river and drops abruptly toward it; and that the area to the south, while having numerous chains of mountains, lies tilted very gradually northward. Thus there are only two main tributaries of the Gila flowing north from the Mexican state of Sonora (with the possible exception of San Simon Creek, although this stream does not rise in Mexico but in New Mexico) and these two main branches from the south are the Santa Cruz and the San Pedro.

From the higher country north of the Gila there are a number of major tributaries, notably, from west to east, the Hassayampa, the Agua Fria, the Salt (with its important substreams the Verde River and Tonto Creek), and the San Francisco (with its own tributary called the Blue). Add it all up, not to mention numerous lesser tributaries, and it is a lot of water.

Up and down the Gila, and on all the branches mentioned, lived the Hohokam people. The date of their arrival in this general area is still archaeological supposition. But it would be reason-able, and even conservative, to say that they had at least 250 cities, towns, or communities in the watershed when William the Conqueror invaded Britain in 1066. The center of population spread out in all directions from a "metropolitan" area near the confluence of the Salt with the Gila, a community that archae-ologist Harold S. Gladwin has called Snaketown. This was the London or the Paris of the Hohokam. The site may be visited readily today as it is not far from Arizona's capital city of Phoenix.

Somewhat farther east, on the main stream, there was a ver-itable chain of communities, and one of the largest was within a few miles of what is the town of Coolidge, Arizona, today. This settlement was on the south bank of the Gila, which was about half a mile or more wide at this point, although not very deep, and the center of the community was, perhaps, a mile or more from the river. Adjacent fields were farmed and the water was supplied by irrigation. The main canal had its intake from the river about seventeen miles upstream (east, in this case) and the flow of water was controlled and guided into various irrigation ditches.

It is to be noted that all the Hohokam towns at this time were composed of one-story buildings. Only traces of these sites remain. But it was throughout this central area—up and down the Gila, the Salt, the Santa Cruz, and the lesser tributaries—that the culture of the Hohokam reached its peak. A number of the larger communities had ball courts where the people apparently engaged in games.

The fact that they had the leisure time to pursue sports would indicate a high degree of culture rather than a hand-to-mouth existence. Early archaeologists thought the courts were used as reservoirs. But Frank Pinkley, the first custodian of Casa Grande, with careful excavation, found floor markers in the center of the court. Further research has revealed about fifty such ball courts throughout the area of Hohokam culture. It is probable that the game was similar to the Mayan *pok-ta-pok*. The present-day Hopi play a kickball game somewhat suggestive of the same sport. Unquestionably the Hohokam games were closely allied to racial ceremonies. The "clincher" on the ball court theory has been the discovery of the actual ball. One was found at Gila Bend and is now in the Southwest Museum in Los Angeles; another was found in a Hohokam site fifteen miles southwest of Casa Grande. The latter has a diameter of 8.6 centimeters, or approximately the size of balls used in Yucatan and Central America. The rubber was not the Brazilian type, but was made from a plant known as guayule, native to northern Mexico, and has all the characteristics of what we know as rubber.

Of all the outstanding Hohokam sites, the best that remain today are the aforementioned Snaketown on the Gila, Pueblo Grande five miles east of Phoenix on the Salt, and Casa Grande, again on the Gila, eight miles west of Florence or two miles from Coolidge.

The culture of the Hohokam people would demand a book in itself. But in brief, the race had as high a degree of civilization, and probably higher, than any other pre-Columbian people in the United States. The culture reached its peak about 1300 from what seems to be its earliest evidence about 300 B.C. By 1300, then, the Hohokam had been on the Gila for sixteen hundred years and had an elaborate series of irrigation canals and grew corn, cotton, pumpkins, squash and beans, and doubtless harvested the fruit of the giant saguaro cactus. Deer were brought down in the mountain country by bow and arrow; and rabbits and other small game of the desert were caught in snares. Dogs had been domesticated, and probably turkeys. They may have had fish, as the Gila was a large river in those days and the skeletal remains of sturgeon have been found in the present-day river bed. They had a variety of tools, utensils, and weapons; and as for pottery they had four types, commonly identified today as Gila Plain, Gila Butte Red-on-Buff, Santa Cruz Buff, and Santa Cruz Red-on-Buff.

The first was pale brown or gray, undecorated, and furnished light utensils used for cooking or storage.

Gila Butte Red-on-Buff was decorated with abstract designs, but more often with figures of birds and animals executed with considerable skill and a strong element of humor. These utensils were scoops, jars, bowls, and plates.

Santa Cruz Buff was undecorated, purely utilitarian, and seems to have been made into thin jars only.

Santa Cruz Red-on-Buff was decorated with red paint on the buff background, consisting of bowls, jars, vases, ladles, scoops, and beakers of many shapes; and the designs varied from abstract lines and scrolls to birds, snakes, animals, and droll human figures usually dancing as in a chorus.

Basketry was definitely a craft but only decayed remains have been found. Unquestionably the Hohokam could weave, and also included woodwork in their crafts. But baskets, textiles, and wooden objects have rarely survived the hundreds of years since the Hohokam disappeared and modern archaeology began.

Pipes were not smoked, but it is believed that the people had a kind of cane cigarette.

As to costume, again time has left little evidence. But cotton garments were surely worn, and fragments of sandals have been discovered.

The dead were cremated. Since this destroyed the skeletons, it is impossible to re-create any physically predominant Hohokam type.

Ornaments were popular. Human figures, usually only heads,

were made of clay. Pottery figurines show eyes, nose, and mouth, but it would be too much of a stretch of the imagination to try to reconstruct the physiognomy of a typical Hohokam from these features. Effigy vessels made in the shape of snakes and animals seem to have been popular, although it is likely that these were more utilitarian than mere objects of art. Among other ornaments there were beads and pendants made of turquoise, bone, and shell. Finger rings and earrings were worn, and of course bracelets.

A primitive metallurgy was developed and research has unearthed a number of copper bells. They are small, something like sleigh bells, and are pear shaped. It is probable that this was the first appearance of the bell in the American Southwest.

Hygiene and medicine may have been primitive, but then it is highly improbable that any Hohokam ever died of cancer or syphilis, or ever suffered from alcoholism, paranoia, or schizophrenia.

Taken in all, life wasn't too bad along the Gila in 1300, in comparison to what it was anywhere else on earth in that year. But up to this time the architectural triumph, the Big House, had not yet been built. The desert is wide and flat, and for the most part Hohokam houses were wide and spread out in compounds, usually walled, but not walled very high, and the houses were never more than one story high. The Hohokam seemed to have little to fear from enemies and their reconstructed history gives every evidence that they were a peace-loving people. They surely had friendly relations with their neighbors of the Anasazi and Mogollon cultures and apparently ranged far and wide over all of southern Arizona, since shells found in the various excavations would indicate the fact that they traveled as far as the Gulf of California in present-day Sonora and may conceivably have traded with the natives of that area.

But the one life-giving property all over the American Southwest was water, and there was never too much of it. Indians who lived along the Kennebec or the Hudson, or the Delaware or the Suwannee, never had to give a thought to their perennial supply of fresh water. In the Southwest there are dry years and wet years, but far more dry than wet. And periodically there will be a great number of very dry years in sequence and a disastrous drought results. A great drought of this type occurred in 1277 and lasted until 1299. It had no devastating effect upon the Hohokam, since they lived along the mainstream itself, the Gila, and along its major tributaries. There the water level went down but did not disappear. But the drought had a ruinous effect upon those people who lived on the lesser tributaries, for these smaller streams were reduced to a trickle or dried up entirely. No family or clan or tribe or race can live without water, and the great drought of 1277–1299 caused a widespread shift in population, particularly in northern Arizona and New Mexico.

In the Gila watershed, people who lived upstream on Gila tributaries found themselves either without water or with the supply so reduced that it was inadequate to support the population. Naturally they moved downstream.

Up on the Salt and the upper reaches of its tributary, the Verde, lived people of the Anasazi culture. Down they moved from their cliff-dwelling type of pueblos—some, as in the instance of Montezuma Castle, being five stories high—from the Verde and upper Salt rivers to the more secure protection of the warm and watered valley of the Gila.

Apparently their invasion of the Gila Valley was without conflict or strife of any kind. This is most unusual when two cultures meet, for more often than not one absorbs the other or a conglomerate results. But it would appear that the Hohokam did not resent the influx of Pueblo people, and the two cultures lived side by side for some years and each preserved its own identity.

But gradually there must have been some interchange of ideas and probably some intermarriage. And some time after 1300, and probably before 1350—1325 would be as reasonable a guess as any—the two races agreed upon a mutual architectural concept and the construction of the Big House was begun. The site was at the approximate center of six contiguous villages, and the whole made a gregarious unit that can be described only as a city.

This Casa Grande was a four-story building, proving the pueblo influence, and the constructive engineering skill of the Pueblo people. Probably its purpose was to serve as a watchtower, granary, and perhaps a kind of municipal or governmental center. The watchtower feature may have been caused by the fact that about this time a new race from the north was beginning to enter Arizona. These new people were wilder, less civilized, and were Athapascans. Their modern descendants are the Navajo and the Apache Indians. These outlanders—Goths and Vandals from the north, so to speak—probably raided villages, stole women, and carried off whatever food supplies they could lay their hands on. As this threat developed, it is likely that the common danger drew the Hohokam and Anasazi closer together. Villages on the periphery of Hohokam civilization may have been abandoned. Population became more concentrated toward the centers such as Snaketown and Pueblo Grande. And at Casa Grande the local Hohokam and the local Anasazi pooled their efforts and built the Big House. These Anasazi were known as Salado Indians, since they came from the Salt River mountain area when the great drought made it impossible for them to remain in their chosen location.

At any rate, Casa Grande was built by the Salado people showing definite factors of Hohokam and Anasazi cultures. The edifice was forty by sixty feet, about forty feet tall, and contained four floors. The ground level was filled in to form a solid foundation, and thus a three-story building stood securely on the broad base of a one-story building. The Big House had sixteen rooms, five of which on the ground level were filled in. The walls were four feet thick at the base and tapered upward so that the walls of the fourth floor were only about two feet thick.

While the building was constructed in pueblo style, it was not made of stone and rock, since none was available, but instead was made of a local adobe mud, a calcareous deposit with a high lime content. There was plenty of it, and there is still plenty of it today. It is known as caliche and is extremely durable. To this caliche (pronounced kah-lee-chay) Casa Grande owes its existence for six hundred or more years. Ordinary adobe would long since have been worn down and eroded away. And even the caliche would be gone in another few hundred years if the government had not erected a huge protective shed which covers the entire building. This is in actuality nothing but a roof supported by four huge posts so that the view of the building from the ground is not impaired, but wind and water erosion are minimized.

Typical of pueblo architecture of the fourteenth century, the building had no stairways. Access was gained to the upper floors by the use of ladders. Unfortunately, the science of dendrochronology (the determining of the age of timbers by tree ring progression, reference, and cross reference) can be applied only sparingly to Casa Grande. This science, developed by Dr. A. E. Douglass of the University of Arizona, can tell with amazing accuracy the age of the beams of many Anasazi pueblos. It is due to the shrinkage of tree rings during the years 1277 to 1299 that we know positively that there was a great drought at that time. But the wood used by the builders of Casa Grande was sparse, and such crossbeams as were in place have almost entirely collapsed and disappeared. Moreover, this wood was not of a coniferous type but was a desert growth of ironwood and mesquite and could not be read by the individual rings or series of rings. Thus a specific date of construction will probably never be determined, and 1325 is as good an estimation as any. At the present writing further work is being done along these lines, and one log has definitely been dated 1354. But whether this coniferous wood was used in the original construction or was imported later for stronger reinforcement is a debatable issue. The construction, of course, might well have been of several, or even many, years' duration. Rome and Casa Grande were not built in a day.

There are a few inexplicable and provocative questions that neither archaeologists nor the government have yet been able to answer.

One is the question of the sun holes. Sometimes these are called "calendar holes." Two of them are small apertures, about an inch and a half in diameter, in the east and center walls. On the seventh day of March a beam from the sun will enter the outer hole on the face of the east wall. It was intended to strike and pass through the hole on the inner wall and thus a beam of sunshine presumably entered the center room of the building. This could be no accident. And it might be that that particular day —our March 7—signified the day of the beginning of the normal spring planting season. And seven months later, on October 7, the sun's beams repeat the performance. This date might well indicate the time of harvest. This primitive clock, or calendar, worked perfectly until a slight settling of the eastern wall threw the penetrating beam slightly out of focus, or out of plumb, in relation to the second hole. But it was none the less ingenious and worked with astronomical perfection for centuries. If the sun holes worked today, on March 6 and 7, and on October 6 and 7, the beam of light would pass through both holes at 6:53 A.M. These dates are significant inasmuch as the former occurs two weeks before the spring equinox and the latter occurs two weeks after the fall equinox. What manner of mind devised this?

But on the other hand, there are other sets of holes that are unaccountable. Through the walls of the fourth story there are nine holes leading to the four cardinal directions. All the scientists and all the king's men have no satisfactory explanation for the purpose of these holes. But they were not put there idly, they must have had some significance, and the twentieth-century intellect has been unable to fathom it. Again, what manner of mind devised this? Or could it be that modern man has not thought to look through these four cardinal points at night? Could it be that from the fourth-floor level one could see certain stars at certain times of the year? And again the significance would be calendarial. If interested, try it sometime—say, when Sirius or Procyon is rising on the eastern horizon in November or December. After all, these people had no electricity to blind them to the night sky. If they used the sun, as they surely must have, isn't it logical that they would also have made a practical use of the stars?

Then there is the unsolved problem of the labyrinthine design on one of the interior walls, a design indicating the legend of Ariadne and the Minotaur. This circular pattern has been etched into the hard caliche with some sharp instrument, and with both skill and portent. It is said that this spiral design coincides with that of a labyrinthine design found on coins in use on the island of Crete about two thousand years ago. Again, modern man has no comprehensible explanation. The only feasible suggestion has been that the work was done for the personal amusement of some peripatetic Spaniard who came by sometime in the seventeenth century—or in the eighteenth. Such an explanation is tenuous enough (Spain is a long way from Crete), but falls to pieces when it is noted that the design was then out of human reach (it was cut into a second-story wall) as the floor of the particular room collapsed long before there was a single Spaniard in North America.

So Casa Grande has its challenges, and is all the more fascinating because of them.

One long-pondered mystery was the reason for its complete abandonment sometime around 1400 to 1425, and the unaccountable and total disappearance of the Hohokam people. Partially satisfactory answers have been advanced, such as religious reasons, disease, and epidemics. But they are not conclusive, and the blame, if any, must be placed on the Gila River itself.

The Gila watershed carries a large saline content—note the name of one major tributary, the Salt—and after centuries of irrigation through 125 miles of canals, the Hohokam engineering and reclamation project came a cropper. The arable land became completely waterlogged. And even if it were allowed to dry out while other areas were irrigated, the dried portions would have accumulated so many salts that the land would be useless for further crops. Alkalization, perhaps, was the Hohokam's greatest enemy, and there was no way for him to combat it. When the good earth will no longer support a people, those people must leave. Famine is a terrible threat.

This explanation is as reasonable as any, albeit not entirely satisfactory. For when the Hohokam left the Gila watershed, where did they go? The Salado people may have returned to their former environment to the north and become absorbed into the Anasazi culture; in other words, reverted to type and become Pueblos again. But the Hohokam certainly did not. They had been desert people for almost two thousand years. It is unlikely they would "take to the hills." So they must have migrated south, probably out of Arizona entirely, to the valleys of Mexico. But this migration cannot be traced or in any way substantiated. The race could not have numbered less than fifteen thousand people by the year 1400, possibly twice that number. Where this multitude went is an archaeological riddle, and there is no more satisfactory explanation other than that they simply stepped off the face of the earth.

When the first of the Spaniards entered Arizona in 1539 and 1540, Casa Grande was a ruin, and the only people living near it were a few groups of Pima Indians whose standard of living was in no way comparable to the Hohokam, and to whom the Big House was untouchable; and about all they could say was that it marked the site of a great city that belonged to the Hohokam—a

Pima word meaning "the ancient ones" or "those who have gone."

It is not on record that the first Spaniards actually saw the house, although they certainly heard of it, and some scouting party off the main safari may have seen it. Pedro de Castañeda, Coronado's historian, makes mention of a large house made of red earth which "appeared to have been a fortress." But this is surely Chichilticalli much farther upstream on the Gila. And it is most unlikely that Coronado's historian ever walked through Casa Grande or spent any of his time drawing reproductions on caliche of the story of Ariadne and the Minotaur. It was not until 1694 that the Jesuit priest Padre Eusebio Francisco Kino wrote in his book *Pimeria Alta* of coming upon a "casa grande—a four-story building as large as a castle and equal to the finest church in these lands of Sonora."

Later, in 1697, Padre Kino visited the ruins again with Lieutenant Juan Mateo Mange, and Mange recorded the first detailed description including measurements. The building was a source of awe and wonder to the two Spaniards.

In 1775 the ruin was visited for a third time by white men. This entrada into the Southwest was made by the Franciscan priest Padre Francisco Tomas Garces. By this time, according to Garces' report, the building was in an advanced stage of deterioration. It was then almost five hundred years old. And on the Atlantic seaboard, the English colonies had not yet asserted their independence, and the United States of America had not yet been born.

The first so-called "Americans" to see the ruin were a party of trappers who were pushing their way down the Gila through hostile Indian country in 1825. In the party were James Ohio Pattie and his father, Sylvester. The younger Pattie later had a book published in Cincinnati in 1831, a book which was full of exaggerations and errors of fact and some plain lies, and in which he mentions his experiences on the Gila. If not in 1825, then within two years of that date, during which time Pattie and other trappers explored the Southwest, the party passed within a mile of Casa Grande. That they did not see this landmark would have been an impossibility, yet in Pattie's unaccountable book he makes no mention of it. But he does say, with the collaboration of his editor, Timothy Flint, a Cincinnati publisher who had never been west of Ohio, that he descended the "Helay" as he identified it, that it was "a river never before explored by white people," which is ridiculous; and that "great quantities of broken pottery are scattered over the ground, and there are distinct traces of ditches and stone walls, some of them as high as a man's breast, with very broad foundations." Vague and clumsy as this may be, it is the first description in print by an American of the culture of the Hohokam people. Pattie, unfortunately, was far more concerned with shooting Indians and animals and making himself out a hero than he was with the pre-Columbian evidence left on the land.

In 1832 another American arrived. His name was Pauline Weaver. His real name was Powell Weaver; and later, for the sake of the Spanish tongue, he called himself Paulino Weaver. This was no happy choice, for while the Spaniards called him Paulino, the contemporary Americans called him Pauline. So Pauline Weaver, a rough and tough tobacco-juice spitting frontiersman, carved his name on a wall within Casa Grande, and it is there today, plain to see "P. Weaver 1832." The "Americans" had arrived.

During the nineteenth century a few other reports were made concerning Casa Grande. Colonel W. H. Emory stated in his *Notes of a Military Reconnaissance*, published in Washington in

1848, that he had visited Casa Grande two years before—1846—
on his journey down the Gila with General Stephen W. Kearny.
He wrote:

> It was the remains of a three-story mud house, 60 feet square,
> pierced for doors and windows. The walls were four feet thick,
> and formed by layers of mud two feet thick . . . it was, no doubt,
> built by the same race that had once so thickly peopled this terri-
> tory, and left behind the ruins.

While this conclusion is hardly original, it is certainly militarily
and unimaginatively accurate.

Colonel Charles D. Poston, a colorful figure in Arizona
history about whom more will be said later, saw Casa Grande
in 1863. About it he wrote:

> The Casa Grande stands alone
> One league from road to old Tucson
> No other nation neath the sun
> Would let this ruin, to ruin run.

The condition deplored by Colonel Poston was on the way to being remedied. In 1892 the first scientific investigation of Casa Grande was made by Dr. J. Walter Fewkes of the Smithsonian Institution. Excavations and studies were made over a period of sixteen years, and at last the people who called themselves Americans began to learn something of the culture of other and earlier Americans who had never heard the word in their lives. The work of the Smithsonian Institution has also been supplemented by further research on the part of the Southwest Museum of Los Angeles and the Los Angeles County Museum. On August 3, 1918, by a proclamation of President Wilson, an area comprising more than four hundred acres surrounding Casa Grande was made a national monument.

In 1903 a roof had been erected to protect the ruin. It was a corrugated iron shelter and was damaged by windstorms until it became a greater ruin than the ruin it presumably protected. In 1932 a larger and better protective covering was built at the cost of almost $30,000.

Approximately thirty-five thousand tourists visit this "Big House" every year. The government has provided guides and a museum and a picnic ground. Most of the visitors leave with a new sense of what life was like along the Gila long before Columbus. And the few who leave in indignation because they have driven out of their way and paid twenty-five cents to see nothing but a ruin made of mud can also leave happily. For, like the one tourist in a thousand who can't see what he is missing, if he will but raise his voice in righteous wrath, the government will give him his quarter back.

5

A BLACK MAN AND A WHITE MAN

THE FIRST emissary of the great white race, the first "European" to set foot in Arizona, was a Negro. Thus the contact between the Arizona Indians and the Old World was a meeting of red and black. It was an African who first explored the Gila watershed, and the first truly white man followed, sometimes at the black's heels but more often three or four days or a week or more behind on the trail.

How this came about is a strange and amazing story, and the telling of the tale is worth a slight digression from the banks of the Gila. For the chain of events that brought a Negro to Arizona began (for the sake of arbitrarily beginning it somewhere) in the port of Sanlucar, Spain, in the year 1527, and to be specific, on the 27th of June. For on that date an expedition set sail for the "New World" led by Panfilo de Narvaez, consisting of five ships and about six hundred men, authorized with a royal commission from King Charles V to occupy, conquer, and colonize the Spanish-claimed province of North America called Florida. Incredible as it may seem, a Negro slave of that expedition named Esteban (Stephen in English), belonging to a man named Andres Dorantes de Carranza, gained a place in history, not by the Florida fiasco but by surviving it and reaching the peak of his thrasonical career by prancing up and down the Gila Valley with a retinue of Pima Indian followers, an assortment of concubines, and two greyhounds in leash. Some of the much-embroidered facts, such as the fierce greyhounds, can be pretty well discounted, but it is none the less true that this huge egocentric black man strutted his hour upon the stage of the Gila until the Zuñi Indians of New Mexico very sensibly shot a few arrows through him just to test his statement that he was a god and was invulnerable. The arrows proved to the Zuñi people, and to history, that he was mortal after all.

The Narvaez expedition was wrecked on Florida's gulf coast. It was ill fated from the start, ill equipped, and Narvaez himself was lost. A few survivors managed to work their way on improvised rafts from Apalachicola Bay in Florida, westerly past the delta of the Mississippi River until they arrived, exhausted, on the coast of Texas at approximately what is the city of Galveston today. This disaster occurred in 1528. Eight years later, only four of the original six hundred arrived overland in the Mexican state of Sinaloa on the Pacific coast. It is one of the most remarkable odysseys in history, and it had a determining effect upon the future of the Gila Valley. The four men who crossed Texas saw a portion of what was to be called the Rio Grande Valley, and trudged on hoping to find their way to the City of Mexico, were Alvar Nuñez Cabeza de Vaca, Castillo de Maldonado, Dorantes de Carranza, and Esteban, the slave belonging to Dorantes. During their eight years of wandering across the American Southwest, Cabeza Vaca greatly impressed the aborigines with his prowess as a medicine man. Whether this was a dodge that worked or whether he himself believed in the efficacy of his cures matters not. The amazing fact was that these four men survived at all. During their prolonged peregrination they occasionally heard of "great cities" that lay to the north. These were surely the pueblos of the upper Rio Grande Valley—towns such as Isleta, Tesuque, Nambe, and Taos. They saw none of them, but the fact that the great cities were there was indelibly impressed on their memories. The fact that a pueblo of mud and wattles housing four or five hundred people was a "great city" to the Indians of west Texas or the deserts of Sonora did not coincide with the Spaniards' conception. They visualized truly great cities such as Madrid and Seville. And somehow or other they heard, or their imaginations supplied, the number seven. Hence these four starved, ragged, unshaven castaways from one of Spain's many fiascos, making contact with their own civilization after eight rigorous years of untold hardships, also brought to Mexico—or New Spain, as it was known in 1536—the story, rumor, or legend of seven rich communities lying somewhere to the north. Each time the story was repeated the seven cities became a little larger and a little wealthier.

This imaginary tale happened to coincide almost exactly with one of the myths of the Spanish Empire, the story of the seven lost cities of the Antilles. The story was born of wishful thinking and was nurtured on hope. There wasn't one jot of truth in it. It came out of the Middle Ages and never died; it was something everyone wanted to believe; it was too good not to be true.

In essence it was this:

In 1150 the Spanish city of Merida was captured by the Moors. Seven bishops of the Catholic Church, each with a group of followers, fled to avoid death at the hands of the Mohammedans. They carried all their valuables and sailed west across the "Sea of Darkness" and established a new civilization in a new land. Each bishop founded a city and each city grew to fabulous wealth. Streets were paved with gold, houses were made of silver and studded with rubies and emeralds. The ignorant masses believed this childish story, and many of the educated people accepted it as well. The thing to do was to find these seven rich cities and make them forever Spain's. And where were they? Somewhere in the New World.

It was thought that Columbus would find them. He didn't. It

was thought that Balboa, or Pizarro, or Ponce de Leon, or Cortes would find them. They didn't.

And then, in 1536, from the mouths of the four who might have died came the story of the existence of seven great cities farther to the north. The Indian word for them was Cibola (pronounced see-bo-la with the accent on the "see") and there was little doubt in the public mind that these Seven Cities of Cibola were the long-lost Spanish treasure trove.

Don Antonio de Mendoza in Mexico City was the viceroy for Charles V. He was a man of great acumen, ability, and cupidity, and he loved luxury. He had sixty servants to jump to his bidding and he never went anywhere without a bodyguard of twenty-five men. He wanted to serve his king well, and he did so, but most of all he wanted to have the credit of discovering Cibola—if it existed.

Mendoza interviewed the four castaways and heard the story of the seven fabulous communities. Mexico City was full of opportunists, climbers, rich men's sons without too much intelligence, parasites, gamblers, and gentlemen seeking fortune. Among this stratum of New Spain's upper social crust ran the rumor of the untold wealth that lay to the north. Everybody wanted to discover Cibola. While people talked, Mendoza went about it with his typical shrewdness. Cabeza de Vaca, Castillo de Maldonado, and Dorantes de Carranza returned to Spain. That was all to the good with Mendoza, but before Dorantes left, Mendoza made a significant purchase. He bought Dorantes' Negro slave named Esteban. Having sixty servants already, Mendoza didn't need this giant Negro, at least not in his domestic service. But the black man could be of inestimable value in locating Cibola, for his health had endured hardships and he had been somewhere close to Cibola already.

Far too canny to start a Spanish gold rush, Mendoza rather discounted the Cibola story publicly, and set off an expedition to find it privately. It was particularly unostentatious. It consisted merely of a 38-year-old Franciscan monk named Fray Marcos de Niza, who was an Italian from Nice in the duchy of Savoy and who had made a good record for himself in Peru and Guatemala. All Fray Marcos de Niza was charged to do was to carry the cross into the wilderness. He could have one or two companion Franciscans if he so desired, and Mendoza would supply Esteban to lead the way. Esteban was to obey de Niza exactly as he would his true owner. The whole project was an advance of Catholicism into the unexplored area to the north. It was nothing to attract attention or to get excited about. It was merely missionary work. Cibola itself? Incidental.

Mendoza sent Marcos de Niza written instructions, nevertheless, and they are unmistakable, and read in part:

You must take great care to observe the people who are there, if they be many or few, if they are scattered or if they live in communities; report the quality and fertility of the land, the climate, the trees and plants and domestic and wild animals which may be present; the type of ground if rough or flat; the rivers, if they are large or small, and the minerals and metals which are there; and of the objects of which you can send or bring specimens, do so, in order that His Majesty may be advised of everything.

. . . You shall arrange to send information by Indians, telling in detail how you fare, and how you are received, and what you find.

And if God, Our Lord, is so pleased that you find some large settlement, where it appears to you there is an advantageous place to found a monastery and to send friars to undertake the conversion, you shall send information by Indians or return yourself. . . . Send such information with all secrecy, in order that whatever is necessary may be done without commotion, because in bringing

peace to the country beyond, we look to the service of Our Lord
and the good of all the inhabitants.

And although all the land belongs to the Emperor, our
Lord, you shall, in my name, take possession of it for His Majesty,
and you shall execute the manifestations of possession that you may
deem necessary for such a case, and you shall give the natives to
understand that there is a God in heaven and the Emperor on the
earth to command and govern it, to whom all must be subjected
and must serve.

Certainly there is no suggestion of cities of gold studded
with jewels, and yet those seven cities were Mendoza's only reason
for purchasing Esteban and sending both the black slave and the
white monk into the unknown.

Fray Marcos de Niza was able to play the game as well as
the viceroy. From Guadalajara (then called Tonala), where he
received his instructions, de Niza wrote back in part:

I, Fray Marcos de Niza, of the order of Saint Francis, affirm
that I received a copy of this instruction, signed by the most illus-
trious lord, Don Antonio de Mendoza. . . . which instruction I
promise faithfully to fulfill, and neither contest nor exceed it in
anything it contains . . . I sign my name, this 20th day of November of the year 1538, in Tonala, which is in the province of
New Galicia, where were delivered to me the said instructions in
the said name.

And so de Niza winked back at the viceroy, and the raising of
the curtain on a drama to be known as the Winning of the
West took place.

Mendoza sat back and relaxed in Mexico City. Now let the
unpredictable Cortes or the ambitious De Soto organize expeditions
to find Cibola. Those rivals for power and royal favor would be in
for something of a surprise. For Mendoza's man would surely get
to the seven rich cities first and take formal possession of them;

and it would be Mendoza himself who would have the honor
and the glory of locating them for his Catholic Majesty Charles
V. And if, by some fluke of circumstance, the whole story turned
out to be nothing but a myth after all, surely nothing would be
lost. The pious viceroy had merely sent a priest into the wilderness to carry the cause of Catholicism to the poor heathen, and
had not squandered the royal exchequer by outfitting an expensive
expedition of several hundred men, arms and armor, servants,
animals, and supplies. Time enough for that if the seven wealthy
cities should be found. Mendoza must have smiled over his
brandy in Mexico City. And as the weeks and months went by
he waited with growing interest and suspense for the report from
the north. (Just what, do you suppose, the Franciscan will find?)

It was November of 1538 when Fray Marcos de Niza left
what was called New Galicia and is now the Mexican state of
Jalisco. The route was not difficult at first. Fray Marcos and
Esteban traveled easily to the city of Compostela, not far inland
from the Pacific Ocean. From there the road followed the coastal
slope north and west to the outpost town of Culiacán. This is in
the present-day state of Sinaloa, and in 1538 it was the last
Spanish settlement to the north. Beyond lay the unknown. One or
two slave-seeking parties had penetrated farther north to capture
Indians and impress them into forced labor, but the only person
who had any ready knowledge of this vast northern hinterland
was Esteban, the Negro slave.

From Culiacán onward the expedition was augmented by a
dozen or more natives who acted in part as guides and interpreters, but were in the main supply bearers; and by one Fray
Honorato, a Franciscan companion of de Niza.

Fray Honorato fell ill on the way, necessitating a three-day
delay at the Indian village of Petatlan (Town of the Mats).
The delay irked Esteban, who was eager to the point of excite-

ment in returning to the mysterious north. Some historians, in view of the later and somewhat incredulous developments, think Fray Marcos and Fray Honorato may have quarreled. At any rate, Fray Honorato returned to Mexico City "sick," but became well immediately. This left the party composed only of Fray Marcos, Esteban, and some Indian servants. They proceeded to an Indian town in northern Sinaloa called Vacapa.

Again Fray Marcos rested for a few days, and again the impatient black man was chafing at the bit. So Fray Marcos sent Esteban on ahead to break the trail that he himself would follow, and with instructions to send back information regarding the value and prospects of the country as he went along. Esteban, of course, could not read or write, and to trust his appraisals as sent back to Fray Marcos by the uncertain expressions of Indian messengers was not sufficiently dependable. So the priest and the slave hit upon a system of communication that was quite simple. If conditions were normal and friendly and the land of moderate importance, Esteban was to send back a cross the size of his husky black hand; if conditions were exceptionally promising, he was to send a cross as large as his two hands. And if he were to find, as Fray Marcos wrote later in his *Relación* of the trip, "something bigger and better than New Spain" (Cibola itself, no less), Esteban was to send a very large cross.

The system worked out to the satisfaction of both parties: Esteban was more or less free and on his own, a condition that pleased no end the ego of this man who had spent all of his past as somebody's slave; and Fray Marcos was able to move forward with unhurried ease, making in one day perhaps only half the distance of his advance scout.

With Esteban was one Mexican-Indian interpreter, but the two picked up other Indians from day to day, some of whom traveled with them to the next native settlement and some of whom continued along from one town to another, forming the nucleus of a retinue. This position of leader flattered Esteban's simple and long-frustrated psyche. In the country of the blind the one-eyed man is king; and in primitive Arizona among the red-skins a black man called himself a god and got away with it—for a while.

Esteban, brimming with childlike vanity, and flaunting his new-found power to a state of bravura, was having the best time of his black life. He decorated his body with feathers, bells, rattles, and carried a magic gourd that gave him (or so he explained to the credulous and awestruck Opata Indians of Sonora and the gullible Pima Indians of Arizona) supreme powers and invulnerable strength. At last the slave was the master, and he demanded and got just about anything the land and the people could offer. One of his appetites was sexual, and the black god enjoyed a different Indian girl every night, unless he found one of superior attraction, in which case he took her along for a few days' journey until he tired of her or until he found a maiden of even more seductive charms. Africa was having its innings, and a goodly share of half-Indian half-Negro babies must have appeared some nine months after the bumptious blackamoor cut his swath down the San Pedro River and up and across the Gila.

Esteban may have been in Arizona, but he would have called it heaven. It is no wonder that he sent back to Fray Marcos a cross the size of his hand, and then another the size of his two hands, and finally, in his ecstasy and hearing of a group of "cities" to the northeast, cities of untold wealth of which the first was called Cibola (!), he sent back to the slowly plodding priest a cross the size of a man. It was so large that two Opata Indians had to take turns carrying it.

Fray Marcos, all this time, was having a much more prosaic journey. A careful reading of his occasionally accurate but usually

far too general and often vague *Relación,* will indicate that his job
was much more an assignment than a labor of love. When the going was tough, the good priest took refuge in describing what
somebody else said instead of making the effort to investigate
for himself. That "somebody else" was always a native Indian,
and at times Fray Marcos wrote a lot of nonsense.

For example, when he was well up into Sonora and approaching what is now the border between the United States and
Mexico, he said that he learned that "the coast turns to the
west." This is correct enough considering his position, since the
Gulf of California does indeed come to its head at that latitude (although he confused it by five degrees or more). Among
other instructions, Mendoza had told him to keep the contour of
the coast in mind and to determine if there were any good har-
bors. At that time California had not been seen, and Lower California (then simply called California) was thought to be an island. Since the priest's main direction had been north, and the
Mexican coast runs to the north and west, the farther he advanced the farther he was getting inland and away from the
coast. He was then, in March of 1539, a good two hundred
miles from the Gulf of California. But he wrote naïvely in his
Relación: "As a change in the direction of the coast was a matter of importance, I wished to learn of it, and so I went to
view it, and saw clearly that, in latitude thirty-five degrees, it
turns to the west . . . and so I returned and continued my
journey."

It is obvious that he thought he was still only fifteen or
twenty miles from the coast. And it proves that his casual "so
I went to view it" is a flat lie. To travel over the two hundred
miles of rugged mountains and raw desert between himself and
the coast would have taken him, at the very least, ten days. That
would be an extremely difficult pace (he was always on foot)

and would require another ten days to get back. In all, twenty
days would be the equivalent of a forced march, and thirty
days would be more reasonable. To anyone who knows Sonora—
even modern Sonora—it is all too palpable, to put it mildly, that
the priest was prevaricating. But this falsehood, born of the fact
that his ignorance of the terrain was his bliss, is quite significant.
In view of his later remarks and casual statements, it throws a
beam of light on a problem that has taxed many a historian for
many a year. Fray Marcos, for all his pioneering courage, never
did anything the hard way if an easier way would suffice. History, unfortunately for his prestige, has caught up with him.

  Apparently the priest received at least three communications
from the slave—a cross, a larger cross, and then the huge man-
staggering cross that could mean only one thing. Esteban was on
his way to Cibola!

  With great enthusiasm to visit Cibola but with little appetite
for further hardships on the road, Fray Marcos continued his
northward journey. His account is remarkably vague as to dates
and it is most difficult to determine exactly where he was geographically at any given time. Since the *Relación* was not a diary,
but was written after his return to Spanish civilization, the vague-
ness was not the result of carelessness, but was apparently there for
a personal and protective reason.

  There is a monument on the Arizona-Sonora line, just inside
the international border on the American side, at the tiny settlement of Lochiel, which commemorates the spot where Fray Marcos de Niza, the first white man, stepped onto Arizona soil. Re-
grettably, it must be said that the monument is not in the right
place by many a mile. There are even one or two historians
who doubt that Fray Marcos ever got as far north as present-day
Arizona, although this criticism seems a little too hard on the pioneering priest. While Fray Marcos in his *Relación* put a bit too

much emphasis on his comfort—what he ate and how the Indians welcomed him and how shelter was provided for him—and not enough emphasis on what he saw or where he was, it is reasonably certain that he entered Arizona (not at Lochiel) by following Esteban's trail through Sonora to the headwaters of the San Pedro River. This stream flows north from Mexico and enters Arizona and joins the Gila.

So sometime in late April or early May of 1539 a Franciscan priest was trudging north down the San Pedro Valley. That he reached the confluence of the San Pedro with the Gila is problematical. Esteban, of course, had found the Gila, crossed it, and continued his royal progress northward until he reached the first of the Zuñi pueblos in New Mexico, the Indian town of Hawikuh.

For the first time his peremptory orders and his highhanded manner did not impress the natives. The Zuñi Indians both mistrusted and resented him. What Esteban said and did at Hawikuh will never be known; but what the Indians did to him is history. Less than a day after his arrival they shot a few arrows through him, and the saga of the black man was over. The Zuñi have no reputation for being a bellicose people, so it is highly probable that Esteban had it coming to him.

Moreover, there is no evidence that the Zuñi killed any of the black man's entourage (although this story of death and mayhem has often been told) and their wrath was satisfied by chopping up Esteban into seven pieces and distributing him among the seven cities. Even this is mere legend and probably fallacious, since the Zuñi towns, as proved by Frederick W. Hodge of the Southwest Museum, numbered only six in the first place. At any rate, the Opata Indians and the Pima Indians who were with Esteban (fantastically numbered by legendry at three hundred or more plus two fierce greyhounds) were not molested but were allowed to return over the trail by which they had come. The interpreter remained peacefully among the Zuñi, and one or two young Opata boys stayed on as well. The others, about twenty to thirty Opatas and Pimas, returned to tell the sad news of the black god's death to Fray Marcos de Niza.

Just where the Franciscan was when he received this startling information will never be known, but it is reasonable to say that he was somewhere near the Gila, if not on it. He was still a long way from Hawikuh (Cibola to him) and he could not have got to it under a further march of about twenty days.

The death of Esteban was such a shock to Fray Marcos that he went into a panic. The only conclusion possible is that the priest was scared stiff. He probably visualized a shrieking horde of maniacal Cibolans brandishing arrows and axes and heading his way.

His trek northward had been slow and tedious. Now it was quite a different story. Apparently he gave away everything that his Indian bearers had been carrying for him to trade with the Cibolans, and he turned tail and fled with all possible speed back along the San Pedro Valley, making far better time than he had ever made on his northbound march.

He'd had quite enough of this awful country and he wanted the safety and security of New Spain just as soon as he could get it.

Out of Arizona and south through Sonora fled Fray Marcos de Niza. And when he had put many a Spanish league between himself and danger he began to breathe easier.

Slowly the country became more familiar. Soon he would be at Vacapa, the Indian town in Sinaloa, and after that would come Culiacán and blessed civilization.

And as the priest neared the Spanish world again, a problem began to develop in his mind.

What was he going to tell the viceroy?

He had failed to carry out virtually all of the instructions passed on to him. He had not seen Cibola; he had not been within two hundred miles of it; he had sent back no information whatever about the lands or the people he had seen. What possible and passable story could he tell? How could he justify accomplishing nothing, and still save his face?

It was a problem, but it was not insuperable. As Fray Marcos approached civilization he made up his mind, and made it up with consideration and care. He collected all the facts and got them in sequence. He marshaled all the data he needed and he told the story to himself. It rang true. It made sense. It was stirring and thrilling. It was incontestable. And then Fray Marcos must have smiled to himself. So the viceroy was eagerly awaiting information about Cibola? Very well. He would get it.

And with a sardonic and determined grin the relieved priest trudged on. Late in June of 1539 he arrived in the capital city of New Galicia, a town called Compostela. And there the newly appointed governor of the province was anxious to know if he had seen Cibola. The governor's name was Coronado.

"What is it like?" he asked excitedly.

De Niza smiled wisely.

"I must report only to the viceroy," he answered.

"Is it so great you can't even tell *me?*" asked the governor.

"Not even you," whispered the priest.

PART 2

Spain Spins the Plot

1540 to 1821

6

THE TIDINGS BROUGHT TO THE VICEROY

Fray marcos de niza, with his story of the Seven Cities of
Cibola still his for the telling, had a few days' rest at Compostela
about the end of June, 1539.

He sent a note south to Viceroy Mendoza in Mexico City
advising his lordship of his safe return and of the fact that the
events and discoveries had been of such significance in the north
that he would not, and could not, reveal them to anyone but
his lordship himself.

As soon as the note had been dispatched by messenger, Fray
Marcos willingly announced to Francisco Vasquez de Coronado,
the governor of the province of New Galicia, in his office at the
capital city of Compostela, that he had indeed discovered the
Seven Cities of Cibola.

Coronado was ecstatic.

Immediately he made arrangements to accompany Fray Marcos to Mexico City. Here was the greatest news since Columbus,
since Pizarro, since Cortes—seven cities of inestimable wealth, and
all Spain's for the taking. But as to details, the Franciscan kept
the governor in the dark. Nothing more could be told until the
round unvarnished tale, the whole truth and nothing but the
truth, could be delivered to the viceroy. Coronado was impa-

tient to be off. De Niza seemed surprisingly cool and in no hurry at all.

By August 1 of 1539, Coronado and de Niza were in Mexico City. The priest and the viceroy were closeted in secret session for a long hour. It is a pity that this conversation can never be history. Nobody will ever know what was said. It is possible, on the one hand, that Fray Marcos told the viceroy the truth—namely, that if Cibola existed he had not seen it, that Esteban had been killed presumably by the Cibolans, and that he himself, in a panic, had fled back to New Spain. On the other hand, it is possible that Fray Marcos manufactured out of the whole cloth of his imagination a tale that he knew the viceroy wanted to hear—namely, that he had been to Cibola, that it was rich beyond all expectations, and that it was only one of many other cities all paved with gold and studded with jewels.

The latter tale, in view of what happened next, would seem the more likely, although there are a number of debatable issues that leave some margin of doubt either way.

Regardless of whether it was due to de Niza's fearless honesty or whether it was due to his outrageous mendacity, the interview sealed the future of the Gila watershed. The might of New Spain prepared to move north. It could have been that Mendoza, chagrined over the fact that de Niza accomplished absolutely nothing, decided to believe in the existence of Cibola anyway and told Fray Marcos that he must swear that he had been there and seen it. This version lets the Franciscan off with his skirts clean. Or it could have been that de Niza told one of the greatest lies in history and completely duped the viceroy. Historians will never know for sure, but it must be said that the weight of evidence is strongly against the veracity of the priest.

That Mendoza was not entirely satisfied with de Niza's report was indicated by an act that was typical of his way of doing things. With no fanfare or publicity whatever, he sent secret orders to a soldier at Compostela named Melchior Diaz. And he ordered Diaz to take fifteen men and investigate at once the area over which Esteban and de Niza had traveled. And apart from Mendoza himself, nobody in Mexico City, including de Niza, even knew of this subsidiary mission.

On September 2, 1539, Fray Marcos completed the writing of his *Relación*. Nobody cared a hoot about anything in it except Cibola. Did it exist? Was it a cache of wealth? Could it be attacked and looted? All of New Spain hung on the answer.

Fray Marcos wrote a plain statement of fact, and in it, after narrating some dramatic details of Esteban's demise, which he had not witnessed, he explained his noble, sacrificing, and death-defying intention of seeing Cibola for himself at all costs. This, we know, was a plain lie. The priest was never within two hundred miles of Hawikuh pueblo, which he took for granted was Cibola, simply because the natives of that village had liquidated Esteban. But he had the effrontery to write (on his own or did Mendoza order him to do it?) this incredible lie:

In the end, seeing that I was determined, two chiefs said that they would go with me. With these and my own Indian interpreters, I pursued my journey until within sight of Cibola, which is situated on a plain at the base of a round hill. It has the appearance of a very beautiful city, the best that I have seen in these parts. The houses are of the style the Indians had described to me, all made of stone, with their stories and terraces, as it appeared to me from a hill where I was able to view it. The city is larger than the city of Mexico. At times I was tempted to go to it, because I knew that I risked only my life, which I had offered to God on the day I began this journey. But finally I realized, considering my danger, and that if I died, I would not be able to make my report of this country, which to me appears the greatest and best of the discoveries. I commented to the chiefs who had accompanied me, on how beautiful Cibola appeared; and they told me it was the poorest of the seven cities, and that Totonteac is much larger, and better than all the seven, and that it has so many houses and citizens that it has no end. Under the circumstances, it seemed appropriate to me to call that country the new kingdom of Saint Francis; and there with the aid of the Indians, I made a great heap of stones, and on top of it I placed a cross, small and light only because I had not the means of making it larger, and I declared that I erected that cross and monument in the name of Don Antonio de Mendoza, viceroy of New Spain, for the Emperor, our lord, as a sign of possession, conforming to my instruction, and by which possession I proclaimed that I took all of the seven cities and the kingdoms of Totonteac and of Acus and of Marata, and that the reason I did not go to these later places was in order to return to give an account of all I did and saw.

There isn't a word of truth in the above quotation. It has been proved by the careful analysis of Cleve Hallenbeck that Fray Marcos was at least twenty days behind Esteban when he, Fray Marcos, reached the Gila River; if, indeed, he got quite that far down its tributary, the San Pedro, while trailing his black scout.

After "seeing" Cibola, Fray Marcos describes returning to the place where he had the news of Esteban's death. Granting that he had even reached the Gila, there were still two hundred miles of difficult mountain terrain between himself and Hawikuh, called Cibola. But he describes this as a journey of two days—one to "Cibola" and one back!

Other falsehoods, such as the erecting of a "heap of stones" and the placing of the "small and light" cross, must also be discounted. If Mendoza made him write these lies, the priest was Mendoza's tool; if Fray Marcos wrote them of his own accord, he may well assume the mantle of the Munchausen of Mexico.

But none of this debate mattered in 1539. Far more significant was the fact that all of New Spain learned that Cibola had
been found. The tidings brought to the viceroy were stunning,
staggering, and exciting beyond all expectation and imagination.
Every young blade of New Spain was eager to join an expedition to advance on Cibola and to attack and exterminate by fire
and sword these decadent, plutocratic, luxury-nursed enemies of
his Catholic Majesty Charles V. Cibola must perish! These das-
tardly enemies of Spain must die to the last man! And all of
this, apparently, was exactly the jingoistic spirit that Mendoza
wanted to inculcate. Whether in his Machiavellian mind he knew
that Cibola was a fraud, or whether he really believed the lies
written by de Niza, or whether he was willing to prepare a major expedition but not willing to send it off until he had received a further report from Melchior Diaz—all are matters of historical speculation. The fact is that he announced to the public
that he would send a powerful and punitive force into the north
to teach these objectionable Cibolans a thing or two.

After all, the viceroy's position toward his king was secure.
If Cibola existed, he had caused it to be discovered; and if it
turned out to be a figment of imagination, the fault was not his
but de Niza's. Mendoza always played everything safe—for himself.

Throughout Mexico City and all of New Spain passed the
glorious news. And every time the story was told Cibola grew
richer and richer. Every able-bodied man wished to be in on
this sixteenth-century gold rush. And as for Fray Marcos de Niza,
because of his brilliant discoveries he would most certainly be
made a bishop.

The expedition was organized and planned by Mendoza in

Mexico City, and its component parts were marshaled at a great rendezvous at Compostela, from which town the official start was to be made.

Mendoza himself financed the major cost. Coronado and a few other leaders of the government or the army made contributions. Coronado was not a wealthy man, but his wife, Doña Beatriz, had inherited a fortune. In order to raise cash, a great amount of her property, both real and personal, was pawned. Nobody was worried. Cibola was such a good thing that nobody could lose. Charles V of Spain put up nothing, and that was highly desirable, for had the king financed the expedition the king would have got all the profits. The thing to do was to keep the king out of it in so far as possible. His percentage, without investing anything himself, would be his royal fifth of whatever should be found. Winks were exchanged among the backers in Mexico City. There was no point in asking the king to risk a penny—of course not. The brains of New Spain could handle this little plum very well among themselves, and keep the king's cut down to one fifth. It has been estimated by Herbert C. Bolton in his *Coronado* that the expedition cost about the equivalent of one million dollars in present-day currency.

Furthermore, the king had no voice in the matter of titular appointments. After all, Madrid was a long way from Mexico City and there was no time to waste. It was largely Mendoza's party and he announced that the leaders would be named at Compostela. And as for those who could not afford to be on the inside but wished to participate, Mendoza announced that he would supply the cash needed to join what might have been called the Great Cibola Looting Company, and from such persons the kind Mendoza would eventually get his capital back and rake in a side percentage. All in all, it was one of the most exciting adventure-business deals of the New World.

About this time, while the soldiers were being mustered and supplies collected at Compostela, Fray Marcos de Niza got an unpleasant shock. Mendoza told him that he must accompany the expedition and lead the way. Fray Marcos was dismayed— his health, perhaps, might not . . . But the viceroy was adamant. Most assuredly, Fray Marcos would go along. He was the only one who had been over the ground before. He could lead the soldiers straight to Cibola.

"But—" began the priest.

The viceroy was impatient. He frowned. Fray Marcos was most eager to go, wasn't he?

The priest had no choice. He agreed. He had no ready alternative. But it was a far from enthusiastic acquiescence.

Since it did not behoove or become the viceroy to abandon his office in Mexico City and lead this crusade for capital himself, he had to find a competent leader to place in supreme command of the expedition. His obvious choice was Francisco Vasquez de Coronado, governor of New Galicia, cofinancier, friend, and partner. Moreover, Coronado, being a gentleman, educated at the University of Salamanca, married to Doña Beatriz who herself was an heiress, would never get out of hand and become a conniving ambitious Cortes or a rascally independent De Soto. Coronado was the right man; not too bright, but not a fool; socially correct, and thirty-five years old.

Unquestionably Mendoza had expected the Melchior Diaz party to return before the major expedition set forth. But all through the fall of 1539 and the winter of 1540 there were no reports from Diaz. He was somewhere in the mysterious north, exact whereabouts unknown. Actually, Diaz had entered Arizona by way of the San Pedro Valley and had reached the Gila. He explored the Gila both east and west of the confluence of the San Pedro. And he discovered the Indian town of Chichilticalli.

Here he was halted by the mountain region to the north. Snows were deep and the range was impassable. And beyond those immense mountains lay Cibola. He was faced with either waiting for spring or returning to New Spain to report to the viceroy. After questioning the Indians of Chichilticalli to learn all he could of and about Cibola (which was merely that the "seven cities" existed beyond the snow-covered mountains, but as to specific details of untold wealth, he could ascertain nothing), Diaz decided that he had done the best he could and had better report back to Mendoza. He started south about January 1, 1540.

Mendoza himself journeyed to Compostela, hoping all the while to hear from Diaz before the great safari could make its historically momentous start. And at that time, for public consumption although it must have already been well known to those on the inside, a great to-do was made over announcing the names of the leaders.

Pedro de Castañeda was the official historian of the expedition, and he wrote:

When the viceroy saw what a noble company had come together, and the spirit and good will with which they all presented themselves, knowing the worth of these men, he would have liked very much to make every one of them captain of an army . . . but he could not do as he would have liked, and so he appointed captains and officers because it seemed that he was so well obeyed and beloved, nobody would find fault with his arrangements.

It was, indeed, very thoughtful of Mendoza. And Casteñeda continued:

After everybody heard who the general was, Francisco Vasquez de Coronado, the viceroy made Don Pedro de Tovar ensign-general, the guardian and high steward of the Queen Doña Juana, our demented mistress—may she be in glory.

Obviously Mendoza wasn't missing tributes to any of the royalty, even the mentally unfit, as long as they didn't cut in for more than the king's twenty per cent. And the historian continued:

It might be clearly seen . . . that they had on this expedition the most brilliant company ever collected in the Indies . . . but they were unfortunate in having a leader who left in New Spain estates and a pretty wife, a noble and excellent lady, which were not the least causes for what was to happen.

Of the 1,100 men, about 350 to 400 were Spaniards and the rest were Indians who acted as porters, burden bearers, stock men, and served any general utilitarian purposes. Many of the Indians brought their wives and families. So there is no exact telling of the number of persons in the expedition. Two Spanish women went along; one who served as a nurse and one, the wife of a tailor, who served as a seamstress.

The average age of these jolly fellows—wearing armor, helmets, visors; brandishing crossbows, harquebuses, lances, swords, and shields; consecrated to what was the rape of a sleepy Indian village made of mud and basking in sunshine—was about twenty-six. It was definitely a young man's gamble. The oldest man in the expedition (among the Spanish) was Juan Gallego, who was fifty and was regarded by the itching-for-a-fight youths of seventeen and eighteen as decrepit. The next oldest man was thirty-seven.

In a previous book, *Listen, Bright Angel,* I have stated: "The values may have been empty and the machinations Machiavellian, but it took brave and hardy men to buck the mountains and deserts of Mexico and Arizona. It must have been a long and impressive safari that departed from Compostela on that 23rd day of February, 1540, colorful to the extreme, with more than eleven hundred people, and twice as many animals, winding slowly northward over this raw land. Coronado took his leadership very seriously, and while he had no talent for this kind of thing, he was not aware of this lack. He considered himself another Cortes."

Mendoza rode with Coronado for the first two days' journey. Then he decided that he could not absent himself from Mexico City any longer. With regret that he was never able to get the double-check from Diaz, Mendoza watched the glorious company pursue its northward march. Everyone was still an eager hero.

There was one individual in the expedition, however, who had his problems. He was the only man who had seen the great unknown land to the north before. He was, of course, Fray Marcos de Niza, and his thoughts as the mightily armed crusade moved forward must have given him many a sleepless night. If the Cibola he had told of could not be found—then what?

7

A GENTLEMAN FROM SALAMANCA

THE IMPORTANCE of the Coronado expedition, not only to the Gila Valley but to the entire American Southwest, cannot be overestimated. Not only were the present-day states of Arizona and New Mexico explored, but so were goodly portions of Texas, Kansas, and Oklahoma. The dog and the turkey were the only animals (if a native bird may be called an animal) that the American aborigines had domesticated. With the Coronado expedition came horses, pigs, sheep, oxen, and most important of all, cattle. The cow, the bull, and the steer, the hallmark of the West, first entered Arizona and the Gila watershed in 1540.

What is more, Viceroy Mendoza, who never did anything by halves, sent a naval expedition from the Mexican west coast port of Acapulco northward into the Sea of Cortez, or what is commonly called today the Gulf of California.

So little was known at that time about the west coast of Mexico that it was taken for granted that a naval expedition would sail generally northward parallel to the land expedition. Mendoza sent three ships north, loaded with supplies for Coronado's army, and this flotilla was under the command of Hernando de Alarcon. Once he had sailed, Alarcon never saw the army again. This was entirely the fault of the *Relación* of Fray Marcos de Niza, who had written that on his first trip to Cibola he had taken a side trip to see where the "coast turned west," or the head of the Gulf of California. De Niza never made such a trip, or he would have learned that, while his route, and later Coronado's, ran steadily northward, the Mexican coast veered sharply to the northwest. By the time Coronado was in great need of the seaborne supplies, there was a distance of several hundred miles between his party and the ships of Alarcon. Contact never was made.

Alarcon reached the head of the gulf and was buffeted about in the tidal bore of the mighty Colorado River. He ascended the river and, with the aid of Cocopah Indians, who believed him when he said he was the God of the Sun, was towed upstream until he discovered the mouth of the Gila River. While he explored the area, and possibly went a short distance up the Colorado above the Gila confluence, and was unquestionably the first white man to set foot on what is now the soil of California, he could find no trace of any scouting party from the Coronado expedition.

At about the same time that Alarcon was in the vicinity of the modern town of Yuma and the lower Gila River, Coronado had reached the Indian town of Chichilticalli, a good four hundred miles up the Gila, due east of his sorely needed supply ships. Thus both land and naval expeditions were on the Gila, but the hundreds of miles of intervening terrain negated Mendoza's carefully laid plans. When questioned, Fray Marcos de Niza had no explanation beyond reiterating that the year before he had seen the gulf that was a good fifteen days' journey from his supposed point of vista.

During this state of affairs, however, the Coronado expedition was slowly advancing northward and suffering the vicissitudes of a few unfriendly Indians and a few casualties such as one or two cases of dysentery, a few broken legs, some animals lost in fording swollen rivers, and the death of the maestro de campo (second in command of the military), a man named Lope de Samaniego, who raised his visor at an untimely moment and was shot in the eye by an unfriendly Indian's arrow which penetrated his brain and killed him immediately. The soldiers hanged half a dozen innocent Indians, decimated an Indian village, and the colorful horde marched on. Coronado appointed Don Garcia Lopez de Cardenas to be maestro de campo, and because of this incident of being promoted to an office of field marshal, Cardenas later became the discoverer of the Grand Canyon.

The stress and strain and the few casualties took the edge off the general enthusiasm long before the entourage entered the Gila watershed. And one other event contributed strongly to the lowering of morale.

Melchior Diaz, returning from the Indian town of Chichilticalli on the Gila River, met the vanguard of the great expedition moving north. In the vanguard, of course, were Coronado and Fray Marcos de Niza.

Everybody wanted to know what Diaz had found, and Diaz, who seemingly was a forthright and honest man, was loath to break the news. But he confided in Coronado and Cardenas and Pedro de Tovar and a few other leaders. The truth of the matter was that what lay ahead was not very promising. True, he had not been able to get to Cibola because of the impenetrable snow in the mountains, and by the time the Coronado expedition reached that last barrier the snow would have melted. But what Diaz had heard of Cibola while he rested at Chichilticalli on the Gila was not exactly exciting. All he could gather was the story that Cibola was a group of seven Indian towns where the people lived much as all Indians did in this tierra nueva. The buildings were two or three stories high and the natives had enough to eat—but of gold and silver, and streets and buildings studded with fabulous gems, he could find no authentication whatever. It *could* be that the story of the untold riches was a case of wishful thinking. To Diaz it began to appear that way.

This news leaked out and all the hotbloods and fortune hunters became indignant. If they were going through this tedious and backbreaking march for nothing, somebody would be called to account. A few critical looks and one or two direct questions were aimed at Fray Marcos de Niza.

Fray Marcos poured oil on the troubled waters. Apparently determined to brazen it out, the priest reassured the skeptical that Cibola was all and even more than he had said of it. "Larger than the City of Mexico" and paved with gold and abounding in precious stones. Hadn't the Cibolans killed poor Esteban in order to protect the secret of their wealth? If all would be patient, all would soon be rich. And Castañeda, the official historian, wrote "and in this way he quieted them so that they appeared well satisfied."

In spite of this assurance, however, there was more than a

modicum of grumbling and discontent as the party moved through what is now the Mexican state of Sonora and reached the Gila watershed and marched into present-day Arizona.

As the days went by it became all too apparent that Fray Marcos de Niza was in a country he had never seen before, and that Melchior Diaz, who had recently been to Chichilticalli, was the only man to guide the expedition. By this time the entire safari was long strung out. Some of the animals, particularly the sheep, could not keep up; and the soldiers whose task it was to bring the three or four swivel guns were far to the rear. When Diaz led Coronado to Chichilticalli on the Gila, the vanguard was a good twelve to fifteen days' march ahead of those who brought up the rear. With food supplies running low, his men exhausted, and the horses jaded, Coronado proclaimed a two-day rest on the south bank of the Gila, which he described as "a deep and reedy" river. In a report to be sent back to Viceroy Mendoza that he was far beyond possible contact with Alarcon and the supply ships, he added his first criticism of Fray Marcos de Niza: "We all now are very distrustful, and feel great anxiety and dismay to see that everything is the reverse of what he told your lordship."

The next problem was the crossing of the Gila, which was too deep at this place to ford. Some of the animals and some of the men could swim, and rafts were built to accommodate the nonswimmers as well as the scant remaining supplies.

From Chichilticalli to Cibola turned out to be a march of sixteen days over high rugged mountain terrain and necessitated the crossing of many mountain torrents, all tributaries of the Gila. But at last the vanguard reached open country, and after one more day's journey, there lay Cibola.

The tired and hungry Spaniards paused, and those in the vanguard received a shock. There was the fabulous and wealthy

Cibola—a small pueblo of mud and wattles, housing perhaps a hundred and fifty poor people.

The Zuñi Indians of this pueblo of Hawikuh, whose scouts had reported the approach of the strangers, stared back at the Spaniards. There was no welcome. Across the no man's land between the two forces there was only hostility.

Coronado, always a gentleman first and a soldier second, naïvely sent word by Indian interpreters that his armed force had come to "protect" the Cibolans, take all their food and wealth, change their mode of life, and give them the great privilege of becoming Christians and subjects of his Majesty Charles V. The gentleman from Salamanca came as a friend and wanted no violence with the people of Cibola. Would they kindly surrender at once?

The leaders of the Zuñi people sent back word that they were entirely satisfied with their way of life, that the presence of the Spaniards was undesirable, and that if these white and bearded men didn't return at once from where they had come they would be driven back by force of arms.

While this parley was going on, the young men of the expedition turned on Fray Marcos de Niza. So that pitiful little poverty-stricken village was Cibola—"larger than the City of Mexico." Castañeda, the historian, stated: "When they saw the first village, which was Cibola, such were the curses that some hurled at Fray Marcos that I pray God may protect him from them. . . . It is a little crowded village . . . there are ranch houses in New Spain that make a better appearance."

But there was no time for further discussion. It was apparent that the Cibolans were stubborn and would not submit to the privilege of being pilfered and looted. War was the only answer. The Spaniards were not demanding gold; they were demanding something more vital—food. Economy determined the next move.

Castañeda continued: "When they refused to have peace on the terms the interpreters extended to them, but appeared defiant, the Santiago [battle cry] was given, and they were at once put to flight."

What Castañeda means is that those Zuñi warriors who had drawn up outside the pueblo immediately retreated into the pueblo. For the style of fighting of the pueblo people was that of Troy; they remained within their protective walls and fought a defensive war.

For one hour the battle raged. The Spaniards, although weary and disillusioned, had the superior strength in armor and numbers; but the Zuñi held the bastion, and more than one son of Spain ceased to be interested in battle when smashed in the chest by a well-catapulted five-pound rock or shot through with a zooming arrow.

Coronado, decked for battle in shining armor and a plumed helmet, commanding his troops in the attack, got too close to the enemy range and was knocked sailing off his horse by a perfectly aimed rock, received an arrow through one leg, and lay senseless on Cibolan soil. While prone, he was still a good target, and would probably have been killed had not Don Garcia Lopez de Cardenas and Don Hernando de Alvarado shielded his body and quickly carried him out of the range of hostilities.

But the defense of the turtle cannot withstand an offensive that can crack his shell. And the hungry Spaniards, in dire need of food for survival, coupled with their overwhelming numbers, eventually stormed the pueblo, swarmed through the one narrow entrance, and "Cibola" capitulated. Perhaps the Zuñi were out of rocks and arrows, but be that as it may, the Spaniards won and a "great" victory was theirs. The first thing they did was to eat all the corn and turkeys the Zuñi could provide. Then ev-

erybody relaxed and peace was declared. Coronado was unable
to stand on his feet and had to be put to bed; but still a gentleman, he forgave the Cibolans for defending their own property, and there was no more violence.

This battle was fought on July 7, 1540. It is seldom mentioned in books on American history. But apart from the slaying
of Esteban the year before, it was the first formal engagement
fought within what is now the continental United States. Esteban
was a case of assassination, but the battle of "Cibola" was war.

Coronado was unable to lead his expedition beyond Hawikuh
pueblo for several months. So he sent out exploratory parties,
which discovered the Hopi villages of northern Arizona, the
Grand Canyon, and the upper Rio Grande Valley in New Mexico. Also he sent the ever-dependable Melchior Diaz back over the
route by which they had come to Cibola. Diaz was to turn west at
a latitude which, presumably, would take him to the Gulf of
California and the ships of Alarcon. In good time Diaz reached
the lower end of the Colorado River, discovered Indians who
had seen Alarcon, and learned that Alarcon had long since given
up hope of making contact with the Coronado expedition and
had returned to New Spain.

Somewhere between the mouth of the Gila and the Gulf of
California the Diaz party found written on a tree: "Alarcon
reached this place; there are letters at the foot of this tree."
Diaz dug up the letters, which explained how long Alarcon
had waited and how he had been unable to proceed farther.

Diaz then went up the east bank of the Colorado until he
found a place where he could cross by building some makeshift
rafts. This may conceivably have been just above the mouth of
the Gila. Here the Diaz party crossed into present-day California.
The exploration proving fruitless in the desert wastes, they de-

cided to return to New Spain. But the dependable Diaz was destined for a tragic end. Summing it up later from hearsay, Castañeda wrote:

A dog belonging to one of the soldiers chased some sheep which they were taking along for food. When the captain [Diaz] noticed this, he threw his lance at the dog while his horse was running, so that it stuck in the ground, and not being able to stop his horse he went over the lance so that it nailed him through the thighs and the iron came out behind, rupturing his bladder . . . he lived about twenty days.

Poor Diaz! His bones lie somewhere near the mouth of the Gila, but the exact site of his grave will never be known.

Coronado had lost one of his most able men, and at the same time he decided to be rid of one who had done more harm than good. From Cibola he sent Fray Marcos de Niza back to Mexico City, and doubtless Fray Marcos was happy to escape the vituperations that were daily heaped upon him. Coronado even feared that some of the more bitterly disappointed fortune hunters might make an attempt to kill the priest. After the arrival at Hawikuh, the Franciscan seemed to take refuge in silence. At least he made no recorded attempt to justify his former statements.

In the fall of 1540 the Coronado expedition, all its component parts clear of the Gila watershed, moved on to search out further rumors of riches at Tiguex and Quivira, and these, like Cibola, turned out to be the mirage of wishful thinking that seemed ever to lie just beyond the blue New Mexican horizon.

The career of Fray Marcos de Niza becomes obscure after his return to Mexico City in the fall of 1540. It is said that he was held in ill repute and often open contempt. He suffered a stroke and retired to the town of Jalapa to rest. Later history

locates him living in a monastery at Xochimilcho, the famous Aztec floating gardens near Mexico City which are today reduced
to a tourist-promotion racket. The priest became gravely ill, and it
is said that the bishop of Mexico, Juan de Zumarraga, provided
him with a cask of wine every month. Zumarraga died in 1548,
but Fray Marcos lingered on, and it is a generally accepted fact
that he returned to Jalapa and died in 1558.

After more than two years of suffering and hardships, and discovering nothing of any exploitable value from the mouth of the
Gila to the plains of Kansas, the great Coronado expedition
straggled back to Mexico City. Nobody had anything, and all
concerned were financially destitute—except for those who left
their bones in the great American Southwest. The entire project
could be counted nothing but a colossal failure. There had not
been one penny of profit, and all investments were a total capital
loss.

And Coronado heard the unhappy news that during his absence his beautiful young wife had fallen in love with another
man. His health broken, out of favor with viceroy and king, the
gentleman from Salamanca made an effort to renew his position
in the government of New Spain. Mendoza still professed to be
his friend, but with Mendoza nothing succeeded like success,
and Coronado, through no fault of his own, had been a failure.
After 1542 his name received only minor notice in New Spain.
He was a has-been. On September 22, 1554, the gentleman from Salamanca went to sleep in Mexico City and never
woke up. His remains lie in the church of Santo Domingo in the
capital city just three blocks north of the great Cathedral of
Mexico on the Zocalo Square.

He died without ever comprehending that his ill-fated and
disastrous expedition had opened the door to one of the most
magnificent and richest areas in all of North America—the great

American West. And all the while the implacable Gila River continued to pour down from the mountains of New Mexico and roll across the Arizona desert, as yet impervious to man.

▼▼▼

8

A SCHOLAR FROM AUSTRIA

Following the curtain-raising act of Coronado, Arizona was such a disappointment to the Spanish that the main show all but failed to go on. The stage was set, but so great was the disillusionment following the Coronado fiasco that no actors cared to tread the boards. The Seven Cities of Cibola had been proved worthless. The curtain, so recently risen, might just as well have been rung down.

It remained for an Austrian to carry the torch, and he successfully kept the plot moving and the play in action.

China was his desire, but Mexico became his reality; later California became his objective, but a huge area known as Pimería Alta became his empire. This last was a general term covering the northern part of the Mexican state of Sonora and most of the Gila watershed. Arizona would not be quite what it is today without the influence at the close of the seventeenth century and the beginning of the eighteenth of this student from Middle Europe. His name was Eusebio Francisco Kino, and he was a Jesuit.

Born in or near Trent in the Austrian Tyrol, on August 10,

1645, Eusebio Kino was a brilliant boy and a highly intelligent youth. His early interests were not religious. Mathematics was his love. He was educated at the universities of Ingolstadt and Freiburg in Germany, and so promising was his scholarship that he was offered a professorship at Ingolstadt. But while a young man he had suffered a serious illness, and seventeenth-century medicine had given him up. Either prayers, or a miracle, or the intervention of St. Francis Xavier, or all three, saved his life. To express his gratitude Kino declined the professorship and entered the Jesuit Order and asked to become a foreign missionary. He added Francisco to his name; and his family name, sometimes spelled Kuhne, sometimes Quino, was thenceforth Kino.

Between Coronado's retreat from the Gila back to New Spain in 1542 and Kino's appearance in Sonora and Arizona in 1687—a matter of almost a century and a half—there were only two entries into Arizona by the Spaniards and neither of these had any lasting effect. Antonio Espejo and a party of soldiers and priests penetrated westerly from the Rio Grande Valley in 1582. As far as is known, the expedition was limited to the northern part of the state and did not enter the Gila Valley, although the members saw the headwaters of a number of Gila tributaries. In 1604 Don Juan de Onate and a party of thirty marched west from the Rio Grande Valley and completely across Arizona until they reached the Colorado River about a hundred and fifty miles above the Gila, at the point where the Colorado is joined by the Williams, or, roughly, the site of Parker Dam today. Onate and his men marched south down the east bank of the Colorado, noted the Gila in passing, which they named El Rio del Nombre de Jesús, and continued on south past the site of the tragic death of Melchior Diaz and the anchorage of the ships of Hernando de Alarcon, until they reached the head of the Gulf of California. Here the party turned around and

marched back over the route by which they had come, bearing
with them nothing of any interest except a better understanding
of the geography of the Southwest.

The next white man to see the Gila was Eusebio Francisco
Kino in 1687.

Kino arrived at Vera Cruz from Spain in 1681. His first efforts were in Baja—or Lower—California, an unpromising land
that had defied colonization since the days of the great Cortes.
It was still a popular belief that California was an island, and
apart from potential wealth in pearl fishing in the vicinity of the
tiny town of La Paz it had little to offer the colonist. The Indians were stubborn, recalcitrant, and even belligerent. Such elements were no deterrents to a man of Kino's zeal, but while in
Baja California he sailed north up the Gulf of California and
discovered the Seri Indians of Tiburon Island and of the Sonoran coast. Not only the Seris, but the entire Sonoran area interested and stimulated him more than the sterile peninsula of
Baja California. He requested and got permission to go to this
little-known northern area. His assignment was to "Pimeria Alta,"
the boundaries of which were more than vague, but which, in
Mexico City, was understood as the northwestern frontier.

Kino arrived in this area—Sonora today—in 1687, and on
March 13 of that year founded the all-important Mission Nuestra
Señora de los Dolores, or Our Lady of Sorrows. This mission,
about a hundred miles south of modern Tucson, was his base, his
headquarters, and from it he ranged far and wide over northern
Sonora and southern Arizona, up and down the Gila River, often
exploring for days at a time a land that no white man had ever
seen. Mission Dolores is just south of the Gila watershed. All that
remains of it today is not its ruins, but only traces of the ruins.
The importance of Dolores, however, was immeasurable, and it is

a pity that the Mexican government has not made an effort to restore this historical monument.

From 1687, for the next quarter of a century, or until 1711, Eusebio Francisco Kino was virtually the pioneer, trail blazer, father confessor, dictator, geographer, cartographer, altruist, architect, and cattle king of the Gila watershed. For the first six years he was the only white man in the entire area, and during this time he founded the missions San Ignacio and Tubutama. These were followed by other missions after 1693 when two black-robed Jesuits were sent as his colleagues, notably the missions Pitiquito, Oquitoa, and Caborca—all in Sonora and all still standing today. Caborca, not far from the Mexican town of Magdalena, is outstanding architecturally and compares favorably with any mission building in Arizona or California. Its twin bell towers are more than four stories high, its façade is definitely Churriguerresque, and few tourists have ever seen it or even heard of it. Caborca—the Magnificent.

In 1700 Eusebio Kino founded a mission that was dear to his heart, second only, perhaps, to his Dolores, and this one, rivaling Caborca, has been visited by countless thousands of tourists. It is San Xavier del Bac, nine miles south of modern Tucson. Here, adjacent to the Santa Cruz River, which flows (when it has any water in it, which is seldom) north and west into the Gila, stands one of the most striking, beautiful, and famous missions in the United States. Somebody has called it the "white dove of the desert," which sounds as if the person who did so was either preparing a chamber of commerce advertisement or was the author of a travel brochure. But apart from euphuism, Mission San Xavier del Bac is well worth a visit, and represents Padre Kino's supreme effort in Arizona.

While the architecture is primarily late Spanish Renaissance,

and the building consists mainly of burned adobe bricks and
plaster, there is a hodgepodge blending of Byzantine, Moorish,
Spanish, Mexican, and native Indian influences that make San Xavier unique. One of its two bell towers has remained incompleted.
There are a number of legends to account for this. One has
it that a priest (not Kino of course) was examining the tower
and fell into it and was killed. As a gesture to him, no further
work was ever done on it. Another story holds that the church
was left unfinished deliberately in order to avoid paying a tax to
the Spanish king. No tax could be levied until the building was
finished, therefore it has never been finished.

San Xavier was not the first church in Arizona. Earlier
Padre Kino founded the Missions Los Angeles de Guevavi (not
far from modern Nogales) in 1692 and San José de Tumacacori in 1696, which is now a national monument and may readily be visited on the road between Tucson and Nogales. Guevavi
is all but gone, but the National Park Service has done a splendid job in saving Tumacacori. This rather difficult word is Pima
Indian meaning "a curved mountain with a sharp peak" and once
an Anglo learns to pronounce it the difficulty vanishes. Call it
Too-mah-cah-cory with the accent on the "cah."

In all, Padre Kino founded twenty-nine missions and sev-
enty-three visitas in Pimeria Alta, with three of the missions and
about a dozen visitas within the Gila watershed. A visita is a
church of sorts but, as the word implies, it was visited by a
priest periodically and there was no permanent father in charge.
At no time did Kino ever have more than ten Jesuit priests
working with him, so it is obvious that even a number of the
missions, in the early days at least, might conceivably go for days
or weeks without a litany. And it should also be stated that
missions such as Caborca, San Xavier, and Tumacacori were not
built in a day or a week or a year. The buildings when first

founded were crude log and brush shelters. The magnificence of San Xavier was not completed until 1797, almost a hundred years after its founding; and Tumacacori was not completed until 1800, or more than a hundred years after its founding. Kino, therefore, never saw the finished buildings as we see them today.

The labor that built these churches was largely Pima Indian, with some help from the Papagos. The wild and warlike Apaches would have no truck with the white man's religion, and the mission ranchos and settlements made a chain of oases in the wilderness where, for Jesuits and Pimas alike, there was a certain amount of safety in numbers. But even this security was not inviolate, for the Apaches swooped down on San Xavier in 1767, or within a year of that date, and completely sacked the edifice so that an entire reconstruction was necessary.

It was this mission system, however, that brought the first civilization (apart from contemporary native races and the more advanced Hohokam people of pre-Columbian antiquity) to the Gila Valley in the late seventeenth century. All the major missions were self-sufficient. Dolores, for example, had—apart from the church equipment such as furniture, bells, chalices, paintings, statues, and ornaments—a well-stocked ranch of sheep, cattle, horses, oxen, and mules; and orchards and gardens of imported Castilian fruit trees—figs, peaches, pomegranates, pears, quinces, and apricots. It had a mill run by water power, wheat fields, corn fields, bean fields, a smithy, and a carpenter shop. Missions and visitas on the periphery of Pimeria Alta were not so richly endowed, but in all there was no problem of survival.

Pack trains were always coming and going between Pimeria Alta and the cities and towns farther south in Mexico. And Padre Kino himself, while devoted to Mission Dolores, seems always to have been coming and going over his vast terrain and well merits the title "padre on horseback" bestowed upon him by historian Herbert E. Bolton. Kino kept a detailed diary which was long lost in the archives of Mexico City, but which Dr. Bolton unearthed and translated. There is nothing like a firsthand account; and to give the measure of the man and the feel of the Gila country in 1700 a few quotations from Kino's own record are in order.

April 26, 1700. Having arrived at this great rancheria of San Xavier del Bac of these Sobaiporis [a part of the Pima nation] I heard the news that some soldiers had gone into the Pimeria of the west, and finding myself with so many Indians in this great valley, who were close to three thousand, and also in view of the many prayers of the natives that I should stay with them, I determined not to go farther. And from this great valley of San Xavier, by way of the Rio [Gila] westward as far as the Cocomaricopas and Yumas, and even to the Rio Colorado, as I desired, I tried to take and did take measures to find out whether the blue shells came from any other region than the opposite coast of California. . . .

During the seven days that we were here . . . we catechized the people and taught them the Christian doctrine every day, morning and afternoon. We killed six beeves of the three hundred they were tending for me here, with forty head of sheep and goats, and a small drove of mares. They also had a good field of wheat which was beginning to head; and during the following days they planted for the church a large field of maize, which they had previously cleared.

San Xavier obviously had been the site of a large Indian town before Padre Kino selected it for the location of a mission. He had first visited the area as early as 1692; and after establishing the Missions Guevavi and Tumacacori, it was inevitable that he would choose this ideal site for the most northerly of his missions, and one destined to survive long after his Dolores.

The "blue shells" he speaks of were of constant interest to him. He had seen such shells on the Pacific coast of Baja California, and if there were blue shells at San Xavier it surely meant that an overland contact with California was possible. It must be recalled that most Spaniards still thought that California was an island. Kino thought otherwise and was anxious to prove it part of the mainland and throw it open to colonization. The diary continues, and Kino gives us a graphic picture of the founding of the Mission San Xavier del Bac.

April 27. On the 27th they gave me five little ones to baptize. *April 28.* On the 28th we began the foundations of a very large and capacious church and house of San Xavier del Bac, all the people working with much pleasure and zeal, some in digging for the foundations, others in hauling many and very good stones of *tezontle* from a little hill which was about a quarter of a league away.

This hill is east of the mission and almost every twentieth-century visitor ascends it for the excellent view afforded of the area. The diary continues:

For the mortar of these foundations it was not necessary to haul water, because by means of the irrigation ditches we very easily conducted the water where we wished. And that house, with its great court and garden nearby, will be able to have throughout the year all the water it may need, running to any place or work-room one may please. . . . On the 29th we continued laying the foundations of the church and house.

On the 30th, at sunrise, various letters from Nuestra Señora de los Dolores were brought me by a courier of this Pimeria, who, it appeared, must have made the sixty leagues which intervenes in a day and a half and two nights. After mass I went down to the rancheria of San Cosme [Tucson], a three leagues' journey, and to that of San Agustin, two leagues farther, to see whether there were any sick, or little ones to baptize. At San Cosme they gave me six children to baptize, and one adult, a sick woman; and at San Agustin I baptized three more little ones. In the afternoon we returned to San Xavier del Bac, and at nightfall various justices arrived from the northwest and from Santa Catalina and from the Rio [Gila] and Casa Grande, among them being the captain and the governor of La Encarnacion, thirty-five leagues away. Immediately, and also at night, we had long talks, in the first place in regard to our holy faith, and in regard to the peace, and quietude, and love, and happiness of Christians, and they promised as we requested of them, to carry these good news and teachings to other rancherias and nations much farther on, to the Cocomaricopas, Yumas, etc. At the same time I made further and further inquiries as to whence came the blue shells, and all asserted that there were none in this nearest Sea of California, [the Gulf of California near the mouth of the Colorado River], but that they came from other lands more remote [meaning California's Pacific coast].

Padre Kino's diary makes a book of well over three hundred pages. But throughout he seems to have got along easily and happily with the Pima people, and most other native tribes, excepting, of course, the uncompromising and intractable Apaches.

On many of his numerous journeys he traveled alone. But the government of New Spain had sent soldiers to Mission Dolores, and in his travels Padre Kino was several times accompanied by Captain Juan Mateo Mange. It was with Captain Mange that the priest came upon the ruin of Casa Grande, and descended the Gila River to its confluence with the Colorado. During his twenty-four years in Pimeria Alta, the thousands of neophytes who were baptized can never be counted.

Kino did not live to see his dream of an overland road to California fulfilled. That project in economy and transportation had to wait for another half century. But he wrote a paper to prove that such a road was a possibility and that California, once and for all, was not an island.

Dr. Frank C. Lockwood of the University of Arizona has called Kino "a great Christian statesman," and it is an admirable summary. For, with all his dedication to the carrying of Catholicism to the pagan, he was at the same time a capable executive, administrator, and virtual benevolent dictator of the Gila country. Apparently nobody seems to know quite what he looked like. Self-effacement, even to physical characteristics, seemed to be part of his creed. But there is no gainsaying that the Pimas loved him and tried in their simple and childlike way to satisfy his every wish. When they discovered that he was interested in blue shells, they sent their best runners to trade for shells with all other Indian tribes who were friendly, and possibly even sent emissaries to the California coast. Without really wanting them, Kino found himself deluged with shells until he had, at Mission Dolores, a collection that was a veritable museum of conchology.

At the age of sixty-six, in 1711, Kino died at Magdalena in Sonora. He had been in good health and was suddenly stricken ill while saying Mass. Little can be gleaned of the man himself from his diary. The account tells what he did and how he did it, but reveals little of the inner man. For a picture of him the best image comes from his successor at Dolores, Padre Luis Velarde, who wrote:

Permit me to add what I observed in the eight years during which I was his companion. His conversation was of the mellifluous names of Jesus and Mary, and of the heathen for whom he was ever offering prayers to God. In saying his breviary he always wept. He was edified by the lives of the saints, whose virtues he preached to us. When he publicly reprimanded a sinner he was choleric. But if anyone showed him personal disrespect he controlled his temper to such an extent that he made it a habit to exalt whomsoever mistreated him by word, deed, or in writing. . . .

After supper, when he saw us already in bed, he would enter the church, and even though I sat up the whole night reading, I never heard him come out to get the sleep of which he was very sparing. One night I casually saw someone whipping him mercilessly [a curious masochistic side angle]. He always took his food without salt, and with mixtures of herbs which made it more distasteful. No one ever saw him in any vice whatsoever, for the discovery of lands and the conversion of souls had purified him.

He neither smoked nor took snuff, nor wine, nor slept in a bed. He was so austere that he never used wine except to celebrate Mass, nor had any other bed than the sweat blankets of his horse for a mattress. He never had more than two coarse shirts, because he gave everything as alms to the Indians. He was merciful to others but cruel to himself. While violent fevers were lacerating his body, he tried no remedy for six days except to get up to celebrate Mass and to go to bed again. And by thus weakening and dismaying nature he conquered the fevers. . . .

He died as he had lived, with extreme humility and poverty. In token of this, during his last illness he did not undress. His deathbed, as his bed had always been, consisted of two calf-skins for a mattress, two blankets such as Indians use for covers, and a pack-saddle for a pillow. When he was singing the Mass of the dedication [for a new chapel] he felt indisposed, and it seems that the Holy Apostle, to whom he was ever devoted, was calling him, in order that, being buried in his chapel, he might accompany him, as we believe, in glory.

And so died Eusebio Francisco Kino, Apostle to the Pimas. He brought his civilization and culture to the Gila Valley, he pushed back the frontier, and he made the first white settlement in Arizona. There can be no greater monument to his memory than the beautiful Mission San Xavier del Bac just nine miles south of old Tucson.

9

THE LOST BELLS OF TUMACACORI

IT WAS a lost age. Not only were the bells of Mission San José de Tumacacori mysteriously lost, but the spearhead of civilization that had penetrated the Gila watershed was all but withdrawn. This was the era from 1711, or the death of Padre Kino, up to the year 1767 when the entire cause of the Jesuits collapsed and was ruthlessly ended.

Kino's great vision had predicated a chain of missions from Dolores, by way of Tumacacori and San Xavier, to the Gila and down the Gila to the Colorado River, thence across California to the Pacific coast. He also wished to establish two or three connecting missions with the Hopi people in northern Arizona, who had been approached by Franciscan priests from the Rio Grande Valley. This dream never quite reached reality, although the Arizona-to-California part of it came close to fruition toward the end of the eighteenth century with the efforts of the Franciscans.

In a sense, the legend of the lost bells of Tumacacori symbolizes this half century—fifty-six years, to be exact—of decay. Several factors contributed to this period of decline, and the most important of them all was the absence of Padre Kino, and the failure of any of his followers even to begin to measure up to his ability. A second factor was the ever-present and constantly growing menace of the Apache Indians, who attacked, looted, stole, burned, and terrified other Indians just as much as they did the Spaniards. And a third factor was the government of New

83

Spain, which sent second- or third-rate men to occupy civil
offices in Sonora and Chihuahua, men who cared nothing about
the future of the country called Pimeria Alta but merely wished
to line their pockets and then get out.

The Apaches, of the Athapascan race, were newcomers among
the aborigines. The first of their kind began to drift down from
the north along with their cousins, the Navajos, about the year
1200. Ethnology cannot name the exact date; possibly they were
in Arizona as much as two hundred years earlier. But their
strength was negligible at first, and it was not until the sixteenth
century that they came into prominence. The Pueblo people were
terrified by them. The Apache was no Indian—he was a fiend in-
carnate. Stronger and more rugged than the Pueblo types, he
preyed first upon the Pueblo's food supplies, and then upon his
women. He was nomadic; he could survive physical conditions
and hardships that were incredible; and he could adapt himself
quickly to new conditions. Apaches were superb archers and very
skillful at close quarters with a knife. They had never seen a
horse or a mule until the Spaniards brought these animals into
the Southwest. And they had never seen firearms. Within one
generation they became excellent horsemen, learned to eat and
relish mule meat, and in good time became very handy with a
rifle. At times they would use a long lance, plunging it into a
victim with both hands while guiding a horse by their knees.
If pursued and outnumbered, an Apache would ride his horse
until it dropped, eat the flesh to sustain himself, and continue
his flight on foot. And as for captives, the cruelty of the Apache
was without equal. The lone Pima or Papago Indian, or the Spaniard, who was captured was lucky to be killed outright.
The Apaches were not interested in scalps. But they did like to
strip a victim, tie him spread-eagled to four stakes over an ant
hill, smear him with a kind of honey made from cactus, and

watch the ants devour him. Or the victim might be tied by his heels, naked, from the limb of a tree, and a fire built under his head. Then the braves would sing and dance about him—or her, sex making no difference—while the squaws cut and peeled long strips of skin from the writhing body. So it is plain to see that the Apaches soon earned for themselves quite a reputation, and an Apache raid struck terror into the hearts of other Indians and Spaniards alike.

After Kino's death, Padre Luis Velarde was the nominal leader of the church in Pimeria Alta. He had Kino's integrity, but not his physical strength, organizational ability, or his sharp intelligence.

A number of new priests were sent north from Mexico City. Many of these were Germans and they were, as the historian Hubert H. Bancroft put it, "more or less discouraged and disgusted." But at least these Germans tried to carry on what their Austrian prototype had begun.

Padre Ignacio Keller led a small expedition north from San Xavier to the Gila in 1743, but was attacked by Apaches, lost most of his horses and supplies, and several of his retinue. He retreated at once to San Xavier. The whir of Apache arrows was quite enough for Padre Keller. He never ventured north of San Xavier again.

Later in 1743 Padre Jacobo Sedelmair, who was in charge of Mission Tubutama in Sonora, led an expedition northward and reached the Gila. His plan was to establish at least one mission and a number of visitas between Casa Grande and the Yuma people who lived far downstream at the mouth of the Gila. He traversed the entire area and returned to Tubutama, but was summoned to Mexico City before he could begin any practical plans. Back again, in 1748, Padre Sedelmair tried once more, but ran into disinterest from a new generation of Pimas who had never known the great Kino, hostility from the Yumas, and open warfare from the Apaches. The whole missionary project seemed to be running into a stone wall.

For a time at Mission Guevavi the priest was Ignacio Pfefferkorn. Altogether he spent eleven years in the missions of Sonora and Pimeria Alta. He had no love for the land, the Indians, the flora, or the fauna—and often stated that he desired a "wider field." His one objective seemed to be to get himself transferred back to Mexico City. Years later, in 1795, at home in his native Germany, Pfefferkorn published a book called *A Description of Sonora*. While it was written with painstaking care, what the author had to say about the country was almost wholly derogatory.

The Jesuit control of the Gila Valley was definitely on the wane. The dominating power was the Apache Indians, and not one of them had ever been inside a church in his life except to loot it and set fire to it. Even the name Pimeria Alta was often referred to as Apacheria.

And not only were the Apaches taking over the valley, but even the Pima and the Papago peoples began to resent the exploitation of their labors by the church. Young Pimas who had never seen Kino resented men like Keller and Pfefferkorn. In 1751 the Pimas rebelled and stole all they could from San Xavier del Bac—vestments, ornaments, horses, cattle, foodstuffs—and disappeared into the desert. Under threats of Pimas, Papagos, and worst of all, Apaches, the few Spaniards retreated into Sonora, and for a year or more there was not a single white man within the Gila watershed. The missions San Xavier, Guevavi, and Tumacacori stood as abandoned monuments to a lost cause.

Then the Spaniards came back. And in 1752 they established a military garrison and a town called Tubac on the Santa Cruz River adjacent to the Mission San José de Tumacacori.

Soldiers, not priests, were now the spearhead. The garrison consisted of fifty armed men. No sooner was it functioning than the
Apaches attacked it. The garrison, needless to say, stayed within
its walls, and the Apaches continued to roam the Gila country at
will.

Nevertheless, the town of Tubac was not without importance.
The previous settlements had been missions and the populace,
apart from the priests and a few soldiers, had been entirely Indians. But to Tubac in 1752 came the first Spanish women
settlers to enter Arizona. Tubac can be called the first white
town in the Gila watershed. Had they come earlier, the Spanish
women might have effected a far stronger hold for Spain on the
area of Pimeria Alta. Somehow, it never seemed to occur to men
like Kino that there could never be a civilization of one sex,
and until the distaff side entered Arizona there had never been
any stronger claim on the land for Spain than the priest and
the soldier. With the few women of Tubac there came another
and even more important claim—the family and the home. The
significance of this is proved by the fact that never again, after
the influx of Spanish women in Arizona in 1752, was the area
"given back to the Indians."

In 1767, however, an event took place in Europe that
ended the Jesuit influence in the Gila Valley and in all of the
three Americas, North, South, and Central. And Pimeria Alta, such
as it existed, was virtually a Jesuit state, politically, economically,
and religiously. Carlos III of Spain had never heard of the Gila
River and could never have located it on a map. But his attack
on the Jesuit Order, pre-emptive as were many of his impetuous
acts, was the result of political peccadillos and greed and graft
and corruption, coupled with the inflated ambitions of some of
the key men among the Jesuits in Europe.. As I have stated in a
book on California called *The Royal Highway*, "This Society of

Jesus was getting out of hand and was just a little too powerful within the Catholic Church. Most Royal Confessors were Jesuits; therefore, they had all the inside information and used it to their own advantage. The rise of deism as a philosophy in Europe after 1750 was definitely anti-Jesuit; men such as Voltaire and Diderot, the intellectualists, united with Pascal and the Jansenists to obliterate the Jesuit Order. They didn't quite do it, but they did rock the society to its very foundations." And the reverberations carried all the way from Paris, Madrid, and Rome to San Xavier, Guevavi, and Tumacacori.

Thus, with one stroke of a pen in 1767, Carlos III put a stop to the Jesuit influence in Arizona. Throughout the Americas the Jesuit priests were placed under arrest and sent to Vera Cruz, later to Europe, and their personal property was confiscated. It was unjust and unfair to the men who were valiantly striving to bring Christianity to the heathens of the Gila country, but it was a royal order, coming from Madrid, and there could be no appeal. All of Padre Kino's efforts of a half century or so earlier came to naught. Or at least so it appeared at the time to Padre Alonso Espinosa, who was officiating at Mission San Xavier, and to Padre Rafael Diaz, who was in charge of Mission Guevavi in 1767. Mission San José de Tumacacori was technically a visita of Mission Guevavi; but the distinction meant little, for if the priest was at Tumacacori then Tumacacori was the mission and Guevavi the visita. The priest didn't follow the mission; the mission followed the priest.

The legend of the lost bells of Tumacacori goes back to 1767, and, being a good legend, goes back another three hundred years to 1467, or at least to some date prior to 1492 and the advent of Christopher Columbus on these American shores called India by him.

Since it is merely a legend, it has never been accepted by historians.

Padres Alonso Espinosa and Rafael Diaz were forced to leave the Gila watershed with the expulsion of their Jesuit Order. But in their breasts was hope. It is a human quality and without it man's life would be the poorer. Their hope was to return to their labors. But they knew that in their absence the mission buildings would be robbed by the no longer friendly Pimas and Papagos and might well be razed by the vicious Apaches. So they gave away everything of monetary value to placate the Indians and left little but the mission buildings themselves still standing. One feature, however, was a treasure they could not carry away, or give away, or bear to leave behind to be despoiled. These were the bells of Tumacacori.

These bells were cast (this is the legend, be warned) in the late fifteenth century sometime before Columbus sailed from Palos, Spain, to seek India across the Atlantic Ocean. How they were brought to New Spain, and when, and how they got to Tumacacori, the legend never tells. But there were four of these bells, ringing never in unison, but in a melodious foursome chime. Obviously the ousted priests could not carry these burdensome treasures along with themselves to their Jesuit exile. And they did not want to leave them behind to be destroyed by Apache vandals. So the last service performed at Mission San José de Tumacacori consisted of the dismantling of the belfry by Padres Espinosa and Diaz.

These two priests, with no neophytes to assist (so that no neophytes would be aware of what was going on), carried the four bells far out into the desert, and there they buried them. Carefully they memorized the location and all the salient landmarks. The four bells were buried deep in the heavy sandy soil, amid the greasewood, east to west—or was it north to south?—so that they were in the order of their chimes. Then the two priests returned to Mission Tumacacori, blessed it for the last time, and turned their heads toward New Spain and the south and marched away to their ultimate exile. They never returned. And only they knew the location of the bells.

The search for these lost bells has gone on for years. Indubitably the legend has some margin of truth; for Tumacacori obviously had a belfry, and in it, obviously again, there must have been four bells. But the bells are not there today. But—and here's the neat little rub—the bells still *ring*!

Many people have believed this legend. More than a few times a clue has turned up purporting to indicate the location of the bells far out on the desert. The clue consists of the story told by generations of Indians who knew the burial place in spite of the precautions of the padres, but who respected the secret and never violated it. Or, from time to time, some old piece of parchment long hidden in the burned bricks of the mission's walls will be found and will indicate (in secret and unreadable code, of course) the location of the missing bells. Or, a heat-crazed, dying prospector will stagger in from the desert and in his delirium will tell of finding not silver or gold but four superb bells buried beneath the ground. Then the old prospector conveniently dies, and the place where he saw the bells can never be found.

The legend has even been debased to the extent that somebody "found" an old map that showed exactly where to dig for the bells. When this document was followed with extreme care, the first spadeful of earth hit a metal object. The searchers were panting for breath, and went on digging with both fury and excitement—and unearthed an old iron bucket which had been planted at that spot, while the pranksters, watching from behind the juniper or the greasewood, howled with glee.

But in spite of padres or pranksters, or treasure seekers or tourists, or scholars or skeptics, there is only one test. Go to the Mission San José de Tumacacori tomorrow night—or any night—and stroll carefully and quietly across the desert, in the Stygian blackness or in the bright moonlight (it matters not), and if you are perceptive, and sensitive, and imaginative, you will hear the chimes of the lost bells of Tumacacori. There will be no doubt about it. The chimes ring one, three, two, four; and then, four, two, three, one. If you don't believe it, listen again. Softly now —and then—hark—you'll hear it:

> One, three, two, four;
> Four, two, three, one.

You don't believe it? Well—that's what the legend says. Go to Tumacacori and test it some quiet desert night, and perhaps . . .

10

BY THE ORDER OF ST. FRANCIS

THE APACHES, several hundred strong, wearing war paint on their nearly naked bodies, danced and whooped and howled and sang and watched the building burn—at least all parts of it that were combustible. They were destroying Mission San Xavier del Bac and they left nothing standing but the charred walls. It was an extremely successful Apache party held in the year 1768.

Because of the edict of Carlos III issued the year before,

there wasn't a Jesuit priest left in Arizona. And the only Spaniards present were the fifty soldiers and their wives and the
sprinkling of civilians at the small garrison and tiny town of
Tubac, forty-five miles away. The soldiers didn't know that
the Apaches were sacking Mission San Xavier, and if they had
known it is most likely that they would have remained within
their garrison walls, and continued to divert themselves by playing
cards or making love; and had a sergeant reported to the comandante, "The Apaches are sacking San Xavier!" the comandante's reaction might well and wisely have been, "Let 'em sack."
The Spanish garrison, as long as it stayed within its walls, was
secure. "Now whose ace was that?" the comandante asked the
dealer. And the sergeant saluted and returned to his quarters.

This implied indifference on the part of the garrison
is hardly a criticism. If the fifty soldiers had ridden the forty-
five miles north to San Xavier, the Apache scouts would long
have known of their coming and the company would have been
ambushed. Or, the soldiers would have arrived to find San Xavier
merely a few walls and hot ashes and not an Apache in sight.
And when they returned, tired and exhausted, to Tubac after a
ride of ninety miles, they might well have found that other
Apaches had attacked the empty garrison and the small civilian
population and had murdered all the men and carried off the
women. It was the better part of valor to remain fifty strong in
an armed camp and while away the time by playing cards than
to make the great mistake of trying to play the Apache's own
game. The odds were ten to one in his favor.

Far to the south in New Spain, at Queretaro, there was a college of the Franciscans. With the expulsion of the Jesuits, the
Franciscans were permitted and encouraged to take over the labor
of carrying Christianity to the wild frontier. Where the black-
robed Jesuits had trod in sandaled feet, there followed the

brown-robed Franciscans, also in sandaled feet, but more often, like Kino, on horseback. Two of the greatest names among the men of this Order were contemporaries: Padre Junipero Serra, in California, and Padre Francisco Tomas Hermenegildo Garces, in Arizona. Without the loyalty, fortitude, strength, devotion, and intelligence of these two men Spain might never have been able to hold California and Arizona for the period of time that she did.

Garces was born in the province of Aragon, Spain, on April 12, 1738. On June 30, 1768, at the age of thirty, he arrived at the burned-out shell of Mission San Xavier del Bac. It was his job to "pick up the pieces," so to speak, and try to revive Catholicism in the Gila watershed. Like Kino, he was able to win the friendship and loyalty of the Pimas and Papagos, and in spite of constant Apache threats the mission was slowly rebuilt, and the construction carried on until 1797, when the building was completed and looked then exactly as it does today. After 1768 San Xavier was Garces' headquarters for eight years.

At this time New Spain had a sorely needed renascence of capable and intelligent leaders in both church and state. Viceroy Francisco de Croix and Visitor-General José de Galvez were both men of ability and vision; and their two leaders in the field, General Gaspar de Portola and Padre Junipero Serra, successfully explored and settled California.

In Arizona, the outstanding man, apart from Padre Garces, was Juan Bautista de Anza. He was given command of the garrison at Tubac and he was a happy choice. In the first place, Anza had been born in Pimeria Alta, had been well educated in Mexico City, and returned to the land of his birth. His father had been killed in battle with the Apaches, and the young Anza was schooled in the problems of the frontier from childhood.

In order to get a firsthand report on New Spain's difficult outpost, the viceroy sent a gentleman with the un-Spanish name of

Hugo Oconor to look over the land and make recommendations. Inspector Oconor arrived in 1775 and quickly saw that the small garrison at Tubac was inadequate to meet the Apache menace. He recommended its removal to a point north of San Xavier by nine miles at the very spot used by Apaches to assemble for their depredations, and he further recommended doubling the size of the garrison. This move was made within a year. Nine miles north of San Xavier Padre Kino had long ago established the visita of San Cosme del Tucson, and not far beyond, another visita called San Agustin, both on the Gila's tributary Santa Cruz. Tubac remained as a civilian settlement, and the army, not doubled but at least increased to seventy-five men, established itself in a new garrison between the two former visitas. The place was called Tucson from a Pima word meaning Place Where the Water Is Dark, or Land of the Dark Spring. The correct pronunciation in English is too-sahn with very nearly equal accent on both syllables. The Indian word cannot be spelled in English, but the nearest approximation is Stjukshon. The city today is Arizona's second in size and is unquestionably one of the most attractive small cities in the United States. Its founding dates from 1776, when it became a walled garrison and town at the instigation of Hugo Oconor.

Thus the Spanish spearhead into the Gila area was pushed well down the Santa Cruz Valley. During these years, 1768 to 1776, Padre Garces was winning back the loyalty of the Pimas and the Papagos, and religious and economic progress, at least in a European sense, were the order of the times.

Viceroy Francisco de Croix was followed by a man of even greater vision. He was Antonio de Bucareli. Viceroy de Croix had been able to seize and hold California by coastal and overland expeditions up the Royal Highway from Loreto in Baja California to an area just beyond San Francisco Bay. Viceroy Bucareli wanted to clinch that control by an all-overland road from Mexico City via Arizona to the Golden Gate.

This idea was met with unbounded enthusiasm from Padre Junipero Serra of the Franciscan missions of California and Padre Tomas Garces of the Franciscan missions of Pimeria Alta. And it struck fire with Juan Bautista de Anza, who visualized a thriving civilization for the Gila Valley, the obvious keystone of this great projected land route.

Padre Garces, from his base at San Xavier, had made three exploratory excursions prior to the Bucareli-backed and Anza-executed California expedition. He had made two trips—entradas in Spanish (a word which seems more accurate without translation) —from San Xavier to the Gila River in the vicinity of Casa Grande. He explored the Gila Valley both east and west with an eye to good sites for future missions. Then, in 1771, he went again to the Gila and followed its course to its mouth. He met the Yuma people for the first time at the confluence of the Gila with the Colorado. And he returned by the way he had come, back up the Gila Valley to the Santa Cruz and up the Santa Cruz to San Xavier. Thus it is plain that Garces was familiar with the terrain before 1774 when the first attempt to reach California by an overland route was launched.

For his first California expedition Captain Juan Bautista de Anza was in command of thirty-four men. The group assembled not at Tucson, which was not yet a garrison in January of 1774, but at Tubac. With them went Padre Tomas Garces and Padre Juan Diaz, one Indian guide, 65 cattle and 140 horses. In spite of the fact that Padre Garces had roamed the Gila Valley on three previous entradas, either alone or with one or two Pima Indians, the first Anza expedition decided to steer clear of the Apache country. They went south in the general direction of

Padre Kino's then abandoned Mission Dolores, rested at Mission Caborca, and proceeded westerly through what is now northern Sonora, approximating the present international border between the United States and Mexico. This route later became known to pioneers and gold seekers as El Camino del Diablo, or the Devil's Highway. Padre Kino had been over it a number of times about a century earlier, but as an avenue to the west it was fraught with danger, lacked water, and crossed several ranges of desert mountains. But it avoided the Apaches, and that was at least a partial guarantee that the party would get through. Reaching the desert plain below what is the present town of Yuma, the party moved north to the junction of the Gila with the Colorado River.

For several days they camped on the banks of the Gila, waiting for the return of the chief of the Yumas, who was away on a hunting trip. At length he arrived. His name, to the Spaniards at least, was Captain Palma. He is an important figure in the Spanish history of the lower Gila River and apparently was a high type of aborigine, although inclined to be at times volatile, and occasionally unpredictable. But he professed a great interest and devotion to the Spaniards; and Anza, professing great interest and devotion to the Yumas, made him a present of a silver medal bearing a likeness of King Carlos III, dangling from a red cord, and himself placed it around the chief's neck. Anza and Palma then embraced, the Franciscan priests blessed the event, and a hundred staring Yuma Indians looked on in a mixture of awe, wonder, and skepticism. Anza was not without an ax to grind—for obviously these Yumas, living at the strategic junction of the Gila and the Colorado, could control, if they wished, this only overland route to California. And Palma was not without an ax to grind—for obviously these foreigners, with their strength in arms, could, if they wished, attack and even subjugate the Yuma nation. So all was love and medals and embraces and kisses on the part of both sides—for the time being.

Anza left some of his supplies and animals with Captain Palma, and the Spaniards crossed the Colorado River by a ford known to the Yumas. This crossing could be used only at low water and was the result of a series of sand bars just above the mouth of the Gila. The Anza party made it successfully on February 9, 1774, and on March 22 of that year they arrived at Mission San Gabriel in southern California not far from the present city of Los Angeles.

It was a momentous meeting. Padre Junipero Serra was there to 'greet this first overland expedition to reach California from New Spain. Anza went on north to Monterey, California's tiny capital, and at long last the road from Mexico City to the Bay of Monterey had been traversed. Padre Garces returned from Mission San Gabriel to the mouth of the Gila. The Franciscans in California had things well in hand, and Garces was more interested in Arizona and the Gila Valley, his own chosen field, than in California. He made a number of exploratory trips up and down the Colorado River while waiting for Anza's return to the Gila, the Yumas and Captain Palma. It was May before Anza got back from Monterey and, as always in the spring, the Colorado was at high water. The ford being impracticable, Palma had his Yumas construct rafts to ferry the Spaniards across to Garces' camp on the Gila. Again there were embraces and jubilation and protestations of undying friendship between the Indians and the Spaniards. Hardly anywhere in history can there be found examples of these two races getting along so well together. It was all one happy family, and it was all too good to last, as history eventually proved.

Good-byes were said again—adiós in this case—and pledges were reiterated and Palma and his Yumas watched Anza depart,

the party being led by Garces up the Gila's south bank. Garces now knew the main portion of the Gila Valley like the palm of his hand. He led Anza upstream and easterly across Arizona, around the Gila's great bend, and on to the point where the Santa Cruz came in, not far from the modern city of Phoenix. All Anza had to do then was to follow the Santa Cruz upstream until he came to Mission San Xavier, and eventually back to his starting place—Tubac. Leaving Anza to complete his last lap, Garces turned north, alone, and braving any hostile forces, particularly Apaches, made a long journey through central Arizona, exploring a great deal of the northern Gila watershed, and unquestionably noting such tributaries as the Hassayampa, the Verde, and the Tonto. It was July 10 before he got back to San Xavier. He had been gone six months, during the last two of which he was alone in a wild and difficult country; he had survived on Indian food, and he estimated that he had baptized twenty-four thousand souls. And he had never been happier in his life.

Things were now looking up for all of Arizona and California. Anza made a trip to Mexico City to report to Viceroy Bucareli the success of the California project. All was enthusiasm and plans for a second expedition were immediately laid. This would be a colonizing and not an exploratory party. Together Anza and Garces had cracked the frontier, and Anza was made a lieutenant colonel.

The second Anza expedition was a minor version of the Coronado safari of the sixteenth century, and while it was not quite so large a group as the would-be conquerors of Cibola, and while its purpose was not loot but the founding of a colony at the Golden Gate to be called Yerba Buena and later San Francisco, it was second only to the Coronado junket in ambition and size. It was made up of about two hundred men and forty-five women, and three of the women gave birth to babies on the way. Garces accompanied the party, which set out from Tubac on October 23, 1775. With Garces were Padre Tomas Eixarch and six servants. This group was to remain at the confluence of the Gila with the Colorado while the main party went on to San Francisco Bay. The official chaplain of the party was Padre Pedro Font, who, of course, remained with it all the way to its destination. The expedition traveled leisurely down the Gila Valley, was made welcome by Captain Palma and the Yumas, crossed the Colorado River and successfully continued its march over deserts and mountains to San Gabriel and up the Royal Highway to the south portal of California's Golden Gate. These were the people who created San Francisco.

Padre Garces and Eixarch remained at the mouth of the Gila. But with Eixarch to continue missionary work among the amenable Yumas, Garces was eager to seek other and more challenging fields. He made his fifth and greatest entrada in 1776 and he visited Indians from the Mojave Desert in California to the Painted Desert in Arizona. Everywhere he was hospitably received until he reached the Hopi people at Oraibi. On his way he discovered the Havasupai Indians deep in their land of the sky blue water in Cataract Canyon, he skirted the south rim of the Grand Canyon and wrote accurately about it in his diary. His travels, on foot or on horseback and often on muleback, and his intelligent writings have been studied and painstakingly translated by Elliott Coues in a book called *On the Trail of a Spanish Pioneer*. It is Arizona literature.

How Padre Garces could survive the hardships of this raw country for weeks and months at a time is in itself a minor miracle. Even some of his compatriots in the Franciscan cause marveled at his achievements. Padre Pedro Font, who was a man who enjoyed his comfort and his ease along with his religion, wrote of Garces with honest amazement:

Padre Garces is so fit to go along with Indians, and go about among them, that he seems just like an Indian himself. He shows in everything the coolness of the Indian; he squats cross-legged in a circle with them, or at night around the fire, for two or three hours or even longer, all absorbed, forgetting aught else, discoursing to them with great serenity and deliberation; and though the food of the Indians is as nasty and disgusting as their dirty selves, the padre eats it with great gusto, and says that it is appetizing, and very nice. In fine, God has created him, I am sure, totally on purpose to hunt up these unhappy, ignorant and boorish people.

It is rather obvious from the tone of Padre Font's words about Garces that Padre Font much preferred the seclusion of a mission, a good meal and perhaps a bottle of wine; and if the Indians had to wait for him to beat the trackless mountains and deserts to Christianize them, they could jolly well stay heathens until hell caught up with them.

But the Hopi Indians would have nothing to do with Garces and Christianity. They had had quite enough of that a hundred years earlier when priests from the Rio Grande Valley in New Mexico had arrived to bring them the light; and with the priests came a few Spanish soldiers who promptly seduced, or possibly raped, a few Hopi girls. The Hopi has always been very protective of his women. The result was that priests and soldiers were slain, and the Hopi would have no relations with the white race after 1680. For once, the efforts of Padre Garces were in vain, and he returned to the Gila Valley, and at last to San Xavier del Bac.

By this time Anza was back from his second successful California expedition. San Francisco had been founded. He met his Yuma friend, Captain Palma, and he took him to Mexico City to meet the viceroy. Apparently Palma was well received in the capital of New Spain and thoroughly enjoyed himself. He was promised mission settlements and education for his people. Upon his return he brought great expectations to the Yumas. Unfortunately this led to eventual disaster. And Palma himself was mistrusted by other tribal authorities, who considered that he had "gone white" by too great a margin. It is not exactly clear why New Spain failed to follow up its advantages with the Yumas at the extremely strategic junction of the Gila and Colorado rivers. One reason may have been the untimely death of Viceroy Bucareli in 1779 of pleurisy. Had he lived, all might have been different. Another cause may have been the transfer of the capable Anza from the Gila watershed to the Rio Grande Valley in New Mexico. Historian Hubert H. Bancroft, groping for an answer, describes it as follows:

Yet for various reasons, including the departure of Anza for New Mexico, the Apache warfare and the consequent difficulty in obtaining men and money, and divers controversies in Mexico, nothing whatever was done for three years. Then Garces went again to the Colorado in 1779, and was soon joined by another friar and a guard of twelve soldiers. Meanwhile the Yumas had become tired of waiting and were disgusted by the petty nature of the mission enterprise in comparison with promises of the past; other tribes were hostile to the Yumas; and Palma had lost something of his authority. In 1780 the formal founding of two mission pueblos was ordered; but the idea of a presidio was abandoned, and a new system was devised, under which each mission was to have ten soldiers and ten settlers. Friars and officials qualified to judge in the matter protested against the system as suicidal, and the result fully justified their fears.

The two missions founded by Garces were both on the California side of the Colorado River: one was directly across from the mouth of the Gila and the other was eight miles downstream on the Colorado. It must be noted that seemingly in the interest

of economy, the Spanish tried to make these two institutions com-
ɔinations of mission, garrison, and settlement, all rolled into one.
The plan failed to work.

Padre Garces called the first one, opposite the Gila, Misión y Pueblo de la Purisima Concepción de la Virgén Santisima,
or Mission and Town of the Immaculate Conception of the Most
Holy Virgin; and the second was the Misión y Pueblo de San
Pedro y San Pablo de Bicuner—Mission and Town of St. Peter
and St. Paul of Bicuner.

Thus there were present soldiers, colonists, and priests, with
the soldiers and the colonists in the majority and making free
use of the Yumas' land. With the Spaniards came their wives
and children. These people had no understanding of the Indians. They expected the Yumas to move out and make way for
them. Captain Palma tried to keep peace and only lost further
authority over his people. Trouble was brewing along the lower
Gila and Garces and his colleagues knew it, but there was little
they could do about it.

The crisis came in June of 1781 with the arrival of Captain
Rivera y Moncada and about forty soldiers. These men had
never seen the Yumas before and cared not a whoop about them.
Indians were simply dirty Indians to Captain Rivera y Moncada.
His was an attitude not unlike that of Padre Pedro Font, except that the officer brandished openly his contempt and superi-
ority. His horses being exhausted, he took the Yumas' horses without so much as a request. When a few Indians came forward
and tried to retrieve their animals, Captain Rivera y Moncada
accused them of trying to steal them (their own animals!) and
had the Indians brutally horsewhipped.

That was the breaking point for the Yumas. Ignoring their
chief, Captain Palma, the young bucks planned an attack on both
the soldiers' camp and the pueblo-missions simultaneously. The cli-

max came on July 17, 1781. So skillful were the preparations and so obtuse were the Spaniards, that every Spanish soldier and male settler was killed, not overlooking Captain Rivera y Moncada whose hacked and beaten body was hurled into the Gila River. All the women and children were taken prisoners. The Mission San Pedro and San Pablo was entirely destroyed and the two Franciscans, Padres Juan Diaz and Matias Moreno, were killed. At Purisima Concepción the assailants spared Padre Garces and his fellow Franciscan, Padre Antonio Barraneche, for twenty-four hours. This may have been done at the command of Captain Palma, although he unfortunately was no longer able to exercise authority over his people.

But on July 18, 1781, the now bloodthirsty and irresponsible warriors attacked Purisima Concepción anew, sacked and burned it, and beat Padres Garces and Barraneche to death with clubs.

There wasn't a Spanish soldier, priest, or settler left. The women and children, however, were spared, held as prisoners, and forced to work for the Yumas. The story is told that Captain Palma wept as he held the body of Padre Garces in his arms. This may or may not be true. It is a pleasant sentimental thought. But the mind and emotions of the Indian are often inscrutable to the white man and the story of Palma's tears may be wholly apocryphal.

So died the second great Christian priest of Pimeria Alta. It may be that Garces welcomed martyrdom as the supreme peak of self-abnegation and service. For the greatest religious leader ahead of him in Arizona, Padre Kino, be it remembered, used to order others to lash him with whips. Kino's masochism never reached the fulfillment of martyrdom. Garces, although it may be totally unfair to call him, psychiatrically, a masochist, did, nevertheless, achieve the masochistic ideal—a painful and violent death in the service of God.

But it is far more pleasant to remember this outstanding Christian in the light of his efforts rather than his cruel end. Francisco Tomas Garces was a little man with a great soul. The details that he preached and the methods that he used and his personal beliefs have nothing to do with this conclusion. Had he been born a Hindu or a Jew he would have preached differently, but he still would have had a great soul.

Before leaving Garces to the history of the Gila River, it seems fitting to quote the man who has been the outstanding student of the Franciscan's career. In his introduction to his translation of Garces' diary, Elliott Coues wrote:

If we follow Garces in his adventures, we shall learn much, and among other things to love the character of the man. Garces was a true soldier of the cross, neither greater nor lesser than thousands of other children of the church, seeking the bubble of salvation at the price of the martyr's crown; his was not his own life, but that of God who gave it. Better than all that, perhaps, this humble priest, like Abou Ben Adhem, was one who loved his fellow men. It made him sick at heart to see so many of them going to hell for lack of the three drops of water he would sprinkle over them if they would let him do so. I repeat it—Garces, like Jesus, so loved his fellow men that he was ready to die for them. What more could a man do—and what were danger, suffering, hardship, privation, in comparison with the glorious reward of labor in the vineyard of the Lord? This is true religion, of whatever sect or denomination, called by whatever name.

With the death of Garces and the absence of Anza, and a new viceroy in Mexico City, the fortunes of the Gila Valley changed again. A punitive expedition was sent to wipe out the Yuma Indians. It arrived almost a year after the bloody uprising of 1781. After more pointless fighting the Yumas were defeated and the Spanish women and children released from bondage.

But the Yumas were never entirely subdued and the value of the
land route to California was lost and then virtually abandoned.
The long-decaying Spanish Empire was rotting from within. The
trouble was not in the Gila Valley or in Mexico City, but in
Madrid. From the death of Garces up to 1821, or up to the
Mexican independence, the history of the Gila River and of all
Arizona is meager. It was a land where nothing happened. The
Apaches continued to run wild; all efforts to Christianize and
colonize the lower Gila were abandoned. The only settlers re-
maining were those at Tubac and Tucson. Missions San Xavier
and Tumacacori kept the spark of Christianity alive. Mission
Guevavi went to ruin in 1784 and only traces of it, as in the case of
Dolores, can be seen today.

Tucson was a walled city and counted itself lucky to be so.
It was a town of adobe mud buildings housing five hundred
timid inhabitants made up mostly of the garrison and the wives
and children of the soldiers. In the mountains of the Gila watershed there were inestimable riches in minerals, and the soil was
productive and ready for planting or the support of cattle. But
the citizens of Tucson scarcely dared venture forth from their
city's walls. The reason—Apaches.

In 1821 came the revolution, and the Mexican Empire
was carved out of the dying body of the once-great Spanish Empire. The emperor of Mexico was one Agustin Iturbide, a Creole
opportunist and upstart who fancied himself another Napoleon.
Almost before this change of government was heard of in far-
distant Tucson, there was another revolution in Mexico City and
his Highness Agustin I was promptly and summarily executed by a firing squad. The Republic of Mexico was then born,
and the long-unstable political circus that was called Mexican government began. It enjoyed seventeen revolutions in the next
twenty-five years. Nobody in Tubac or Tucson knew who gov-

erned what. It was the nadir of Spanish civilization and culture.

But something new was coming. In spite of the fact that the Gila Valley was no longer Spanish, but was Mexican, and in spite of the fact that the Apaches considered all the area their own, things were happening toward the east.

The Santa Fe trail had been opened, and tall, fair, blue-eyed men had reached the Rio Grande Valley, coming all the way from the Mississippi and the Missouri. Some of them wondered what lay beyond New Mexico to the west. Some of them decided to see. . . .

PART 3

Mexico Casts the Play

1821 to 1856

11

THE INTERLOPERS

"INTERLOPER—ONE who thrusts himself into a place without right, or one who traffics in trade legally belonging to others. In other words," completed the governor of New Mexico at Santa Fe—"Americans."

Governor Manuel Armijo was not exactly contemptuous toward the few Americans he met, but he simply didn't like them or approve of them. The vanguard of Americans moving west didn't know about and were not interested in international boundaries. Most of these men were rough and tough; some couldn't read or write. But all were men of daring and courage, perfectly capable of coming to grips with a grizzly bear, ruthless in their aims as the Apaches, able to live by the rifle in any wilderness, and totally unconcerned about whose land they were trespassing.

After the culmination of the Louisiana Purchase in 1803 the United States suddenly found itself doubled in size. And the western frontier was no longer the Mississippi but the Rocky Mountains. The white men in this huge area were almost exclusively trappers. The western boundary of the Louisiana Purchase was perfectly plain—on paper. But it had never been surveyed and nobody could say for a certainty, beyond the indefinite "west to the Rockies," just where American claims ended and Spanish soil began. The trapper didn't care. Men such as Bill Williams, Ewing Young, James Pattie, Pauline Weaver, Jedediah Smith, and Kit Carson were at home in the wild West, and if some fine pelts were to be taken and a small fortune made in furs, it was "just too damn bad" if they were beyond the hypothetical border of the Louisiana Purchase. Who the hell were these Spaniards anyway? The attitude of the burly tobacco-juice spitting mountain-man was not conducive to the creation of international friendship.

But Washington was deeply interested in its new acquisition. Second only to the famous Lewis and Clark Expedition of 1804–1806 was that of Zebulon Montgomery Pike. Major Pike and his party moved west up the Arkansas River to the Rockies, and then south into New Mexico and arrived in Santa Fe with fifteen soldiers on March 3, 1807. Pike was definitely beyond the borders of the United States but he either winked at this intrusion or pretended that he had arrived without intention of invasion but merely exploration. Since no expedition had preceded his, it was inevitable that he might have strayed into Mexican territory. But he "strayed in" a mighty long way and the governor of New Mexico in Santa Fe (which included Arizona) didn't like it.

In his book, published in Philadelphia in 1810, Pike recounts his conversation with Governor Joaquin Alencaster, who kept him waiting a long time before receiving him, and the tenor of the talk makes it worth quoting briefly. Pike could not speak Spanish and the governor could not speak English, but both were men of education and both could speak French. The following is Pike's version:

Governor: Do you speak French?
Pike: Yes, sir.
Governor: You come to reconnoiter our country, do you?
Pike: I marched in to reconnoiter our own.

Governor: In what character are you?

Pike: In my proper character, an officer of the United States Army.

. . . . . .

Governor: How many men have you?

Pike: Fifteen.

Governor: When did you leave St. Louis?

Pike: Fifteenth of July.

Governor: I think you marched in June.

Pike: No, sir!

Governor: Well . . . come here at seven o'clock and bring your papers.

The tone does not augur well for a long-standing friendship. But Pike behaved like a gentleman and the governor's coolness lifted considerably. With true Spanish courtesy he invited the American major to dinner. There, as Pike tells it, conditions became more agreeable.

The dinner at the governor's was rather splendid, having a variety of dishes and wines of the southern provinces, and when his Excellency was a little warmed with the influence of cheering liquor he became very sociable.

But the Spaniard's parting adiós that night to Pike was the cryptic "Remember Alencaster, in peace or war." And the following day he refused to let Pike and his men return by the route they had come. He insisted that Pike would have to travel down the Rio Grande Valley to El Paso and on into Chihuahua and report to General Salcedo, commander in chief of the army of New Spain. Pike had no alternative but to accede to what amounted to the governor's orders. He left under protest, but saw a lot more of the Spanish territory than he originally intended. And he learned that not far to the west, in south-central New

Mexico, in the Mogollon Mountains which were plainly visible before he reached El Paso, were the headwaters of a great river which flowed west all the way to California. Pike never saw the Gila, but he learned of its existence and he understood that if an army needed to do so it could ascend the Arkansas, invade New Mexico from Colorado as he had done, take Santa Fe (as he had not), and bisect all of Arizona by descending the Gila to California. It was something to think about—just in case . . .

In the Mexican state of Chihuahua, Pike was formally and courteously received, his papers confiscated, and sent home by way of the lower Rio Grande River and Texas into Louisiana. The journey had no further international significance, but Washington at least learned of a way west to the Pacific. And it was unquestionably the first time that Washington knew that the Gila River existed. And Pike added a subtitle to his book which was called rather inaccurately *Sources of the Mississippi and Through the Western Parts of Louisiana,* and the subtitle was *And a Tour Through the Interior Parts of New Spain in the Year 1807.*

Following the advent of Pike, who merely learned of the river's existence, it is impossible to say for a certainty exactly who was the first American to see the Gila. It may have been the boastful and somewhat baleful egoist, James Ohio Pattie. He and his father, Sylvester, were in New Mexico in 1824, and with a party of trappers came upon the Gila northwest of the present town of Silver City, New Mexico. There is a good likelihood that this group can safely be called the American spearhead.

These so-called "mountainmen," who were the first American civilians to reach the Gila Valley, left no permanent settlements. They brought no women, although a number of them took Indian wives. For the most part they were illegal entrants to a nation not their own and they cared not a hoot about that fact. No Mexicans could tell them anything short of the muzzle of a gun, and any Mexican with a gun better not be bluffing or he'd get a bullet through his chest in a hurry. These men left scant records. In a sense, however, they were the movers and the shakers between the years 1824 and 1846. A lot more would be known about them had one of their number been a writer. But most of them had very likely never so much as read any books in their extroverted lives. They came into the Gila Valley from its headwaters, and they trapped beaver and otter up and down the Gila, and its tributaries, the Salt, the Verde, the San Francisco, and the San Pedro.

From Pike's expedition up to 1822 only a few Americans arrived at Santa Fe. Those who had any merchandise sold it at an immense profit. The result was the opening of the Santa Fe Trail from Independence, Missouri, to New Mexico's capital city, in 1822. The governors at Santa Fe .charged an ad valorem duty on such goods, and the money went, almost without exception, into their own pockets, since these derechos de arancel (tariffs, and nothing else) were assessed by the governors at whatever rate they thought they could get without too much protest. Five hundred dollars a wagon was average. After that precedent was established there is no record of any New Mexican governor resenting the arrival of a caravan of goods from Missouri. And you can be well assured that the men from Missouri weren't losing a dime either. Economics, not romance, created the Santa Fe Trail.

One of those who came overland was James Ohio Pattie of Kentucky. With him came his father, Sylvester Pattie, and their objective was trapping for furs and possible trade with the natives and Indians. The two Patties arrived at Taos with a caravan in 1824, and then proceeded down the Rio Grande to Santa Fe, arriving in the capital city on November 25.

For the next six years the younger Pattie covered an immense amount of ground from the Rio Grande Valley and the Gila Valley to such distant spots as Mexico City and the Russian colony fifty miles north of California's Golden Gate. He seems to have had a finger in everything that was going on from revolutions and vaccinations to the rescuing of imprisoned maidens, and the exaggerations of his story are mountainous. Nevertheless, his account of his six years in the West is based on truth, regardless of the fantastic superstructure, and what he had to narrate was of immense interest to the eastern public, who wanted to know all about the West. Pattie's story made a best seller of its day, but Pattie, of course, didn't write it. He "recalled" it and the book was ghostwritten by its "editor," who was Timothy Flint of Cincinnati. *The Personal Narrative of James O. Pattie of Kentucky* was published in 1831, in Cincinnati, and is one of the most curious and spurious pieces of frontier literature.

Pattie made an effort to get permission from Mexican authorities to trap beaver in Arizona. His own account (or editor Flint's by reflected light) offers some vivid pictures of life along the Gila in the late 1820's. At Santa Fe he approached the governor, and tells it thus:

We asked the governor for permission to trap beaver in the river Helay [the Gila]. His reply was that, he did not know if he was allowed by the law to do so; but if upon examination it lay in his power, he would inform us on the morrow. Accordingly, to this request, we went to the place appointed the succeeding day. . . . We were told by the governor, that he had found nothing, that would justify him, in giving us the legal permission we desired. We then proposed to him to give us liberty to trap upon the condition, that we paid him five percent on the beaver we might catch. He said, he would consider this proposition, and give us an answer the next day at the same hour. The thoughts of our hearts were not at all favorable to this person, as we left him.

Before a decision could be reached by the governor, Pattie's story is interrupted by an episode involving robbery and murder and shooting and chasing, in which he plays the hero, and none of which has anything to do with his Gila expedition. Most of his book is interlarded with such preposterous adventures to the point of monotonous reading. But eventually he gets back to the business of the day. The governor, of course, decided he'd like to have his five per cent, so the license to trap was granted. Pattie and his father and partners (an unspecified or unidentified group) set out for the Gila River by way of the Rio Grande Valley, the Mimbres Basin, and the Santa Rita copper mines. These famous mines are near the present town of Silver City, New Mexico, and were the last outpost between New Mexico and Tucson, Arizona. Pattie's narrative continues:

We were here but one night, and I had not the leisure to examine the mode, in which the copper was manufactured. In the morning we hired two Spanish servants to accompany us; and taking a northwest course pursued our journey, until we reached the Helay on the 14th. We found the country hilly and somewhat barren with a growth of pine, live oak, *pinion,* cedar, and some small trees, of which I did not know the name. We caught thirty beavers, the first night we encamped on this river. The next morning, accompanied by another man, I began to ascend the bank of the stream to explore, and ascertain if beaver were to be found still higher, leaving the remainder of the party to trap slowly up, until they should meet us on our return. The first day we were fatigued by the difficulty of getting through the high grass, which covered the heavily timbered bottom. In the evening we arrived at the foot of mountains, that shut the river in on both sides, and encamped.

On the morning of the 13th we started early, and crossed the river, here a beautiful clear stream about thirty yards in width, running over a rocky bottom, and filled with fish. We made but

little advance this day, as bluffs came in so close to the river, as to
compel us to cross it thirty-six times. We were obliged to scramble
along under the cliffs, sometimes upon our hands and knees,
through a thick tangle of grape-vines and underbrush. Added to
the unpleasantness of this mode of getting along in itself, we did
not know, but the next moment would bring us face to face with
a bear, which might accost us suddenly. We were rejoiced, when
this rough ground gave place again to the level bottom. At night
we reached a place where the river forked, and encamped on the
point between the forks. We found here a boiling spring so near
the main stream, that the fish caught in the one might be thrown
into the other without leaving the spot, where it was taken. In
six minutes it would be thoroughly cooked.

This description of the upper Gila River, high in New
Mexico's Mogollon Mountains, although seen in the summer of
1825, describes the country exactly as it exists today. Pattie's
walk upstream may be duplicated, but it would have to be done
exactly as he did it, on foot, or with pack animals. It is some of
the remotest country in the United States, and the white race has
touched it only slightly. It is now preserved as the Gila National
Forest. Since this part of Pattie's narrative is obviously honest, what happened to him next is worth quoting.

The following morning my companion and myself separated,
agreeing to meet after four days at this spring. We were each to
ascend a fork of the river. The banks of that which fell to my lot,
were very brushy, and frequented by numbers of bears, of whom
I felt fearful, as I had never before travelled alone in the woods.
I walked on with caution until night, and encamped near a pile
of drift wood, which I set on fire, thinking thus to frighten any
animals which might approach during the night. I placed a spit,
with a turkey I had killed upon it, before the fire to roast. After
I had eaten my supper I laid down by the side of a log with my
gun by my side. I did not fall asleep for some time. I was aroused

from slumber by a noise in the leaves, and raising my head saw a panther stretched on the log by which I was lying, within six feet of me. I raised my gun gently to my face, and shot it in the head. Then springing to my feet, I ran about ten steps, and stopped to reload my gun, not knowing if I had killed the panther or not. Before I had finished loading my gun, I heard the distinct charge of one on the other fork, as I concluded, the two running parallel with each other, separated only by a narrow ridge. A second discharge quickly followed the first, which led me to suppose, that my comrade was attacked by Indians.

I immediately set out and reached the hot springs by daybreak, where I found my associate also. The report of my gun had awakened him, when he saw a bear standing upon its hind feet within a few yards of him growling. He fired his gun, then his pistol, and retreated, thinking, with regard to me, as I had with regard to him, that I was attacked by Indians. Our conclusion now was, to ascend one of the forks in company, and then cross over, and descend the other. In consequence we resumed the course, I had taken the previous day.

Some days later Pattie and his unnamed companion rejoined the main party of trappers and they proceeded downstream, having poor luck and even worse luck as they progressed west. In the area of what is now eastern Arizona, Pattie describes the Gila as "beautiful, running between banks covered with tall cottonwoods and willows. This bottom land extended back a mile on each side. Beyond rose high and rather barren hills."

The group of trappers continued downstream to a point where the Gila is joined by the Salt, or a short distance southwest of modern Phoenix. Then they decided to retrace their steps. They made a cache of the furs that they had accumulated, and worked their way back upstream into New Mexico to the Santa Rita copper mines, enduring physical hardships and running into incidents such as:

We found a man the Indians had killed. They had cut him
up in quarters, after the fashion of butchers. His head, with the
hat on, was stuck on a stake. It was full of arrows, which they had
probably discharged into it, as they danced around it. We gathered
up the parts of the body, and buried them.

After a series of adventures including Indian fighting and
bear hunting, Pattie made two more trips to the Gila, and these
took him to its mouth at the Colorado.

On the second such trip Pattie and his party moved downstream from the river's mouth along the Colorado's east bank until they were out of Yuma Indian country and in the land of
the friendly Cocopahs. These Indians had been glad to welcome
Hernando de Alarcon in 1540 and Padre Kino in 1690. The
present generation in 1828 had never seen a white man, according to Pattie's story, although this is probably not true as elderly
members of the tribe must have recalled occasional Spaniards from
Anza's expeditions and other Spanish pioneering parties.

But for once Pattie found a group of Indians he liked.
They were so hospitable that they prepared a feast for the white
men. This banquet consisted of a stew made by "killing a number of fatted dogs." Before this communal and canine dinner,
the chief of the Cocopahs, who went around naked, as did all
the rest of the tribe, made a long speech of which his white
guests understood not a word. But it was all a matter of "keys"
to the Cocopah "city," and when the talk was over dinner was
served. Pattie describes it:

The oration finished, a large dish of the choice dog's flesh
was set before us, and signs were made for us to eat. Having
learned not to be delicate or disobliging to our savage host, we fell
to work on the ribs of the domestic barkers. When we had eaten
to satisfaction, the chief arose, and puffing out his naked belly,

and striking it with his hand, very significantly inquired by this sign, if we had eaten enough?

The white men assured him, by what signs Pattie does not say, that the feast had been sumptuous. But the chief's hospitality did not end with food. A number of Cocopah girls were brought forth, in the nude of course, and displayed for the admiration of the visitors. Propriety came first on the part of the white men, but it is not necessary even to read between Pattie's lines to learn that when in Cocopah land it seemed best to do as the Cocopahs did:

We gave the women some old shirts, and intimated to them as well as we could, that it was the fashion of the women to cover themselves in our country, for these were in a state of the most entire nudity. But they did not seem rightly to comprehend our wish. Many of the women were not over sixteen, and the most perfect figures I have ever seen, perfectly straight and symmetrical, and the hair of some hanging nearly to their heels. . . . The night which we passed with them, passed away pleasantly, and to the satisfaction of all parties.

Pattie's long narrative continues with numerous other adventures, many outside of the Gila watershed. But he had indeed seen more of the Gila country than any other American except those who were along with him. He was familiar with its flora and fauna, and the Apaches, Pimas, Maricopas, Yumas, and Cocopahs.

By 1828 only Padre Kino and Padre Garces had traveled up and down the Gila Valley as much as this self-sufficient young Kentuckian. Inexplicable as his book may be, there is no discounting the fact that Pattie did, in the main, just about all he claims, less numerous extravagant statements of superheroics in attacking and slaying Indians, the encountering of 220 grizzly bears in one day in Arizona, and the vaccinating of twenty-two thousand people in twelve months in California. He killed Indians, he fought bears, and he vaccinated citizens of California, but either Pattie or his editor and ghost writer, Timothy Flint, let proper figures soar to astronomical proportions. Perhaps Flint thought such amazing statements would help sell the book, and probably they did. There is no evidence to prove that Pattie wrote any of the narrative. Certainly after his day-to-day struggle for survival he was not carrying any manuscript when he finally arrived back in Kentucky in 1830 by way of Vera Cruz and New Orleans. The odd and persistent use of the comma throughout is certainly Flint's; and tautological expressions such as "We killed her dead" are surely Pattie's, and suggest that some of the composition may have been taken by dictation. Sylvester Pattie, the father, died in jail in San Diego when authorities of that California town imprisoned the two interlopers, and no longer figured in the latter part of the story. Pattie himself seems to have completely disappeared shortly after his return to Kentucky. There is a story, or unauthenticated rumor, that he went to California in the gold rush and perished somewhere in the Sierra Nevada Mountains in a snowstorm. But for this there is no verification. So James Ohio Pattie remains one of the colorful characters of Gila Valley history—if not the first American to see the river, at least the first one to tell about it—and in his way, incongruously perhaps, must be reckoned with Esteban de Dorantes, Fray Marcos de Niza, Padre Kino, and Padre Garces.

Following Pattie there were a number of trappers who worked the Gila and its tributaries through the 1830's and 1840's. The fact that there was such an amazing combination of predecessors from dinosaurs, through pre-Columbian engineers, and athletes on ball courts, to Christian fathers, was never within the ken of the frontiersmen of 1828–1846. Rough and tough, often illiterate, some have been lost to history and others are merely names. Most of them had no right to be in Mexican territory and few of them gave it a thought. Some, such as Ewing Young and Kit Carson, were men of stature and ability, but others were hardly more than outlaws. Their total effect on the Gila Valley up to 1846 was transient and negligible. The towns of Tubac and Tucson continued to doze, the Pimas and the Papagos were reasonably friendly, the Yumas controlled the area at the mouth of the Gila, and the roving and marauding Apaches were eager to dismember any unfortunate travelers they could capture.

But in 1846 there occurred an event that was to change the course of civilization along the Gila in a way that nobody could have foreseen. For on May 11, 1846, President James K. Polk, speaking in Washington, asked the Congress of the United States, on the basis of acts of unprovoked aggression along the lower Rio Grande, for a declaration of war on the Republic of Mexico. On the 13th day of May the American Congress declared war. The days of the trapping interloper were over; he was soon to be followed by the American soldier.

12

GENERAL KEARNY LOSES HIS PATIENCE

IN HIS *History of Arizona and New Mexico* Hubert H. Bancroft states with admirable candor: "In 1846 the United States began a war against Mexico for the acquisition of terri-

tory." The historian is at least honest, but the majority of those
who saw the territory felt that it was a wasted war. After a difficult crossing of the Gila Valley the average American soldier
would have said, "Let Mexico have it, and I hope I never see it
again."

California, of course, was the real objective in the western
campaign, with New Mexico of secondary importance and Arizona
of so little importance that Washington neglected to grab all of
the Gila Valley and had to pay ten million dollars for it a few
years later. This was due to a lack of understanding of the importance of southern Arizona as a connecting transcontinental link
between Mississippi Valley points and California.

At the first outbreak of hostilities California seemingly fell
to Commodore Robert F. Stockton and Colonel John C. Frémont without a struggle. So delighted were these two with the
abject helplessness of the area and the collapse of any military resistance on the part of the Californians that they sent the frontiersman Kit Carson overland with dispatches for Washington to
inform the War Department that California had capitulated. They
were somewhat premature.

Carson, making record time and exhausting mules, crossed
the Colorado River and followed the Gila upstream across Arizona easterly, into New Mexico, and then by way of the Santa
Rita copper mines to the Rio Grande Valley. He was heading for
Santa Fe and was within a hundred and fifty miles of it when
he met General Stephen W. Kearny, who was in command of
the Army of the West, over three hundred strong, on his way to
seize and occupy California, a thousand miles away.

Kit Carson told Kearny and his dragoons that the war was
already over. It was a big disappointment to Kearny to learn that
Stockton and Frémont had stolen his thunder. But he believed
Carson (much to his later regret). His credence is reasonable inas-

much as he himself had recently taken Santa Fe, New Mexico's
capital, with no resistance whatever.

Kearny had started from Fort Leavenworth, Kansas, in June
of 1846 about a month after war had been declared. He entered Santa Fe on August 18 and the affair was bloodless. Governor Manuel Armijo fled and acting-Governor Juan Vigil had
his troops fire a friendly salute to the raising of the American flag
over the governor's palace. On August 27, Kearny gave a grand
ball for the officers of both armies, prominent citizens, and their
wives. Everybody ate and drank too much. It was a most pleasant
war. A month later, with everybody happy, Kearny set out for his
ultimate objective, California, only to have Kit Carson meet him
south of Albuquerque and tell him the bad news that the war
was over on the Pacific coast.

Kearny, nevertheless, was happy to meet Carson. In truth, he
was just the man he needed to guide him to California. He listened to Carson's description of the difficult terrain that lay
ahead, virtually a thousand miles of grim mountains or raw desert
with only the Gila as a guaranteed source of water. He heeded
Carson's advice that wagons could make it—maybe—but if so it
would take six months to get there. And he decided that Kit
was never going to deliver his dispatches to Washington. Any
courier could do that, but Carson alone knew the country that lay
ahead, had trapped beaver along its streams years before, and had
only now crossed it again. Kearny commanded Carson to turn his
dispatches over to another man. Carson was reluctant to obey.

While Kit was considering his position and debating
with himself how to act with the best integrity, Kearny sent over
two hundred of his soldiers back to Santa Fe along with the
cumbersome wagons, and kept one hundred men with horses and
pack animals for the forced march that lay ahead. Since California had already been conquered, a token force for occupation was

all that he would need. This would considerably increase the speed of the expedition. With these picked one hundred men he also kept two 12-pound bronze howitzers which turned out to be the bane of everybody's existence. Incidentally, they were the first wheeled vehicles to cross Arizona—two gun caissons.

Kit Carson's name stands high in the annals of the American West, and justly so. He was born in Kentucky in 1809, which would make him thirty-seven at the time he met Kearny. In contrast to most trappers and mountainmen—large, loud, and boastful—Kit was five feet six inches tall, soft spoken, clean minded, and somewhat of a paragon of virtue in a land where virtue was not considered important. He had been of inestimable aid to Frémont as a "pathfinder," although this term is usually tacked on to Frémont himself. Disappointed over Kearny's command to return to California as his guide, Kit decided, nevertheless, to obey this general of the army. He turned his Washington-bound dispatches over to another messenger, provided by Kearny, and the Army of the West headed for the Gila.

This force, though primarily military, was in part a scientific expedition as well. Apart from the long-lost Hohokam engineers and the erudite Padre Eusebio Kino, it marks the first attempt to study the Gila Valley in terms of topography, botany, zoology, and ecology. Several men kept daily reports, and these journals later proved valuable to the government in comprehending the peculiar problems of the Gila watershed.

One of these men was Lieutenant Colonel W. H. Emory, whose records were published in 1848 as a Senate report called *Notes of a Military Reconnaissance from Fort Leavenworth, in Missouri, to San Diego, in California.* Fort Leavenworth is, of course, in Kansas on the west bank of the Missouri River, but the name "Kansas" was not in use at that time.

Another journal, which was not for governmental purposes but which was simply a personal diary, was kept by John S. Griffin, M.D., attached to the Army of the West. Dr. Griffin's account was published by the California Historical Society in 1943 as *A Doctor Comes to California*. Many people believe that Dr. Griffin was the first qualified medical man to enter Arizona and California, and technically this is true. But he was preceded by John Marsh in 1835, who crossed Arizona by way of the Gila to California and settled in Los Angeles. Marsh had fled from an unsavory past in the Black Hawk War of 1832. There was a warrant in St. Louis for his arrest. Whether he was innocent or guilty is beside the point. He had a degree of Bachelor of Arts from Harvard and he presented it to the Spanish authorities in Los Angeles as a medical degree. Since they couldn't read Latin, it worked, and from 1835 on he was Dr. Marsh, California's first physician and surgeon, with an A.B. degree! So Dr. John Griffin was the first accredited medical man to pass through the Gila Valley to California, but Dr. John Marsh had been practicing in Los Angeles for eleven years when Dr. Griffin arrived.

Kit Carson led the Army of the West to the Santa Rita copper mines and then to the upper Gila in New Mexico. Both Colonel Emory and Dr. Griffin have left firsthand and often colorful accounts of this stage of the trip. Emory wrote:

Some hundred yards before reaching this river the roar of its waters made us understand that we were to see something different from the Del Norte [the Rio Grande]. Its section, where we struck it, 4,347 feet above the sea, was 50 feet wide and an average of two feet deep. Clear and swift, it came bouncing from the great mountains which appeared to the north about 60 miles distant. We crossed the river, its large round pebbles and swift current causing the mules to tread wearily.

And Dr. Griffin, in his diary, described it:

We followed down a branch of the Gila today, and about three o'clock came to that stream. It is a fine, bold, beautiful mountain stream but with no land about it that can be cultivated, cottonwood timber, fine fish, plenty caught this evening. No game, though I found plenty of deer sign.

Colonel Emory was attracted by both the flora and the fauna, and he described them carefully:

We heard fish playing in the water, and soon those who were disengaged were after them. At first it was supposed they were the mountain trout, but, being comparatively fresh from the hills of Maine, I soon saw the difference. The shape, general appearance, and color are the same; at a little distance you will imagine the fish covered with delicate scales, but on a closer examination you will find that they are only the impression of scales. The meat is soft, something between the trout and the catfish, but more like the latter. They are in great abundance.

We saw here also, in great numbers, the blue quail. The bottom of the river is narrow, covered with large round pebbles. The growth of trees and weeds was very luxuriant; the trees chiefly cottonwood, a new sycamore, mezquite, pala (the tallow tree of our hunters,) a few cedars, and one or two larch. There were some grape and hop vines.

16 circum-meridian observations beta aquarii, and 9 of polaris, give the latitude of this camp 32° 50′ 08″. Its approximate longitude is 108° 45′ 00″.

The howitzers did not reach camp at all.

From that first camp on the upper Gila the Army of the West began its long and tedious journey down the Gila to California. It is interesting to note that if a visitor will go to Colonel Emory's carefully taken latitude and longitude today he will

find the river, the flora, and the fauna exactly as the scholarly
colonel described them. There has been no change in the country in over a hundred years. Man has hardly touched it.

Dr. Griffin's description of the first day's journey downstream
is typical of many days that the army pushed onward in the
mountain area. He describes it as follows:

Oct. 21, 1846. This has been a long and fatiguing day's journey. When we left camp this morning we had two difficulties
presented to us—the one a most steep and rugged mountain, the
other a canyon of the river, we took the latter as the lesser evil,
followed down the Gila some five or six miles and finally turned
the steepest point of the mountain. In following the course of the
river, we were obliged to cross it every half mile or so, the mountain jutting down to the very edge of the stream, making a very
picturesque affair of it—but damn bad roads—the fact is we have
so much of the grand & sublime scenery that I am tired of it. After
turning the flank of the mountain we ascended it, and found it
bad enough even at that. Carson said this was a turnpike road in
comparison to the other route. We struck the river about four or
five o'clock in the evening and found the country quite open.
More fish have been caught this evening. I tried my hand but
could not even get a nibble—plenty of deer and turkey sign today—none seen. I had to take a *pleasant* (!) ride of some miles on
the back trail to see a sick man—this made me late in getting into
camp. Our march today some 18 miles by my computation. The
Howitzers have not come up yet, and it is now 8 PM—poor Davidson [the officer in charge of the cannon], he has a sweet time of
it—these are the only wheeled vehicles we have along, and they
are about as much trouble as all the packs put together. Our pack
animals begin to suffer dreadfully from sore backs, and the beef
cattle are becoming so tender footed that they are driven along
with the greatest difficulty. Some Indians came up shortly after we

started this morning. We have seen nothing of them since. The rascals are loafing along after us to steal some mules, I suppose.

For the first day's journey down the Gila this was not too pleasant. But the worst, as always, was yet to come. Dr. Griffin continues:

Oct. 23. This morning we left camp about 9 o'clock, crossed the River, and marched down the bottom on the north side of the stream, the road was quite level, but ye gods the dust. I never suffered or saw men suffer more from any trifling annoyance in my life. The grass and weeds indicated quite strong soil, and might be cultivated by proper irrigation. We saw one or two wild geese & two or three flocks of ducks—the advance guard saw the black quail and the common quail of the United States. No other game was seen, the fact is Carson says he never knew a party on the Gila, that did not leave it starving, this I am fearful will be our case before we leave—Marched about 16 or 17 miles.
[No howitzers.]

The entries in the doctor's diary follow in this general vein, and at length he notes the evidence of the Hohokam people which interested him only as a side commentary on the contemporary Indian population:

. . . passed the ruins of several buildings in some places the cedar posts were standing. The buildings evidently were quite large—and pieces of crockery were scattered about in great profusion—we have found these ever since we got on the Gila. Some pieces are plane, some painted black & white, & red & black. Who could have done this—there is no record or tradition that I have heard of, of the Mexicans having lived in this country, and the present race of Indians never either built so extensively or made the crockery—that they may have smashed it is quite likely as they seem to have a genius that way, in common with all the red skin rascals I have ever seen yet. The river at this point is some 60 yards broad and very rapid and quite deep.

The "red skin rascals" referred to by Dr. Griffin were Apaches. Since the expedition was well armed and one hundred strong, the Apaches did not attack. If they had, Dr. Griffin would certainly have had an even stronger adverse opinion. The toll on the animals was very high and the Army of the West was sorely in need of new mounts. They made offers for fresh animals to the occasional Apache who rode by, and some of the Apaches, going by the code "if you can't kill them, trade with them," showed a willingness to open negotiations. But every time this happened the Apaches brought only broken-down animals or those of the army which they had already stolen. To General Kearny the whole expedition was becoming a bigger and bigger headache. And the two howitzers were often so far in the rear that the party was forced to wait a day or two for these utterly useless weapons to be brought up. Sometimes they had to be dismantled and carried piecemeal around, up, over, and down cliffs and canyons. It was Lieutenant Davidson who had charge of these guns; and he also had the patience of Job. General Kearny was not so patient. He could visualize Commodore Stockton and Colonel Frémont organizing and governing the prostrate Spanish California, and he knew it was his military business to be there and to do it. There they were, the happy conquerors, and here he was, assigned to such a job, and still battling his way down this blasted Gila River.

At last a definite agreement was reached with some Apaches that they would bring into the American camp some fresh animals to trade. Kearny hoped such new livestock would help to speed up the junket. It was not a success, but the outcome had at least a semicomic aspect, and both Griffin and Emory recorded it. Emory's account is as follows:

Nov. 3—Our expectations were again disappointed, the Indians came, but only seven mules were the result of the day's labor, not a tenth of the number absolutely required.

Our visitors today presented the same motley group we have always found the Apaches. Amongst them was a middle-aged woman, whose garrulity and interference in every trade was the annoyance of Major Swords, who had charge of the trading, but the amusement of the by-standers.

She had on a gauze-like dress, trimmed with the richest and most costly Brussels lace, pillaged no doubt from some fandango-going belle of Sonora; [what the horrific fate of the Spanish girl who originally owned the dress might have been is anybody's speculation] she straddled a fine grey horse, and whenever her blanket dropped from her shoulders, her tawny form could be seen through the transparent gauze. After she had sold her mule, she was anxious to sell her horse, and careered about to show his qualities. At one time she charged full speed up a steep hill. In this, the fastenings of her dress broke, and her bare back was exposed to the crowd, who ungallantly raised a shout of laughter. Nothing daunted, she wheeled short round with surprising dexterity, and seeing the mischief done, coolly slipped the dress from her arms and tucked it between her seat and the saddle. In this state of nudity she rode through camp, from fire to fire, until at last, attaining the object of her ambition, a soldier's red flannel shirt, she made her adieu in that new costume.

Comic or not, the day's trading gained only seven fresh mules and one horse. Again General Kearny was impatient. But they had to wait another day for the howitzers to catch up to them. Two days later, as they were nearing the confluence of the San Pedro with the Gila, where the town of Winkelman stands today, Dr. Griffin described the area as "the Hog River because of the number of wild hogs found on it—the country passed over barren mountains, and utterly worthless." But the doctor was within a short distance of what was later to be the famous Christmas mine, a copper strike which earned, in future years, far more for its stockholders than he ever made from his professional services. Also this is the location, or very close to it, where Fray Marcos de Niza learned of the death of Esteban in 1539. Emory recorded it thus:

Nov. 6—For the double purpose of allowing the howitzers to come up, and to recruit our mules, it is decided this shall be a day of rest. The grama [grass] is good but sparsely scattered over the hills, and it is necessary to loosen every animal and let them graze at will. . . . Strolling over the hills alone, in pursuit of seed and geological specimens, my thoughts went back to the States, and when I turned from my momentary aberrations, I was struck most forcibly with the fact that not one object in the whole view, animal, vegetable, or mineral, had anything in common with the products of any State in the Union.

This, of course, must be taken as the point of view of a man from Maine taking his first good look at Arizona. And he continues with:

The only animals seen were lizards, scorpions, and tarantulas. . . . About two miles from our camp the San Pedro joins the Gila just as the latter leaps from the mouth of the canyon. The place of meeting is a bottom three miles wide . . . seamed with tracks of deer, turkey, beaver, and one trail of wild hogs.

For the same day Dr. Griffin recorded:

Nov. 6, 1846. This has been a most weary day, the Howitzers being left in the mountains and the great difficulty of getting anything along with wheels, caused the loss of another day—and the lord knows when they will arrive—though I have no doubt that Davidson and his party have worked like devils to get the cursed things ahead. . . . Every bush in this country is full of thorns—and every piece of grass so soon as it is broken becomes a thorn at both ends—every rock you turn over has a tarantula or a centipede under it, and Carson says in the summer the most beautiful specimens of rattlesnakes are scattered around in the greatest profusion. . . . The fact is, take the country altogether, and I defy any man who has not seen it—or one as utterly worthless— even to imagine any so barren. The cactus is the only thing that does grow, and we saw some of them yesterday—I should say 50 feet high—yesterday our rear met a party of Indians. The red rascals would have nothing to do with the soldiers. . . . The Howitzers have *got in,* so we leave in the morning bright and early.

On the 9th of November conditions began to look a little better. The Army of the West had reached the point where the Gila emerges once and for all from the mountain area and begins its long flow across the desert plain. The observing Colonel Emory described it thus:

The Gila at this point, released from its mountain barrier, flows off quietly at the rate of three miles an hour into a wide plain, which extends south almost as far as the eye can reach. . . . In one spot we found only a few bunches of grass; more than four-fifths of the plain were destitute of vegetation; the soil, a light brown loose sandy earth, I suppose contained something deleterious to vegetation.

We made our noon halt at the grass patch. At this place were the remains of an immense Indian settlement. [Colonel Emory now has his reaction to the Hohokam.] Pottery was everywhere to be found, but the remains of the foundations of the houses were imbedded in dust. The outlines of the acequias [irrigation ditches] by which they irrigated the soil, were sometimes quite distinct.

At this point they were about sixty miles northwest of the Mexican garrison at Tucson on the Gila's tributary, the Santa

Cruz. But the Mexican soldiers did not venture forth. Perhaps they didn't even know that Kearny was on the Gila. And Kearny's objective was not Tucson, but California. Slowly and steadily the western march continued. For November 9 Emory recorded:

> After leaving the mountains all seemed for a moment to consider the difficulties of our journey at an end. The mules went off at a frolicsome pace, those which were loose contending with each other for precedence in the trail. The howitzers, which had nearly every part of their running gear broken and replaced, were perhaps the only things that were benefitted by the change from the mountains to the plains. In overcoming one set of difficulties we were now to encounter another. In leaving the mountains we were informed [by Kit Carson] that we bid adieu to grass, and our mules must henceforth subsist on willow, cottonwood, and the long green ephedra.

Continuing downstream to the point where the Salt River joins the Gila, the Army of the West made contact with the Pima Indians, who were friendly and co-operative and the going did become a bit easier. Colonel Emory was fascinated with the various ruins, plethora of pottery, and the obvious fact that a large and civilized race of people must have dwelt along the river. The word "Hohokam," of course, he did not know. On inquiry from one of the more intelligent Pimas he got, in explanation, a Pima legend which he carefully recorded.

> I asked him, among other things, the origin of the ruins of which we had seen so many; he said, all he knew, was a tradition amongst them, that in bygone days, a woman of surpassing beauty resided in a green spot in the mountains near the place where we were encamped. All the men admired, and paid court to her. She received the tributes of their devotion, grain, skins, &c., but gave no love or other favor in return. Her virtue, and her determination to remain unmarried were equally firm. There came a

drought which threatened the world with famine. In their distress, people applied to her, and she gave corn from her stock, and the supply seemed endless. Her goodness was unbounded. One day, as she was lying asleep with her body exposed, a drop of rain fell on her stomach, which produced conception. A son was the issue, who was the founder of a new race which built all these houses.

November 11—Leaving the column, a few of us struck to the north side of the river, guided by my loquacious friend, the interpreter, to visit the ruins of another Casa Montezuma. In the course of the ride, I asked him if he believed the fable he had related to me last night, which assigned an origin to these buildings. "No," he said, "but most of the Pimos* do. We know, in truth, nothing of their origin. It is all enveloped in mystery."

The casa was in complete ruins, one pile of broken pottery and foundation stone of the black basalt, making a mound about ten feet above the ground. The outline of the ground plan was distinct enough. We found the description of pottery the same as ever; and, among the ruins, the same sea shell; one worked into ornaments; also a large bead, an inch and a quarter in length, of bluish marble, exquisitely turned.

This ruin may have been Pueblo Grande on the Salt River adjacent to modern Phoenix, or possibly the site that is today called Snaketown, south of Phoenix. At any rate, Colonel Emory had a good look at the remains of the Hohokam civilization.

From this point on downstream to the Colorado River the army traveled without untoward incident. Dr. Griffin summed up the lower Gila as follows:

Nov. 17th & 18th. One days march on the River is so much like unto another that one description will do for all that is to say

---

* Pimo and Pima are arbitrary forms of the spelling of the name of this tribe of Indians. Pimo is now generally considered archaic.

—sand, dust, & a black stone, so blistered from the effects of heat that they look like they had hardly got cool—no grass, nothing but weeds & cactus. The River here is some 60 or 80 yards wide—on an average three feet deep and rapid. On the night of the 17th we had considerable frost. The mountains still continue on our right and left, and if anything more jagged and forbidding in appearance than any we have passed yet. Some of them have the most fantastic forms. I neglected to note a stone we passed on the 16th, or rather a hill of stone, all carved up with Indian hieroglyphics—the sun moon & stars—horned frogs—attempts at the human form divine, were the most frequent forms—they seem to be of recent date—whether cut in sport or to commemorate some great event we could not tell.

On November 22 the Army of the West reached the junction of the Gila with the Colorado, and here an incident occurred which increased General Kearny's impatience to a state of acute irritation and indignation. The howitzers, as always, brought up the rear and didn't get into camp until nine at night. The men in charge reported seeing campfires across the Gila along its north bank. General Kearny had to know at once just who and what was there. He sent Colonel Emory and fifteen dragoons to reconnoiter, and this group ran into a camp of Mexicans who were taking a band of five hundred horses from California to General José Castro in Sonora. Unbeknown to the Americans, Castro was to organize a cavalry troop and lead it back to California. But the Mexicans said they were merely employees of some wealthy Californians who were sending horses to the markets of Sonora. Incredibly, the Americans believed this, although the leader of the group was, in reality, Colonel José Maria Leguna, of the Mexican Army. Colonel Emory took four of the Mexicans to General Kearny. When they were each examined separately their stories didn't jibe. Kearny kept them all night as prisoners. The next day Colonel Emory rode to the confluence of the Gila with the Colorado. Just beyond the Gila lay the Mexican camp. He described this important scene as follows:

The day was stormy, the wind blowing fiercely from the north. We mounted a butte of feldspathic granite, and, looking 25° east of north, the course of the Colorado was tracked by clouds of flying sand. The Gila comes into it nearly at right angles, and the point of junction, strangely chosen, is the hard butte through which, with their united forces, they cut a canyon, and then flow off due magnetic west, in a direction of the resultant due to the relative strength of the rivers. . . . The Gila, at certain stages, might be navigated up to the Pimos village, and possibly with small boats at all stages of water.

Near the junction, on the north side, are the remains of an old Spanish church, built near the beginning of the 17th century, by the renowned missionary, Father Kino.

Emory is in error. What he saw was the ruins of Mission Purisima Concepción, founded by Padre Tomas Garces in 1776 on the California side of the Colorado River. He continues:

On our return we met a Mexican, well mounted and muffled in his blanket. I asked him where he was going; he said to hunt horses. As he passed, I observed in each of his holsters the neck of a bottle, and on his croup a fresh made sack, with other evidences of a preparation for a journey. Much against his taste, I invited him to follow me to camp . . . his anxiety to be released increased my determination not to comply with his request. I took him to General Kearny and explained to him the suspicious circumstances under which I had taken him, and that his capture would prove of some importance. He was immediately searched, and in his wallet was found the mail from California, which was of course opened.

And then General Kearny got a shock. For this mail was composed of military dispatches from General José Maria Flores in
Los Angeles to General José Maria Castro in Sonora. Instead of
the war in California being over, it indicated that it had only
just begun. Moreover, the Mexican dispatches told of the defeat
and surrender of Captain Archibald H. Gillespie at Los Angeles, the routing of 450 American soldiers and sailors from the
USS *Savannah* who had tried to retake Los Angeles and failed,
and the fact that Stockton and Frémont had not subdued California at all, but were themselves under pressure. The red, white,
and green of Mexico flew from San Diego to Santa Barbara. A
new government under General Flores had been organized and
Los Angeles was its capital. In the north there were insurrections
harassing Stockton and Frémont; Californians were united and
aroused at last, and while the gringos still held Monterey, it
was only a question of time until every Yanqui in California
would be driven into the sea.

This was amazing news to General Kearny. And it tried his
patience to the breaking point. Because of the stupidity of Stockton and Frémont in sending Kit Carson east to report the war
over when it hadn't begun, General Kearny had left two-thirds
of his fighting force back in Santa Fe! These men, now sorely
needed in California were one thousand miles away and it would
appear to be Kearny's fault for not leading his complete Army
of the West to California, which had been his orders from
Washington. And where was Kearny now? Faced with a desolate
desert to cross before he could reach San Diego and relieve the
town, if, indeed, his one hundred weary dragoons would have the
strength to do it. What Kearny said and thought about Stockton
and Frémont must have made the air blue around the mouth of
the Gila that 23rd day of November, 1846.

On November 25 the Army of the West crossed the Colorado into California and thereby left the Gila watershed. But a few words in postscript are in order to bring the story of General Kearny's strained patience to an end.

After a grueling desert journey, the Army of the West reached Warner's Ranch in the mountains northeast of San Diego. Shortly thereafter they made contact with a California force under Flores' general, Andres Pico. In his exhausted condition Kearny was unwise to attack, but attack he did at first sight of the enemy. Rankling inside and spoiling for a fight after this long march from Fort Leavenworth, the American move was hasty and disastrous. The Californians fled at the first volley and the Americans pursued them. This turned out to be an ambush and the Californians counterattacked with the benefit of fresh mounts and the long lance, a nasty weapon in the hands of an experienced horseman. The Army of the West took a forty per cent loss in men after an engagement of one hour, the first half of which was a decoy retreat on the part of General Pico and the balance of which was vicious and bloody fighting at close quarters. General Kearny himself was badly wounded, and had the Californians had any real talent for strategy, as had the Sioux at a later date against Custer, they would have wiped out Kearny to the last man. That they didn't do this was, in the end, fortunate for both sides. But in its first and only engagement as a fighting unit the Army of the West was badly defeated. This is known historically as the Battle of San Pasqual and a monument commemorates the site today in San Diego County.

And for the final ironic touch, the bothersome, agonizingly difficult howitzers, dragged and pushed and pulled and carried all the way from the Missouri River, were, as always, too far in the rear and never got into the battle at all.

13

THE MORMON BATTALION

Presldent James K. Polk was not a man to do things by halves. Neither was Brigham Young. It is not on record that the Scotch-Presbyterian president of the United States and the Mormon president of the Church of the Latter-day Saints ever held any great fraternal love for each other, but each was quick enough and shrewd enough to recognize a good business deal when he saw one.

In 1846 the Mormons had been cruelly persecuted in Illinois and Missouri; they could not remain there, and Brigham Young needed a place for them to go. In 1846 American colonists were needed for California; it was difficult for them to get there unless James K. Polk could send them under a military guise. These factors made a mutual deal possible between the titular heads of the Mormon Church and the government of the United States.

Church and state put aside their individual grievances and worked for their united advantage. Brigham Young wanted Mormons in the West—preferably California (this was before the founding of Salt Lake City). James K. Polk wanted soldiers in the West—preferably California. The result was the creation of the Mormon Battalion of 1846, mustered in at Council Bluffs, Iowa, for a period of enlistment of one year. The battalion's orders were to go overland to California by way of Santa Fe, and in so doing establish a wagon road to the Pacific coast. The men, for the most part, started out with their wives and children.

General Kearny and the Army of the West had already departed. His was a combination of military and scientific aims, but primarily military. It was to be followed by the Mormon Battalion, a combination of military and colonizing aims, but in name at least primarily military.

At first there were a number of deterring elements that had to be worked out. The government furnished military equipment and supplies, but nothing domestic. Since there could be no fighting short of the Gila watershed, the battalion was far more in need of domestic supplies for families—food, clothing, and medicine. And to top it off, the commander died before the expedition got beyond Fort Leavenworth. To complicate things further, there were in the expedition, apart from the enlisted members of the battalion, women, children, old men, adolescents, and a sprinkling of the lame, the halt, and the blind. And this organization, it was naïvely assumed by Washington, would form a wagon train to California over a terrain that had never been crossed by a wagon, or even seen wheels, until the arrival of General Kearny's useless howitzers only a few months before.

Lieutenant Colonel P. St. George Cooke was appointed the new commander, and Colonel Cooke had a job on his hands that was no sinecure. The diverse members of the Mormon Battalion arrived in Santa Fe between October 9 and October 13, 1846. The New Mexico capital was not hostile; on the contrary, it was happy to receive this new and motley group of Yanquis about five hundred strong. The Army of the West, presumably breaking the trail, was at this time approaching the Gila, well on its way beyond Santa Fe. Kearny, as shown in the previous chapter, had his own problems, and the trials and headaches caused by the Mormon Battalion were exclusively those of P. St. George Cooke. And he resolved them expeditiously indeed.

Wisely, Cooke went over the roster and excluded the women

and children, and also those too old, too young, or too feeble. This group of about 150 people he sent north from Santa Fe to Pueblo, Colorado, and eventually, in the next year, they arrived at the newly founded Salt Lake City.

With a train of wagons, horses, mules, and about 340 men, and five women, who were the wives of officers and who were reluctantly permitted to accompany their husbands, Colonel Cooke led the Mormon Battalion from Santa Fe westward on October 19, 1846. On January 21, 1847, the men and the five women arrived at Warner's Ranch in the mountains northeast of San Diego. During that interim they had a remarkable trip and several remarkable experiences.

They took an armed Mexican fort and town (Tucson) without firing a shot, and their only battle was with attacking animals, not men; they were the first travelers to go boating on the Gila, and they proved that wagon wheels could roll from Iowa to California, something that wheels of various kinds have been doing ever since.

Colonel Cooke's problem differed from Kearny's. Kearny had an "army" mounted on mules; Cooke had a wagon train, and it could not follow the trail set by Kit Carson. But Cooke had a guide of Kit Carson's ability. He was the western frontiersman Pauline (Powell) Weaver, and Weaver and Cooke made a long and circuitous loop from the Santa Rita copper mines southwest to a point that is just about the southeastern corner of Arizona today. Here, at the San Bernardino ranch, abandoned by Mexicans due to Apache attacks, the battalion found plenty of beef on the hoof, and a pass through which the wagons could move west. Making fifteen to twenty miles a day, the Mormons reached the Gila's tributary, the San Pedro, which they described as a "pleasant stream" with "fish in abundance" and "black walnut timber" along its banks. Turning north toward the Gila, the battalion followed the route of Esteban and Fray Marcos de Niza, and Melchior Diaz and Coronado.

Each day's journey had its difficulties and incidents, and a typical entry in the diary of one of its members, Henry Standage, reads:

Dec. 8. Clear and cool this morning. Men detailed to go with the pack mules and gather up the beef killed yesterday. Laid by to rest the teams. . . . Sister Brown came to our tent and informed us of the death of Br. Elisha Smith. He did not belong to the Battalion but came along with Cap Davis to drive his team and act as waiter, they being old acquaintances. He had been unwell for several days. His wife left the Battalion at Santa Fe for Pueblo. Some few dug his grave and buried him while the rest prepared for a start. 8 o'clock found us once more on our way to California. . . .

A few days later, while moving north downstream along the San Pedro, the battalion engaged in its first and only battle. Incredible as it may seem, the wagon train was attacked by a herd of wild bulls. This incident wasn't taken seriously at first as it was assumed that a few shots would scatter the animals. But the sound of the muskets seemed only to infuriate the bulls. Colonel Cooke wrote later: "I had to direct the men to load their muskets to defend themselves . . . the animals attacked without provocation."

The battle began early in the morning and lasted several hours. A number of men were seriously wounded, and in his excitement Lieutenant George Stoneman shot himself in his left thumb (almost forty years later this same George Stoneman became governor of California). Horses and mules were gored and disemboweled. Private Amos Cox was gored and tossed ten feet in the air, suffering wounds "four inches long and three inches deep." The historian of the expedition, Daniel Tyler, described the unaccountable battle in his *History of the Mormon Battalion* as follows:

The roar of musketry was heard from one end of the line to the other. One small lead mule in a team was thrown on the horns of a bull over its mate on the near side, and the near mule, now on the off side and next to the bull, was gored until he had to be left with his entrails hanging a foot below his body. Pack mules were also killed. The end-gates of one or two wagons were stove in, and the sick, who were riding in them, were of course, frightened. Some of the men climbed upon the wheels of the wagons and poured a deadly fire into the enemy's ranks. Some of them threw themselves down and allowed the beasts to run over them; others fired and dodged behind mesquite brush to re-load their guns, while the beasts kept them dodging to keep out of the way. Others, still, climbed up in small trees, there being now and then, one available.

After an engagement of several hours "the enemy" withdrew. The estimate of the number of bulls killed varies in different accounts, with fifty being the minimum and eighty-one the maximum. The reason the "battle" lasted so long was due to the fact that the bulls were extremely difficult to kill. One good shot would normally stop an Apache brave, but a mad bull could take, as Colonel Cooke noted, "two balls through its heart and two through its lungs," and still charge and gore man or beast.

When the battle was over, the Mormon Battalion moved forward. A few miles beyond the scene of the engagement Colonel Cooke recorded: "We crossed a pretty stream, which I have named Bull Run." In later years the words "Bull Run" became famous for another battle (two, in fact) in Virginia. Arizona's Bull Run has been eclipsed by the march of history.

The Battle of the Bulls occurred on December 11, and on December 15, in contrast, the battalion proceeded to take an armed Mexican town without a shot being fired on either side.

Leaving the San Pedro and veering west at what is the town of Benson today, the battalion approached Tucson on the Gila's tributary, the Santa Cruz. The presidio of Tubac had been abandoned, and Tucson, the only Mexican town and garrison in Arizona, stood squarely in the way of the Mormon Battalion. And a state of war existed between Mexico and the United States.

Short of Tucson, the battalion met half a dozen Mexican soldiers. Cooke was told that he would not be permitted to pass. So Cooke sent forward the terms for which he would accept Tucson's surrender. Every man and musket in the battalion was ready for a fight. The battalion moved cautiously forward, with the women and the ailing bringing up the rear. As the company neared the town, a single Mexican soldier rode out to inform Colonel Cooke that the comandante had refused his demand for surrender. The soldier was permitted to return to the town, and then the Mormon Battalion advanced to take it by force.

This combination of tough talk and direct action on Cooke's part worked. It so frightened the Mexican garrison that the comandante and his army fled south toward Mission San Xavier del Bac, and a goodly portion of the populace went with them. The Mormon Battalion marched into Tucson in fighting formation only to find a scant hundred people left in the town, all of whom were civilians and all of whom welcomed the "victors" and wanted to do all they could to assist them.

Thus the potential Battle of Tucson never took place. The Mormon Battalion remained in the town only two days. During that time all was peaceful. The officers found a large supply of wheat stored in a granary, and they took as much of that as the wagon train could carry. From the remaining citizens the privates purchased fruit and beans, and were given tortillas. These round

flat Mexican cakes they eagerly devoured, having tasted them before in Santa Fe.

While spending forty-eight hours in Tucson the alert Colonel P. St. George Cooke learned that the Mexican state of Sonora, of which Arizona was a northern outpost, albeit still a part
of New Mexico, had a governor who was well disposed and
friendly toward the United States. Since Santa Fe had welcomed
Kearny and his dragoons, and later Cooke himself and his Mormon Battalion, Cooke sensed that there was a good chance
of grabbing off all of New Mexico, Arizona, and Sonora for the
United States, not to mention California, which was destined to
be Americanized at any cost. So he wrote a letter while in Tucson and left it in care of the absent (in terror) comandante, to
be delivered to Governor Manuel Gandara in Sonora. Cooke's
strategy is interesting to read in the light of what finally happened
and the ultimate necessity of the Gadsden Purchase, which, since
this was a so-called war, should never have had to come about.
As a diplomatist, Cooke took a good shot in the dark with his
letter to the governor of Sonora. Had there been any plausible way
to follow it up, it might have saved a lot of later annoyance
and given the United States control of the Gulf of California.
At any rate, the quick-thinking Cooke wrote:

> In Camp,
> Tucson, Sonora.
> December 18, 1846

Your Excellency:
The undersigned, marching in command of a battalion of United
States Infantry, from New Mexico to California, has found it con-
venient for the passage of his wagon train to cross the frontier of
Sonora. . . . I have found it necessary to take this presidio in my
route to the Gila.

Be assured that I did not come as an enemy of the people

whom you represent; they have received only kindness at my hands. Sonora refused to contribute to the support of the present war against my country, alleging the excellent reasons that all her resources were necessary to her defence from the incessant attacks of the savages; that the central government gave her no protection, and was, therefore, entitled to no support. To this might have been added that *Mexico supports a war upon Sonora*. For I have seen the New Mexicans within her boundary, trading for the spoil of her people, taken by murderous, cowardly Indians, who attack only to lay waste, rob and fly to the mountains, and I have certain information that this is the practice of many years; thus one part of Mexico allies itself against another.

The unity of Sonora with the States of the north, now her neighbors, is necessary effectually to subdue these Parthian Apaches.

Meanwhile I make a wagon road from the streams of the Atlantic to the Pacific Ocean, through the valuable plains, and mountains rich with minerals, of Sonora. This, I trust, will prove useful to the citizens of either republic, who, if not more closely, may unite in the pursuits of a highly beneficial commerce.

With sentiments of esteem and respect, I am your Excellency's most obedient servant,

P. St. George Cooke,
Lieutenant-Colonel of the United States Forces,
to his Excellency, Sen. Don Manuel Gandara,
Governor of Sonora, Ures, Sonora.

The letter was a matter of love's labors lost. Perhaps Governor Gandara couldn't read English. And if he couldn't, surely nobody else in his constituency could. But it serves to show the foresight and intelligence of Colonel Cooke. He would have made a wise and benevolent military governor of the entire Southwest.

Leaving his letter and hoping for the best results, Cooke

led the Mormon Battalion on down the Santa Cruz River and reached the Gila on December 21. After his big swing to the south he was now back on General Kearny's trail. Here he was greeted by the friendly Pima Indians and later downstream by the Maricopas. Cooke was pleasantly surprised by the behavior of the Pimas. In all, they were the best Indians he had ever met. In his report he gives no faint priase to these aboriginal citizens of the Gila Valley.

The Pimas are large and fine looking, seem well fed, ride good horses, and are variously clothed, though many have only the center cloth; the men and women have extraordinary luxuriance and length of hair. . . . But innocence and cheerfulness are their most distinctive characteristics.

Several miles short of the village, groups of men, women and girls were met, coming to welcome the battalion. These last, naked generally above the hips, were of every age and pretty, walking often by twos with encircling arms; it was a gladdening sight, so much cheerfulness and happiness. One little girl, particularly, by a fancied resemblance, interested me very much; she was so joyous that she seemed very pretty and innocent; I could not resist tying on her head, as a turban, a bright new silk handkerchief, which I happened to wear today; the effect was beautiful to see—a picture of happiness.

The camp is full of Indians, and a great many have some eatables, including watermelons, to trade; and they seem only to want clothing or cotton cloth, and beads. I am sorry they will be disappointed. It reminds me of a crowded New Orleans market. There must be two thousand in camp, all enjoying themselves very much; they stroll about, their arms around each other, graceful and admirable in form; their language certainly sounds like ours, their honesty is perfect.

Below the Pima villages the battalion met the Maricopas. These Indians had eight mules which had been abandoned by

General Kearny. They turned the animals over to Colonel Cooke, and again he recorded his admiration of the Gila Valley inhabitants:

They live in cordial amity . . . and their religion consists in a simple belief in a great ever-ruling spirit. This seems to have proved a foundation for a most enviable practical morality. . . . Their dwellings are domed shape wicker work, thatched with straw or cornstalks, and from twenty to fifty feet in diameter; in front is usually a large arbor, on which is piled the cotton in the pod for drying; horses, mules, oxen, chickens, and dogs seem to be the only domestic animals; they have axes, hoes, shovels, and harrows. The soil is so easily pulverized as to make the plow unnecessary. . . .

They have the simplicity of nature, and none of the affected reserve and dignity characteristic of other Indians, before whites. At the sound of a trumpet, playing of a violin, the killing of a beef, they rush to see and hear, with delight or astonishment strongly exhibited.

With all this happiness of environment, Colonel Cooke made his first mistake of the trip. He took a look at the Gila River, which was at this point, and would be today if there were any water in it, about four or five feet deep and 150 yards wide.

He decided to construct a boat, to be made of two wagon beds lashed together, and ballasted by two long cottonwood logs.

Lieutenant George Stoneman, whose self-shot thumb had now healed, was put in command of this first ship to attempt to run the Gila. The clumsy craft was overloaded. Colonel Cooke's thought was to lighten the burden of the wagon train, and to utilize water power by letting the Gila pull his boat downstream as if it were a raft. That plan might have worked on eastern rivers, but not on the unpredictable Gila.

Lieutenant Stoneman became the first skipper on the Gila River—and he regretted it. The improvised boat carried mostly meat and flour. At times the craft caught on sand bars and spun crazily. Once it was half submerged and Stoneman and his crew of three had to hustle the cargo ashore. Then the boat was freed of the sand bar and they had to moor it and reload. Irksome was the word for it. For in less than a mile it snagged on another sand bar and the same tedious process had to be repeated. As this kind of thing became the routine of the day, Stoneman decided he'd never get to the mouth of the Gila. So he lightened his ship by making a cache of half the cargo and eventually guided, pushed, and poled her to the lower end of the Gila, and beached her just in time to prevent her from being sucked into the more mighty Colorado. Here he met his commanding officer. Boating on the Gila, he reported to Colonel Cooke, was definitely not to be recommended to Washington. Cooke, being a man of adaptability, dropped the subject. And, without making an issue of it, he sent four men and four mules back upstream to salvage the cached meat and flour.

The battalion didn't find the Yuma Indians quite so co-operative as the Pimas and the Maricopas, but at least there was no hostility. It took three days to get the expedition across the Colorado to the California side. But by swimming the animals and fording the wagons it was finally accomplished at the site of the present city of Yuma, a point virtually the same as when Kearny had crossed. And the cumbersome first ship to navigate the Gila saw useful service at last as a ferryboat.

West of the Gila, across the dreaded Colorado Desert of California, the battalion met its greatest hardships. Mules and horses collapsed and some of the weaker members could not keep up with the advance guard. The party became strung out, and for a while it appeared that lack of water would take a heavy toll. But those in the lead, finding a spring in the mountains, sent back water to the stragglers, and at last the Mormon Battalion reached the security of Warner's Ranch and from there on their troubles were over.

And so was the war in California. Shortly before the battalion arrived in San Diego, Stockton and Frémont, plus what was left of Kearny's Army of the West, managed to crush the last vestige of native strength at Los Angeles. As a military force the battalion was no longer necessary, but it could indeed function as a colonizing force. In July of 1847, one year after its organization in Iowa, the battalion was marched to Los Angeles and its members honorably discharged.

The importance of the Mormon Battalion in southwestern history was institutional rather than active. It brought the Mormon culture through the Gila Valley to California, it proved that wheels could move west; and it instilled the idea in some men's minds that where wagon wheels could go so might, some future day, a railroad. It demonstrated that the Gila River was not practical for navigation, and it added considerably to the knowledge of remote Arizona. Because of the success of the expedition other wagons prepared to move west. Americans were on the march.

14

It was Hilaire Belloc who wrote, "Readable history is melodrama," and the story of the Oatman case is both. Although this tragedy with a happy ending for only two of its nine participants occurred on the banks of the Gila River in 1851, it was not until 1857 that it received national publicity, became of national news value, and made its printed account a best seller of its day. *The Captivity of the Oatman Girls* by the Reverend Royal B. Stratton sold thirty thousand copies in eleven months, a remarkable sale for nonfiction in 1857. The opening of a wagon road west by the Mormon Battalion, bad advice, and an ignorance of Indians on the part of the father of the family, Royce Oatman, and the murderous lust and inherent cruelty of the Apaches—all were the causes of this story that swept the nation.

With the end of the Mexican War in 1848 and the discovery of gold in California that same year there began a great immigration of Americans moving west. The Treaty of Guadalupe Hidalgo, formally terminating the Mexican War, gave the United States all of California, New Mexico, and that portion of Arizona north of the Gila River. In other words, the Gila from its mouth to the western boundary of present-day New Mexico formed the international line. For the United States, at least, it was an unsatisfactory choice; but Washington still didn't understand the topography of Arizona sufficiently in 1848 to see the need of grabbing more of it. North of the Gila, in central and

eastern Arizona, the land was mostly mountainous, south of the
Gila it was largely desert. To get to California by the southern
route it was, therefore, still necessary to pass through Mexico, and
Tucson was still a Mexican city. Kearny's route, for the most
part, had been on the south bank of the Gila; the Mormon Battalion had moved west far south of the Gila until it reached
the river at the confluence of its tributary, the Santa Cruz, and
then had marched along the south bank all the way to the Colorado. After the peace treaty, Major Lawrence P. Graham led a
battalion of dragoons from occupied Chihuahua to California,
and was south of the Gila all the way, and was therefore in
Mexican territory until he crossed the Colorado River. So it was
evident to those who had been on the scene that it was not possible to travel to California without staying south of the Gila.
And in that case, you were in Mexico and outside the jurisdiction of the United States.

When the gold in California's mountains lured people west,
few of those who took the southern route cared if they passed
across a part of Mexico or not. Between the end of the Mexican War in 1848 and the Gadsden Purchase in 1853, which
moved the international boundary south from the Gila to its
present location, there is no possible accurate estimate of the number of Americans who followed the Gila Valley to California.
There were at first, in late 1848, a few emigrant parties. In
1849 the real rush was on. For an account that was not written
for military reconnaissance or for scientific research, but merely
as a day-to-day report of the vicissitudes of crossing Arizona
as a civilian, a pioneer, and a gold seeker, the Huntington Library has published a book called *Mexican Gold Trail*, which is
the diary of George W. B. Evans who started from Ohio in
February of 1849 and arrived at the "Mariposa Diggings" in California in November of that same year. It is a painstaking record

of incidents, good and bad, and the occasional blessings and the minor tragedies of an argonaut who followed the Gila to the land beyond the rainbow. It must be typical of many such diaries, most of which have been lost. For a normal run of emigrant events it makes casually interesting reading.

None of the members of the Oatman family, which followed much the same as Evans the Gila route to the west, kept a diary. But their story is unique inasmuch as nothing like it had happened before, or has ever happened since.

The Oatmans were far from destitute emigrants moving west on a pittance and living on hope. Royce Oatman, the father (sometimes spelled Boyce and sometimes Roys), had a good education and was married to a girl whose maiden name had been Mary Ann Sperry, of Laharpe, Illinois. Oatman himself was a native of New York State. He was nineteen when he married Miss Sperry, who was one year his junior. This was in 1828. Twenty-two years later, at the ages of forty-one and forty, respectively, Royce and Mary Ann Oatman had a family of seven children. History finds them in Independence, Missouri, in 1850 with their seven children and a covered wagon, about to depart for the West—California, of course—with a number of other emigrants forming a wagon train. There were fifty people in the party made up of nine wagons.

With the normal run of pioneering adventures the wagon train moved farther and farther west by way of the Arkansas River, across the Texas panhandle, New Mexico, the Rio Grande Valley, the route of the Mormon Battalion, and eventually arrived at Tucson in February of 1851.

By this time the fifty people, less one or two who had died en route, but plus one child born (not to the Oatmans), were weary and greatly in need of a rest. They planned to remain in Tucson for one month, and during that time the leaders of the party were appealed to by the citizens of Tucson to stay in their town indefinitely. Or, if they remained for only a year, they could have a good rest, plant and harvest grain, fatten their animals, and then be in fine fettle to continue their arduous journey to California. This argument was of strong persuasion to the majority of the party. But at the end of one month in Tucson Royce Oatman was restless and anxious to be on his way west. Two other families, the Wilders and the Kellys, agreed with the Oatmans. So the wagon train was divided. Six wagons and six families remained in Tucson (which they called "Tukjon") and three wagons and three families proceeded down the Santa Cruz to the Gila. Here they met the Pima people, and as always these Indians were friendly and hospitable.

But beyond the Pima villages (and the Maricopa) lay almost two hundred miles of desert country before the emigrants could reach the Colorado and Fort Yuma. This government post had been established in 1850 at the strategic merging of the Gila with the Colorado. It was at first on the Arizona side where the city of Yuma is today, but in 1851 was transferred to the California side and occupied the exact site of Padre Garces' Mission Purisima Concepción. The three emigrant wagons could follow the south bank of the Gila, which would lead them straight to Fort Yuma. Water was no problem, as the Gila supplied that. Food was the major problem. Food, and of course Apaches.

The Wilders and the Kellys were discouraged, and were admittedly in favor of returning to Tucson. But at this time the emigrants met Dr. John Lecount, who, with a Mexican guide, had only just come by horseback through the desolate area from Fort Yuma to the Pima villages, and he reported no sign of any Apaches. Lecount was scouting the area for possible mineral wealth and he told Royce Oatman that he would return, with his guide, to Fort Yuma within a few days.

Oatman had to face a decision. Should he return to Tucson, stay here with the Pimas as the Wilders and the Kellys planned to do, or make an effort to reach Fort Yuma? Since Dr. Lecount had recently come over the lonely and dangerous road ahead and seen no Apaches, and since a stay with the Pimas meant starvation rations, and since his objective was California to the west and not a return to Tucson to the east, Royce Oatman made his choice. It was west.

It was about two hundred miles to Fort Yuma, and the Oatman wagon made a hundred miles of it confronted with every possible difficulty. They were then in the neighborhood of Gila Bend. At this time Dr. John Lecount and his Mexican guide caught up to them. Realizing that the family could never make the next hundred miles (actually about ninety) to Fort Yuma, the doctor advised them to move forward slowly. He, being on horseback, would reach Fort Yuma in four or five days and would ask the commanding officer to send men and supplies out to meet the Oatmans and lead them to the mouth of the Gila and Fort Yuma.

This was a breath of life to the exhausted Oatman family, with their scanty food supply and their jaded and dying animals, and they thanked the good Dr. Lecount and watched him and his companion ride on into the promised West.

But two nights later while camping and eating dinner, Dr. Lecount and his Mexican guide were suddenly confronted out of the night by half a dozen Indians. And they were Apaches.

Dr. Lecount met them by drawing a cocked revolver. The Mexican guide drew his knife. But the Apaches protested nothing but friendship and they managed to converse in pidgin Spanish. The six Indians and the two white men talked for about fifteen minutes. Then the Apaches left. All were friends —between a cocked gun and a brandished knife—and when the

Indians had disappeared into the darkness, both Dr. Lecount and the guide breathed a sigh of relief. They took turns sleeping that night, but the Apaches did not return.

And there was good reason.

While the six had been distracting Dr. Lecount and his guide, other Apaches had been stealing their horses. In the morning there was not an Apache in sight, and they had no animals to carry them to Fort Yuma. Dr. Lecount sent the Mexican ahead, on foot since there was no other way, and considered returning east toward the slowly oncoming Oatman family. He decided that nothing could be gained by this. So he printed a sign and tied it conspicuously to a tree, warning Royce Oatman that Apaches were in the vicinity and to take every precaution. He also said that he would continue on to Fort Yuma on foot and send back aid as soon as possible.

By the 18th of March, 1851, the family was exhausted—husband, wife, children, and animals. On the 19th the road—or trail, as it should be called—ascended a bluff above the river, and it took the family all day to make about four miles. They made a dreary camp late in the afternoon, and just before sunset they were startled by the sudden appearance, as if they had sprung from the earth, of a band of Apache Indians, said to have been nineteen in number. These were unquestionably the same Indians who had accosted Dr. Lecount and stolen his horses.

Apparently the Oatmans had not seen Dr. Lecount's warning sign. It is unlikely, however, that they could miss it on the trail, and it is possible that Royce Oatman found it first, read the message, and then concealed the fact from the rest of the family so as not to add terror to their trials and tribulations.

The Apaches confronted the frightened family and used at first the same approach as they had with Dr. Lecount. They professed friendship and they asked for food. Oatman tried to explain that the family didn't have enough for its own members. The Indians seemed to think that he was lying and gave evidence of belligerence. To placate them, Oatman gave them a little of his scanty supply of flour. As soon as they received this, they demanded more. Oatman explained that there was no more. Grumbling, they withdrew from the family and stood apart in a group, talking in Apache, which the Oatmans couldn't understand, and giving the white family occasional hostile looks. The Oatmans, on the orders of the father, went about their camp chores and made an effort to appear at ease. It was the wrong technique, although what else Oatman could have done is problematical. He might have fired a shot just over the heads of the Indians and ordered them to leave, thereby scaring them away. But Apaches weren't easily scared. He might have fired deliberately into their ranks, killing two or three, and threatening the rest with the same medicine if they didn't let him alone. This might have worked, but it might only have resulted in a later vengeful attack.

Before anything could be done, in a matter of a few minutes, the Apaches suddenly turned on the family, and wielding knives and clubs, and yelling piercing war whoops, killed six of them in the space of a minute or two. Oatman was slain immediately, his wife and youngest child only seconds later. Three other children were quickly murdered, and Lorenzo, the eldest boy, who was sixteen, was knocked senseless and left for dead. For some reason the Apaches spared two of the children, Olive and Mary Ann. Olive was either thirteen, fourteen, or fifteen at the time (accounts disagree, but fourteen would be reasonable) and Mary Ann was seven.

Several Apaches held the two girls while the rest looted the camp and wagon and corpses and prepared to carry away everything they could transport. Lorenzo, when searched, seemed to be alive. Instead of knifing his throat, the Apaches, threw his body

over the bluff down toward the Gila. Satisfied that they had everything they wanted, and forcing the two screaming and terrified children to accompany them, they trooped off into the dusk toward their horses.

It is far from a pretty scene; but it is history and it is true. It is often told in far more lurid detail than narrated here.

In time, Lorenzo Oatman regained consciousness. He lay beside the Gila all night, and in the morning, suffering from shock, he staggered back toward the Pima country. He would surely have died had he not been found by two Pima hunters who carried him part way toward the nearest Pima village until they met two covered wagons coming toward them. They were the Wilders and the Kellys, who had decided to emulate Royce Oatman's courage and follow his route to Fort Yuma.

These two families took care of the hysterical and suffering boy, and they returned to the Pima village. Here they waited for several days. Lorenzo recovered. After another week he was well enough to travel west with the Wilders and the Kellys to Fort Yuma, and eventually on to California.

It must have been a grueling moment for Lorenzo when the two covered wagons reached the scene of the massacre. Six bodies were found and buried. Some of the animals had died and some had strayed away and were lost in the desert. The covered wagon still stood where Royce Oatman had brought it to a halt that fateful afternoon of the 19th of March, 1851. It was decided to abandon it.

And of Olive and Mary Ann there was no trace.

There was nothing more that could be done. Sadly the Wilders and the Kellys turned their teams to the west; and the tearful Lorenzo rode on with his friends.

The two wagons reached the mouth of the Gila about the

middle of April. They were barely able to cross the Colorado River in spite of the fact that by this time there was a crude ferry—a flatboat that had to be controlled by poling it against the current from the mouth of the Gila across, and downstream with the current, to the California side and Fort Yuma. One wagon was damaged and almost lost. At Fort Yuma they met the officer in charge, who was Major Samuel Heintzelman.

The purpose of Fort Yuma was to establish a garrison at this strategic location for the protection of the emigrants. But when Dr. John Lecount had arrived at the fort on foot after the Apaches had stolen his horses, and had explained the dangerous plight of the Oatman family, not only from the ordeal of crossing two hundred miles of desert in a covered wagon but that he knew from personal contact that Apaches were between the Oatmans and the fort, and that the family consisted of only one male adult and all the others were a wife and seven children—with all this information Major Heintzelman refused to send soldiers and supplies to assist the emigrants. Why? Because they were on the south bank of the Gila and were therefore in Mexico. He had no authority to send soldiers of the United States into Mexico. The two nations were now at peace. Didn't Dr. Lecount know that? Had the Oatmans been on the north bank of the Gila, that would have made a difference. They would have been in their own country. Dr. Lecount explained that no emigrants could approach Fort Yuma from the north bank of the Gila. They all had to start south of the Gila and would perforce stay on the south bank. But to Major Heintzelman the south bank was in Mexico. And as for the Oatmans—too bad.

Lorenzo made a personal appeal to the major and the major received him reluctantly. He explained his reluctance later as being due to his hesitancy to tell the boy the truth. But the fact was that any captives taken by the Apaches would be slowly tor-

tured to death within twenty-four hours. And Major Heintzelman shrugged the whole episode off with "That's the way with
Apaches."

A man identified in history only as Dr. Hewitt met Lorenzo
at Fort Yuma and treated the 16-year-old as his son. He took
him to San Diego and later to San Francisco and found him a
job. Within six months personal affairs took Dr. Hewitt to New
York, and Lorenzo was left in San Francisco, a brooding and
melancholy youth who wished to know only one thing—what
had happened to his two sisters and could they still be found
and rescued.

What actually happened to Olive and Mary Ann Oatman will
never be known in complete detail. Mary Ann died during her
ordeal of captivity and Olive, when finally rescued five years
later, was merely the physically wrecked and mentally numbed
shadow of a white girl. For many days she could do no more
than cry; and it was several weeks before she could again speak
in English. At this time she was probably nineteen years old.

In the Reverend Royal B. Stratton's best seller, *The Captivity of the Oatman Girls,* the author goes on at great length to
describe the ordeal of hardships, beatings, constant brutal treatment, and menial tasks that became the girls' daily life. The author takes many words to describe their pitiful sufferings as slaves
to the Apaches, and he waxes periphrastic with continuous expressions such as "these miscreant wretches" [Apaches], who were
"human devils of savage ferocity lurking for prey," and "this
hellish deed" and "a country infested with these miserable
brutes" who were "prowling banditti," and "the ghastly demon
of horrible famine," and Olive's "fate worse than death" until
in his book even the Gila River comes in for a load of adjectives
and is described as "that ceaseless, mournful, murmuring, mordant
Gila." So it is plain to see that his Reverence had a grand

time writing the book, and not only did it sell many copies but the Reverend Mr. Stratton must have swayed many a congregation by his telling oratory. But one thing he always did: he kept his eyes well averted from any possible sexual outrages. And possibly he was quite correct so far as the Apaches were concerned.

In his account of the massacre he describes the Apaches as painted and nearly naked except for wearing wolfskins about their middles. All of a sudden they attacked with clubs, and he explains these as "war-clubs which had hitherto been concealed under their wolfskins." To hide a war club under a pair of wolfskin shorts would be quite a feat of concealment. But statements such as this, along with numerous other impossibilities, are the result of the Reverend's writing the book from newspaper accounts and hearsay. It is true that Lorenzo Oatman did supply him with many details, but the Reverend's imagination lent a colorful, if often inaccurate, embroidery. Apaches, incidentally, used habitually the bow and arrow and the knife—but hardly ever a war club.

After a year or more of misery as Apache slaves, the two girls were traded to the Mojaves for two worn-out horses and a few beads. The Mojaves lived, and live today, along the Colorado River in the general vicinity of what is the town of Needles. This is a long way from the Apache country and the girls were forced to endure a fearful march. Their life with the Mojave Indians was perhaps a little better than with the Apaches. One of the things that fascinated the Mojaves was to sit around a campfire and listen to the two white girls sing hymns. Although the girls were still slaves and assigned to menial tasks, the Mojaves did not abuse them as had the Apaches, and one old Mojave woman was kind to them and treated them as if they were her own daughters.

There was a drought in 1853, and the Mojaves suffered for

food. In this famine the younger girl, Mary Ann, died, but Olive somehow survived. In the telling of this episode the Reverend Mr. Stratton's book is full of torturings and burnings and even a crucifixion of a "beautiful Cocopah girl" who was captured by the Mojaves. She had tried to escape to her own people and was put to a painful death by the Mojaves as a warning to Olive Oatman, who was forced to witness it, that a similar fate would be hers if she also tried to escape to the white civilization. And obviously the author thoroughly enjoyed writing this sadistic episode. It is probably largely imaginative, although it is true that the Mojaves did engage in war and marauding raids against the Cocopahs, who lived below the Gila on the lower Colorado River.

So Mary Ann was dead and Olive lived on to the age of nineteen with the Mojaves. During this time Lorenzo Oatman grew up, and at the age of twenty was still valiantly striving to find assistance in learning the whereabouts or fate of his two sisters. The story made newspapers, but never headlines up until 1857, and nothing constructive was done about the problem. But from time to time rumors drifted from Indians to trappers and miners that there were two captive white girls living with the Mojaves. At length rumor had it that there was only one white girl still a captive. And this was true. In 1856 the persistence of the rumor caught the interest and imagination of Henry Grinnell, who was employed as a carpenter at Fort Yuma. He had arrived at the post in 1853. That a white girl should be held captive among Indians and that white men did nothing about it was to him outrageous.

Lorenzo, during these years from 1853 to 1856, had appealed for help to public-spirited citizens, to newspapers, and even to Governor Neely Johnson of California. The California governor said the matter was out of his jurisdiction and referred Lorenzo to the Indian Bureau in Washington. Lorenzo's pleas were involved in buck passing and red tape, but Henry Grinnell at Fort Yuma, unbeknown to Lorenzo, went about it in a far more practical way. And fortunately the commanding officer of Fort Yuma was now Colonel Martin Burke, who, though skeptical, was willing to assist Grinnell. And since Grinnell was a private citizen employed at the fort, he had a right to make any efforts he wished.

As more rumors reached the fort from the Indian country of a white girl captive of the Mojaves, Grinnell let a few rumors drift back. He told all the Indians he saw, mostly Yumas, but occasionally a Mojave who might have come down the river to trade with the Yumas, that a great reward in horses, blankets, and food would go to the Indian who brought the girl to Fort Yuma. The results were painfully slow. Indians showed no interest. But at length one of the more intelligent Yumas came to Grinnell and began furtive negotiations. This Yuma's name was Francisco, and he said he might be able to get the white girl from the Mojaves by trading something for her. He was willing to go up the river and try, with the understanding, of course, that he himself would get the "great reward" if the scheme worked.

At that moment Grinnell had an inspiration. He picked up a copy of the Los Angeles *Star* and pretended to read from it, translating into Spanish, which Francisco could comprehend. The article may have been a weather report, or a series of want ads, but Grinnell, making it up as he went along, read slowly aloud in Spanish about a great army of thousands of men being mustered in Los Angeles to attack and wipe out to the last man the entire Mojave nation. So, concluded Grinnell, the Mojaves didn't know it yet, but if that army found a white girl among them or didn't find her because the Mojaves had killed her—in either case, there wouldn't be a Mojave left alive on earth. About the only thing they could do to save themselves would be to trade that white girl to somebody else as fast as they could. And Grinnell put down the paper and looked at Francisco.

The Yuma was deeply impressed.

Grinnell suggested that Francisco warn the Mojaves. And with that he went back to his work.

Francisco thought about it overnight. In the morning he returned to Grinnell. What he said then so impressed Grinnell that he took Francisco to Colonel Martin Burke and had the Yuma repeat his story to the commanding officer.

Francisco promised that if he were supplied with two horses, some food, four blankets, and plenty of beads, he would bring the white girl to Fort Yuma in exactly twenty days.

How would he do it?

Francisco refused to say anything more except, "In twenty days, when the sun is there," indicating where a shadow would fall at four o'clock in the afternoon.

Fortunately it was Burke and not Heintzelman who was in command at Fort Yuma. Francisco was given the supplies he requested and later that day he left the post.

Nineteen days went by and nothing happened.

But on the twentieth day three Yumas appeared about noon and told Grinnell, "Francisco is coming."

"Is the girl with him?" demanded Grinnell.

"Francisco will come when the sun is there," replied the Yumas. And they left.

Henry Grinnell and Colonel Burke paced the floor for four hours, straining their eyes peering to the north, across the Gila, and up the Colorado. And at four o'clock Francisco arrived, coming down the east bank of the Colorado on foot, crossed the Gila, and then was ferried across the Colorado to Fort Yuma. He was alone.

"I came for the great reward," said a weary but placid Francisco.

"Where is the girl?" demanded Grinnell and Burke in unison.

"She is alive. She is well," said Francisco. "She is hidden in the willows just beyond the Gila. She has no white clothes."

An officer's wife provided clothing and Grinnell and Francisco set out at once for a clump of willows a short distance north of the mouth of the Gila. And there Grinnell found Olive Oatman—the first white person to see her in five years.

This dramatic scene was described by Grinnell to J. Ross Browne, who later included the Oatman story in his *Adventures in the Apache Country*. Here is Grinnell's account as related by Browne:

She was sitting on the ground, as he described the scene to me, with her face covered by her hands. So completely was she disguised by long exposure to the sun, by paint, tattooing, and costume, that he could not believe she was a white woman. When he spoke to her she made no answer, but cried and kept her face covered. It was not for several days after her arrival at Fort Yuma that she could utter more than a few broken words of English.

Grinnell finally persuaded Olive to put on the dress of the officer's wife, and with coaxing and kindly words he led this wreck of a white girl to the army post. Olive was dazed and numbed, and hardly seemed to realize that the terrible Indian ordeal was over.

Major Burke and Henry Grinnell were ecstatic over the rescue. Francisco got his reward in full, and the fort fired a salute of four cannons. Everybody cheered, flags were waved, rifles cracked, and only Olive Oatman seemed to be unaware of what it was all about.

Officers' wives took her in charge and after several days Olive began to come out of her mental apathy. Morbid tears flowed less often and at length she managed to smile. Slowly but surely she was returning both mentally and physically to the white world. At fourteen her mother had taught her to sew. And her recovery manifested itself when she asked for a needle and thread. For several days she sewed by the hour. This was a clear case of applied occupational therapy, and was unrecognized as such in 1856. But it worked. Olive was busy and happy. Finally she spoke more freely, and at last a smile became laughter. She was a white girl again. Only the marks of tattooing on her arms and chin remained to remind her of her captivity. These marks could not be removed and she bore them to her grave. They consisted of five vertical blue lines, or cuts, filled with dye, and running from her mouth down her chin to just below the jawbone. On each of her upper arms there was one long line, also made of blue dye.

The sensational rescue became news value at once, and the Los Angeles Star was the first paper to print the story. This was merely the briefest account, in only twenty-two words headed "American Woman Rescued from the Indians!" and followed by "A woman, giving her name as Miss Olive Oatman, has been recently rescued from the Mojaves, and is now at Fort Yuma." That was all that was known at first. And in Los Angeles, Lorenzo Oatman was stunned by this news.

He went to the editor at once and the editor assured him that the report was reliable since it had come from Colonel Burke at Fort Yuma. With a friend to accompany him, Lorenzo set out immediately for the mouth of the Gila River. It was March 10, 1856. It took him ten days to reach Fort Yuma. And there, five years and one day after the Apache attack, Lorenzo and Olive met and embraced. It was a touching scene indeed, and there were tears in the eyes of those present. The Reverend Mr. Stratton described it in his book:

Not an unmoved heart nor a dry eye witnessed it. Even the rude and untutored Indian, raised his brawny hand to wipe away the unbidden tear that stole upon his cheek as he stood speechless and wonder-struck!

Two weeks later Olive and Lorenzo were in Los Angeles. Their story was eagerly read by the public, and the *Star* printed a detailed account of it that covered most of its front page. Other California papers copied it and then eastern papers picked it up. For a while Olive and Lorenzo were national news. People rushed to see them and the *Star*, carrying on the story, hastened to inform the public that Olive had not "suffered a fate worse than death," and scotched such a rumor and couched the denial in such decorous prose as, "She has not been made a wife." And it went on to assert that "her defenceless situation [was] entirely respected during her residence among the Indians." The *Star* further complimented her on her "lady-like deportment," her "pleasing manners," and her "amiable disposition." And the paper continued by informing the public that Olive Oatman was more delicate and courteous than the sensationally curious who, open mouthed, came to gawk at her.

Be that as it may, the tattooing on a Mojave girl's chin is usually indicative of marriage. Just as the Hopi girl changes her hairdo when she weds, so the custom among the Mojaves was for the married woman to have tattoo marks placed upon her face. In Olive's case this probably was an exception, for if she had had a Mojave husband she would never have been allowed to escape with Francisco, the Yuma intermediator.

Olive was most eager for education, and for several months she attended school in California. Later she and Lorenzo visited a distant relative in Oregon. And about this time the Reverend Royal B. Stratton met them and from their verbal accounts and from newspaper reports wrote his extremely popular book.

There are conflicting stories about the remainder of Olive's life. One has it that she became more and more depressed, was unable to adjust to the white world from which she had been alien during such important formative years, and at last became a manic-depressive (called a condition of melancholia in those days), took interest in nothing, and finally became a mental case and died in 1877 in an asylum after having gone completely insane.

How this story got about it is difficult to ascertain unless it is the kind of thing that the public wanted to think should be the tragic end of a girl who endured Olive's 5-year ordeal.

But there is no truth to it, which may be happily stated once and for all. Olive went on to live a normal and happy life. In March of 1858, two years after her return to her own world, she sailed with Lorenzo and with the Reverend Mr. Stratton from San Francisco to Panama, crossed the isthmus, and sailed again from the port of Aspinwall to New York. In November, 1865, when she was about twenty-eight, she married John B. Fairchild in Rochester, New York. She had a happy married life, and it is believed she bore two or three children. She died, at the age of sixty-six, in Sherman, Texas, on March 20, 1903. This statement can be corroborated by the files of the Sherman, Texas, *Daily Register* for March 21, 1903.

And thus ended the life of Olive Oatman Fairchild, certainly the only white girl to survive a 5-year captivity among the Apaches and the Mojaves; and it brings to an end one of the strangest stories to come from the banks of the Gila.

After almost a hundred years the Oatman case is well buried in history. But Arizona historian Sharlot M. Hall did some careful research on it, and it is due to her efforts that the true ending of Olive's career has been verified. The name "Oatman" exists today in two places in Arizona. Just below the bluff on which the family camped on that fateful 19th of March, 1851, there is a plain along the south bank of the Gila which is known as Oatman Flat. And in the Black Mountains of northwestern Arizona, in the country of the Mojave Indians, there is the mining town of Oatman. The town was named for a nearby spring, still known to old residents of the area as the "Ollie Oatman Spring" because the Mojaves hid the girl there for some months after purchasing her from the Apaches. U.S. Highway 66 curves through the town of Oatman, and probably not one tourist in a thousand knows that the town received its name from a 14- or 15-year-old girl whose dramatic story began several hundred miles away, and a hundred years ago, on the Gila River.

15

MR.   GADSDEN MAKES A PURCHASE

MR. GILA HOWARD is not a name readily identified in history. But in a sense Mr. Howard made his contribution to history without knowing it. For he was the first child born to American parents in Arizona, and he was delivered by an unidentified doctor on a flatboat as it drifted down the Gila River on October 21, 1849.

Two important historical events preceded the young Howard's arrival. On January 24, 1848, gold had been discovered in California; and on February 22, 1848, the Treaty of Guadalupe Hidalgo ended the Mexican War and made the Gila a part of the international boundary.

The lure of gold in California brought Edward Howard and his wife west in 1849. And the Treaty of Guadalupe Hidalgo made it impossible to say for a certainty whether the Howard baby was born in the United States or in Mexico. The international boundary was the middle of the river, theoretically; although the river often shifted its main channel and it was impossible to identify an unconstant and ever-changing boundary. The Howard baby arrived on one side or the other of the imaginary line down the middle of the river; and his parents, totally unconcerned whether their son was born in Mexico or the United States, promptly named him Gila. He is probably the only child ever delivered on the river, for navigation of the Gila proved utterly impractical. Very few emigrants even attempted to flatboat from the Pima villages to Fort Yuma, although the Howards, and a doctor and a clergyman, tried it and made it. Four people embarked on the flatboat, and where the Gila met the Colorado five went ashore. And doubtless young Gila was squalling lustily.

The identity of the Gila's southern watershed, where all the streams flow north, had always been more or less politically nebulous. For 150,000,000 years it had belonged to the ruling class of life on earth—dinosauria. After the extinction of the great reptiles the area was dominated for 60,000,000 years by mammalia. And with the advent of man on earth, it was the home of some slowly evolving forms of the human race for probably 25,000 years up to its first civilization, the Hohokam, who appeared about 2,500 years ago and gradually developed their culture up to about A.D. 1400.

Its first white political identification was Pimeria Alta with no determined boundaries. Eventually, when Mexico became independent of Spain, Pimeria Alta became a part of the Mexican state of Sonora, but at the same time was generally considered to be part of New Mexico north of the Gila River. And as the Apaches became stronger the land became theirs and a goodly portion of it was so designated—Apacheria. It was not until well into the nineteenth century that Arizona became the popular designation.

The name "Arizona" posits a problem. There is little or no basis for believing that Coronado in his disappointment called it "arida zona"—arid zone—for the words don't make sense in Spanish. But this is one version of the source of the name, and it persists.

Another explanation accepted (but rarely) is that Arizona came from the Aztec word "Arizuma," meaning "rich in silver."

Historian James Harvey McClintock states that, "There is no doubt that Arizona was named after some springs near Banera, eight miles south of the border, and about eighty-five miles below Tucson." These springs are called "Aleh-zon" by the Papagos, meaning "small spring." This explanation is now accepted by most contemporary historians. The word itself first came into use about 1755, and because its euphony allows it to roll easily off Spanish or English tongues, it gradually supplanted the more clumsy Pimeria Alta and Apacheria.

In 1854, when it was first suggested that the area be made a territory in its own right apart from New Mexico, three possible names were suggested: Pimeria, Gadsonia, and Arizona. The last was selected. But the bill to create such a territory died in Congress in 1855. People identified the area as they wished, and in time the pleasant-sounding Arizona supplanted all others.

In fact, everything south of the Gila, and the northern wilderness as well, might have been called Peralta. This was due to a curious claim, possibly legitimate so far as its grant goes, but certainly unable to maintain itself in view of subsequent political and international developments. The Peralta Land Grant, if it ever was a reality, created the Baron of the Colorados. This impressive title was bestowed upon Don Miguel Peralta de Cordoba by his Majesty Ferdinand VI of Spain on December 20, 1748, as a reward for Peralta's services to the crown. Following instructions from the king, the viceroy made the grant. It consisted of an area 75 miles long from east to west following the Gila in the region of the Pima villages and the confluence of the Salt. From north to south the grant extended for 25 miles on both banks of the Gila. Thus Don Miguel, newly created Baron of the Colorados, owned about 3,750 square miles of the heart of the Gila Valley, or an area about the size of the state of Connecticut. When Carlos III followed Ferdinand VI, the baron requested royal confirmation of the grant—and got it. Peralta died in 1788 and bequeathed his estate, and presumably his title, to his son, Miguel Peralta II. This second Baron of the Colorados was living in San Diego, California, in 1853. He believed he was in imminent danger of losing his demesne because of the Mexican War. Actually, it is unlikely that this title of Baron of the Colorados, created by the favor and whim of a Spanish king, would have had any validity after the Mexican break from Spain in 1821. But nobody wants to give up a good thing, understandably, and the Peralta family, led by the second baron, pressed its claims. The president of the Republic of Mexico, Antonio Lopez de Santa Anna, sensing, or knowing full well, that the United States would eventually grab all of Arizona and possibly a good piece of Sonora, was happy to substantiate the Peralta claim, and executed a certified title, guaranteeing its propriety, integrity, validity, and sufficiency.

The second baron died in 1864 and the title to the fabulous Peralta Grant passed to an American relative, George M. Willing, Jr. He held it only three years, and then the title went to James A. Reavis in 1867. Mr. Reavis made efforts to es-

tablish his claim to a fortune in Arizona real estate and enlisted
the assistance of Mexican authorities such as the governor of the
state of Jalisco and a Guadalajara court. Mr. Reavis even stated
that he had located the boundary marks of his grant. If so, such
markings were never recognized by the government of the United
States.

Under what circumstances Mr. Reavis obtained this title was
at first not clear, although amply clarified later. He may have inherited it (as he claimed); he may have purchased it; or he may
have taken it in payment for a debt, deeming it worth a specula-
tive effort. At any rate, Mr. Reavis had the old, foxed, stained,
and torn Spanish documents to substantiate his claim. If authentic,
this Peralta Land Grant would supersede all other titles, for the
United States, in the Treaty of Guadalupe Hidalgo in 1848, had
promised to recognize all former land grants and to hold such
claims inviolate. Mr. Reavis's grant comprised about 3,750 square
miles of some of the most desirable land in Arizona and was
not to be sneezed at. Mr. Reavis was so assured of his validity
and sufficiency of title that he retained Robert G. Ingersoll as
his legal representative, and an attorney of Mr. Ingersoll's stature
and national reputation frightened many a small property owner
in the contested area. The Peralta Grant included land worth
over one hundred million dollars. Mr. Reavis wanted it all. And
Mr. Ingersoll set out to get it for his client.

Mr. Reavis traveled to New York and to Spain. He invoked
the aid of the American minister in Madrid and the Spanish
ambassador in Washington. His appeals to the Republic of Mexico were further substantiated. There was no doubt about it—
James A. Reavis owned the heart of Arizona.

And then the whole case collapsed like a pricked balloon
when it was pointed out by an investigator of the old Spanish

documents that when merely held up to the light they showed the unmistakable watermark of a paper mill near Appleton, Wisconsin.

Mr. Ingersoll was no longer interested in the case.

And Mr. Reavis promptly spent a number of years in a suit of black and white stripes with a cap to match and a convict's number properly displayed. When the case was finally subjected to all possible analysis and study, it was discovered that Mr. Reavis, the pretender Baron of the Colorados, had been a horse-car conductor on a St. Louis, Missouri, public carrier, who tired of his job, came west, and married a girl who was a half-breed Indian. Somehow he learned of the fabulous Peralta Land Grant and spent several years carefully preparing his claims. But he entirely overlooked the fact that fine paper has such a talisman as a watermark.

Since the demise of James A. Reavis nobody has carried on the claim of the Peralta Grant. But it is on record that there is no Baron of the Colorados today.

All former claimants of the Gila Valley from prehistoric dinosaurs to spurious barons came to an end on December 30, 1853. For on that date the United States concluded an agreement with Mexico for the acquisition of an area known as the Gadsden Purchase, which established the international border along its present-day and highly arbitrary boundaries.

James Gadsden was a native of Charleston, South Carolina, and was graduated from Yale in 1806. He served as soldier and diplomat, and in 1853 President Franklin Pierce appointed him minister to Mexico. His job was to rectify the shortsightedness in the framing of the Treaty of Guadalupe Hidalgo which, while it terminated the Mexican War in 1848, didn't give the United States control of that important avenue to the west, the Gila Valley. Washington at last realized that it hadn't grabbed enough from a helpless and prostrate opponent. It had been so anxious to get California that it had overlooked other plums.

The first plan was to "buy" all of the land south of the Gila that is now Arizona; a good piece, if not all, of Sonora in order to include the port of Guaymas on the Gulf of California; and all of Baja (Lower) California. This purchase was to be made from Mexico, but Mexico had nothing to say about it. It was a case of "You want to sell it, don't you? For if you don't, we'll start shooting again and simply take it. You'll accept twenty million dollars for this area and you'll ratify the purchase quickly. We have no time to waste." The quotation is apocryphal, but it does illustrate Washington's attitude toward Mexico City.

Mexico said yes.

Washington sent Mr. Gadsden to conclude the job. It also explained that this purchase was to clarify the international boundary, which had been in dispute in spite of the fact that the Gila River, forming a natural line between the nations, left little for the first surveyors to dispute about. But the more clouded the issue the more important would be the clarifying Gadsden Purchase. And what the first surveyors of the area had pointed out—men such as John R. Bartlett, Andrew B. Gray, Captain Lorenzo Sitgreaves, W. H. Emory, and A. W. Whipple—was the obvious fact that if a railroad was to connect the lower Mississippi Valley with California, it would, for topographical reasons, have to have a right of way south of the Gila River. And, incidentally, another attractive but not necessarily emphasized element in the prospective purchase was the fact that there were rumors—and even evidence—that the area in question would prove rich in mineral wealth, particularly in gold, silver, and copper. That, too, was an aspect to be reckoned with.

It is probable that under pressure, if not duress, and greatly in need of money, the Mexican government might have accepted the first offer and collected twenty million dollars. But the project ran into trouble in Congress, not in Mexico City. The coming breach between North and South was growing more apparent day by day. Senators and representatives from northern states were not willing to see huge areas such as Sonora and Baja California come into federal control, for such lands meant an expanding southern economy and the pushing of the institution of slavery all the way to the Pacific coast. Moreover, if a railroad was to reach the Pacific, the northern adherents wanted it in northern territories—say west from Council Bluffs rather than west from New Orleans. For a while it looked as if the projected Gadsden Purchase would be debated to death, but eventually a compromise was reached. The border was set where it is today, allowing ample room for a wagon road and a railroad to cross Arizona south of the Gila to California. But the rest of the land grab was quashed, and Mexico was allowed to keep her Sonora and Baja California. Also, she was told she would take ten million instead of twenty in view of these magnanimous changes.

Again Mexico accepted.

And on December 30, 1853, the Gadsden Purchase became a reality. To the public it was a seemingly useless expenditure, and the ever-ready critics ridiculed Congress for being so addle-pated as to buy a worthless desert. The Gadsden Purchase was considered idiotic by much of the press of the nation and was described as "our national cactus garden" and "rattlesnake heaven." This shortsightedness soon ran its course. Would that the adverse critics of Congress could see the area a century later—and what a howl would go up if somebody suggested selling it back to Mexico for what we paid for it—or even for a thousand per cent profit.

So with the beginning of 1854 all of present Arizona (still

a part of the territory of New Mexico with administrative head-quarters in Santa Fe) was open to the American colonist. Tucson, with a population of about one thousand, and Tubac, with about three hundred, were still the only towns of any consequence, but a new order was soon to come. The Gila Valley, and virtually all of its watershed with the slight exception of the head-waters of the San Pedro and the Santa Cruz in Sonora, was now under the red, white, and blue. And with a route to the West assured, a boundary issue settled, an immense area for coloniza-tion available, and untold wealth in minerals for the taking, the U.S.A. also acquired something that nobody from President Pierce and James Gadsden to the most antipathetic critic had even con-sidered—the Apache Indians.

PART 4

The U.S.A. Produces the Show

1856 to 1870

16

A PENNSYLVANIA Dutchman became the first mayor of an Arizona town that didn't exist. He was mayor simply because he was the only citizen. His name was L. J. F. Jaeger and although thirty thousand or more people passed through his "town" there wasn't a house standing. The "town" at the mouth of the Gila had something more important to passing emigrants; it had a ferry across the unpredictable Colorado River and that ferry put them in California.

The establishment of a practical workaday ferry came into existence because of the business sagacity of Jaeger. There had been ferries of various kinds from Yuma Indian rafts to the family raft that Edward Howard floated down the Gila in 1849 and on which Gila Howard was born. These were makeshift. There was no permanent ferry business until 1850. A man identified only as Hartshorne ran a ferry of occasional and irregular service—a raft made of cottonwood and willow logs—in July of 1850, and that same summer sold out the business to Jaeger. The Pennsylvania Dutchman (really a German and not a Hollander) had left Philadelphia in 1848 and had sailed around the Horn to San Francisco. After a short stay there he arrived as a cook on one of the first steamers to try to run the Colorado, and reached the Gila's mouth in July, 1850.

The Yuma Indians were anything but friendly and Jaeger had to live in a stockade near the ferry just south of the mouth of the Gila. But he had been in San Francisco and had seen the excitement caused by the gold rush of '49. He reasoned that at first hundreds and then thousands of people would be coming west. If they followed the natural avenue of the Gila Valley they would have to cross the Colorado at the Gila's mouth. So Jaeger rebuilt the awkward raft, made it large enough to accommodate a wagon and team, and had for himself a nice little monopoly. The number of emigrants who crossed the Colorado at the Gila between 1850 and 1856 has been estimated at sixty thousand. This is probably an exaggeration. But the number was certainly not less than thirty thousand, all attracted by gold in California, and Jaeger charged them $2 each to cross the river. Thus, at this desolate and apparently unproductive location, the ferryman made at least $60,000 in six years.

But he ran into a type of Kentucky Bluegrass shrewdness equal to his Pennsylvania Dutch acumen. In July of 1854 Charles D. Poston, twenty-nine years old, with a party of four topographical engineers, had come down the Gila Valley to the Colorado. They were bound for San Diego and must, perforce, cross the Colorado. Jaeger sized them up. Doubtless they were on government expenses. And whatever fare he exacted they would have to pay. They couldn't cross any other way, and they had to get to San Diego. They were on orders. It looked very attractive to Jaeger; here was a chance to make the most of a good thing. He bided his time.

After a few minutes Poston approached and asked him how much it would cost to ferry his party to the California side of the Colorado. The party consisted of five men and seven mules.

"Well—" Jaeger smiled. "It will cost you only fifty dollars."

"Well—" The gentleman from Kentucky smiled. "It must be a very wide river."

"Look at 'er," said Jaeger. "She's good and high now. It's a half-a-mile ride to the California side." And he added pointedly, "No other way to get across but my ferry. Let me know when your party's ready."

And he started to walk away.

Poston thought the price outrageous, but he gave no reaction.

"No hurry," he called to Jaeger. "We don't want to cross today. We're going to camp here beside the Gila for a while— on business."

"What business?" inquired Jaeger, looking over the empty desert.

"Haven't you heard?" asked Poston. "We are laying out a city—right here."

"Here?" asked the incredulous Jaeger. He walked back to Poston.

"Certainly," said Poston. "The future capital of Arizona."

"Here?" asked the amazed Jaeger again.

"Where else?" asked Poston. "Where two great rivers meet is bound to be the site of a big city. You're from Pennsylvania: consider Philadelphia at the Delaware and the Schuylkill; consider Pittsburgh at the Allegheny and the Monongahela. Consider this spot at the Gila and the Colorado. Why you're standing right now on the most valuable land in the entire West. Well, my boys and I have to go to work."

And with that the engineers began their survey. Maps and equipment were produced, instruments and charts were brought from the packs on their mules, and the men proceeded to lay out a town. There were two stakes for main street; another stake indicated first street; over there would be Central Avenue.

Jaeger was confounded. But this soon changed to incredulity and finally to delight. For here he was, already on the scene as the ferryman for the traffic of a great city—to be. He could visualize a mighty metropolis rising from the greasewood and the cholla cactus. And there was no doubt about it, for Poston and his engineers were really going to it. Their preliminary survey included 926 acres, quite enough for a townsite.

"Those city lots are going to be worth a lot of money someday soon—aren't they?" half stated and half asked Jaeger.

"Fabulous," said Poston.

"Who owns 'em now?"

"Government," said Poston.

"What government?"

"The U.S.A."

"Since when?"

"Since the Gadsden Purchase was completed a year ago," said Poston. "Ever hear of it?"

"Ja, ja," said Jaeger. "I'm an American citizen."

"From Pennsylvania," added Poston.

"Where you from?" asked Jaeger.

"Kentucky," said Poston.

"I like the looks of this town-site," said Jaeger, "now that I come to think about it."

"Worth a fortune in a few years," declared Poston.

"Now *there's* a choice lot," said Jaeger, indicating a flat sandy area free of cactus and greasewood.

"They're all choice," said Poston.

"How can a private citizen get one?" asked Jaeger.

"Buy one," said Poston.

"What do the lots sell for?" asked Jaeger.

"Well—" Poston hesitated— "that desirable corner lot at Main and Central, right there where the cactus is thickest—that lot—" and he hesitated again.

"Yes?" prompted Jaeger.

"That desirable corner lot sells for only fifty dollars."

"I'll take it," said Jaeger.

"Sold," said Poston.

"How do I get a guarantee of title?" Jaeger asked. And his crafty eyes watched Poston.

"When we get to San Diego, I'll register the townsite there. Those are my orders. Your lot will be included in the original registry. Then, when Arizona gets a stable and organized government, the registry of townsites will be returned to the capital city of this great territory."

"Which will be this city right here?"

"Exactly," said Poston.

"Here's fifty dollars. Spot cash," said Jaeger. "You register that corner lot for L. J. F. Jaeger."

"Thanks," said Poston, accepting the money. "I'll do it." Then he called to his engineers. "We're all through here, boys. Let's pack up!"

Jaeger examined his new lot while the engineering party prepared to resume their journey to San Diego. In a very short time they were ready, and marched to the ferry. Poston paid Jaeger $50 for the fare for the party, and Jaeger guided the ferry by poling it with the current and tied it up on the west bank next to a sand bar and some willow trees. The soldiers, looking down from Fort Yuma, waved to the engineers. And then the party debarked.

Poston had an interview with the commanding officer, and then the engineers proceeded west across the dangerous Colorado Desert.

"Wait a minute!" called Jaeger from the ferryboat. "What might the name of that new town be?"

Poston looked back.

"Oh—ah—Arizona City," he called, naming the first name he could think of.

The engineers moved on west, and presently they were beyond hearing distance of the ferryman.

"Arizona City," mused Jaeger.

He looked at the $50 he had received for his ferry fare. It was, of course, the same $50 he had paid for his lot. Somehow he felt that something was rotten in the fair city to be called Arizona. But for the life of him, he couldn't say exactly what or why.

And Poston, jogging west on his mule, was smiling in spite of the desert heat. "You know, men," he said to his engineers, "there's more than one way to cross a river."

17

"PIONEERS! O PIONEERS!"

IT WAS not until 1856, or nearly three years after its purchase, that the United States took formal and military possession of the area south of the Gila that had been relinquished by Mexico for ten million dollars.

At this time the Apache Indians controlled most of the Gila watershed. There were only three towns in the area: Tucson,

Tubac, and Arizona City. The latter was only a government survey, but one lot in the survey was owned by a private citizen. He was L. J. F. Jaeger. Charles D. Poston had been as good as his word. Jaeger's title was assured. He owned a plot of ground 150 feet by 200 feet which consisted of a number of greasewood bushes and a variety of cactus, mostly the sharp, spiny cholla (pronounced in Spanish, choy-a). As to buildings, Arizona City had none.

But things were looking up for speculator Jaeger. By 1858 Arizona City had a population of eleven, and Jaeger himself made it twelve. And it was the third largest white city in Arizona. The "buildings" then consisted of one stockade, one lean-to, three shacks, and a few tents. All the citizens went about town armed. The reason for this protection was the presence of sullen and sometimes openly hostile Yuma Indians. As to becoming the capital city of the territory of Arizona, the settlement had a fair chance. There were only two ahead of it—Tucson and Tubac—but the territory itself had not been formally organized in 1858. Nevertheless, several important events occurred in that year.

First, and most sensational, gold was discovered on the Gila River about twenty-five miles upstream from its mouth. The pioneer prospector who made the strike was Jacob Snively. When his pick turned over a few nuggets of gold, what was to become Arizona's great mining industry was born. Actually mining in Arizona had begun four years earlier at the Ajo (Spanish for garlic) copper mine, about fifty miles south of Gila Bend. But it was gold that captured the imaginations of men. Copper at Ajo was not sensational news to the fortune hunters, but gold on the Gila meant a miniature gold rush. Following Snively's strike, other prospectors found nuggets of coarse gold all along the stream, from "Arizona City" easterly to Snively's diggings. This area rapidly became a town of a few adobe houses, a few sa-

loons in shacks or tents, and a dozen brush shelters. The name
was Gila City. A post office was established in December of 1858,
and Henry Burch became the first American postmaster in Arizona. Within a year, Gila City had a population of one thousand, and bid fair to outstrip Tucson, Tubac, and Arizona City
for the honor of being the capital of the territory—if ever a
territory should come into existence. But Gila City's boom was
short-lived. By late 1859 the placers had been pinched out. There
was gold there, indeed—and there is gold all along the lower
Gila today—but its yield is so slight that it isn't worth the ex-
pense of mining for it. Panning for it would be a better description, for it turned out that the whole Gila strike was made
up almost entirely of coarse gold in alluvial deposits, and required merely panning, washing, or placer rocking. Once that
had been completed, the cream—two million dollars in two years
—had been skimmed from the Gila's gold crop. Gila City, therefore, became Arizona's first ghost town. It is virtually impossible
to find any trace of it today, for in 1862, such shanties as
were left were destroyed when the Gila flooded its banks and
washed away the town.

But J. Ross Browne, who saw what was left of the town
in 1864, wrote a vivid account of its history while on his way
from Fort Yuma to Tucson and other Arizona points. In his
book *Adventures in the Apache Country* he states:

We camped at Gila City, a very pretty place, encircled in the
rear by volcanic hills and mountains, and pleasantly overlooking
the bend of the river, with its sand flats, arrow-weeds, and cottonwoods in front. Gold was found in the adjacent hills a few years
ago, and a grand furor for the "placers of the Gila" raged throughout the Territory. At one time over a thousand hardy adventurers
were prospecting the gulches and canyons of this vicinity. The
earth was turned inside out. Rumors of extravagant discoveries

flew on the wings of the wind in every direction. Enterprising men hurried to the spot with barrels of whisky and billiard-tables; Jews came with ready-made clothing and fancy wares; traders crowded in with wagon-loads of pork and beans; and gamblers came with cards and monte-tables. There was everything in Gila City in a few months but a church and a jail, which were accounted barbarisms by the mass of the population. When the city was built, bar-rooms and billiard-saloons opened, monte-tables established, and all the accommodations necessary for civilized society placed upon a firm basis, the gold placers gave out. In other words, they had never given in any thing of account. There was "paydirt" back in the hills, but it didn't pay to carry it down to the river and wash it out by any ordinary process. Gila City collapsed. In about the space of a week it existed only in the memory of disappointed speculators. At the time of our visit the Metropolis of Arizona consisted of three chimneys and a coyote.

But a thousand men scrambling for gold along the banks of the Gila had a definite effect upon Arizona City at the mouth of the Gila. It became a supply point, not only for the gold seekers along the Gila, but for others who found gold farther upstream along the Colorado.

All this activity meant big things to one L. J. F. Jaeger. He built a store and a hotel on his lot—at least he called them such. And by 1859 Arizona City had a population of two hundred, or possibly three hundred, most of whom were goldseekers, some of whom were merchants and saloonkeepers, and a dozen or so of whom were women who were commonly and properly called whores. And the bewildered and bellicose Yuma Indians looked on at this increasing invasion of their land and wondered what it was all about.

What had been Jaeger's one-man town continued to grow slowly. When a few steamers began to ply the Colorado as either exploratory ventures, such as the government expedition under Lieutenant J. C. Ives, or private enterprises, such as the commercial steamer owned by Captain George A. Johnson, Arizona City became a port of call. Somehow the name was awkward. Men often referred to it as "that Yuma town," identifying it with the local Indians. The latter name, short and to the point, caught on. In 1873 the name was officially changed from Arizona City to Yuma by the territorial legislature, which, by that date, had come into existence; although Yuma never achieved Charles Poston's idle boast to impress Jaeger—namely, the honor of being the capital of the land.

With the influx of American pioneer settlers came men of all sorts, some good, some bad, some indifferent. Some came for adventure; some for fortune; some came to change their names and start life anew. Some came for no reason except that they were habitual drifters, staying awhile and then moving on. And one pioneer who is called by historian Frank C. Lockwood "the most potent character who ever came to Arizona" was John Barleycorn. In his book, *Pioneer Days in Arizona,* Lockwood states:

John Barleycorn came early and long survived, and few were the men of that day upon whom he did not set his mark. It is not strange that men drank and gambled almost universally at that time, for human existence was as arid as surrounding nature, and it was far more pleasant and practicable to irrigate the human system with alcohol than to bring water to the land. As for gambling, it was easier than mining, more exciting, and almost as profitable. At any rate, many a daring pioneer was laid low by drink and gaming, and few, indeed, however capable and stalwart, were able to get fully upon their feet and demonstrate their real fighting power. Judge Edmund Wells tells how at Fort Whipple, when he was a youth there furnishing government supplies, a barrel of whisky, with a tin cup attached, invited every weary and thirsty comer or goer. He said that "it proved very democratic, as it placed every one on a level."

John Barleycorn, however, could not break down the will and determination of men like L. J. F. Jaeger and Charles D. Poston. Jaeger remained at Yuma—Arizona City—and ran his ferry fares up to a fortune. This he invested in mining ventures and again was successful. He became the tycoon of Yuma and had a finger in many a pie. The copper, for example, mined at Ajo, had to be transported to Yuma for shipment. Jaeger supplied a pack train and received $100 a ton for hauling ore from the mine to a waiting steamer. Later his teams hauled ore from the famous Vulture Mine, one of the richest gold mines in the West, located near Wickenburg on the Hassayampa River (sometimes called a creek), one of the Gila's tributaries from the north. Still later he held government contracts to haul supplies to various army posts in Arizona. He enlarged his store in Yuma and sold hay to the army for $60 a ton. With all this, he kept his ferry in operation, and by 1877 he was said to be worth well over half a million dollars. He married a Mexican girl from Magdalena, Sonora, and they had three children. The son of this union, L. J. F. Jaeger, Jr., inherited his father's energy and enterprise. He built and owned the Montezuma Hotel in Nogales and the Santa Rita in modern Tucson.

Thus an interesting chain of events began with the meeting of Jaeger and Poston at the Gila's mouth in July of 1854; and if Poston could say of their meeting, "There's more than one way to cross a river," Jaeger could look back and add, "I had a damn good reason for buying that lot." After a lifetime in Arizona, Jaeger made a trip to Washington, D. C., and died there on June 30, 1892. This man who had arrived as a cook on the river steamer *General Jessup* at the confluence of the Gila with the Colorado in 1850 made the most of opportunity where to many there seemed to be none. He epitomizes, to a large degree, the American pioneer.

While Jaeger was making a business career for himself, based primarily on a town that came into existence only because of an engineer's jest, the engineer was doing equally well in his own way.

Charles D. Poston was sure that Arizona had a great future. Leaving the Pennsylvanian to his ferry and his new town, the Kentuckian went to San Diego, San Francisco, and finally New York. With him was Herman Ehrenberg, who had been one of the original surveyors of Arizona City, and whose name was later associated with early mining history in Arizona. There, based on what they had seen, what they believed, and what enthusiasm they could instill into the minds of others, they organized the Sonora Mining and Exploring Company, with a capitalization of one million dollars. Poston and Ehrenberg returned to Arizona by way of Texas, and in 1856 engaged in mining operations with headquarters at Tubac. At this time Tubac had a population of a little over eight hundred, and almost all of these people were Mexicans. Few of the natives could read or write, there were no schools, and the nearest mission, San José de Tumacacori, three miles away, was falling into ruin. So far removed from Mexico City or Washington was this town that it is probable that not one of its citizens knew of or could comprehend the ultimate significance of the Gadsden Purchase that made them American citizens. And to stray far from town meant risking an Apache attack. To them a man like Poston was a kind of "great white father," although at the time Poston was only thirty-one years old. His own account of his life as an American pioneer at Tubac is worth a few quoted paragraphs from his story written nineteen years later, for the *Prescott Miner* of May 7, 1875:

We had no law but love, and no occupation but labor. No government, no taxes, no public debt, no politics.
Sonora has always been famous for the beauty and graceful-

ness of its senoritas. The civil wars in Mexico, and the exodus of
the male population from northern Mexico to California had dis-
turbed the equilibrium of population, till in some [Sonoran]
pueblos the disproportion was as great as a dozen females to one
male . . . Consequently the senoritas and the grass widows sought
the American camp on the Santa Cruz River [Tubac]. When
they could get transportation in wagons hauling provisions they
came in state; others came in on the hurricane decks of burros,
and many came on foot.

This accretion of female population added very much to the
charms of frontier society. The Mexican women were not by any
means useless appendages in camp. They could keep house, cook
some dainty dishes, wash clothes, sew, dance, and sing. Moreover,
they were expert at cards, and divested many a miner of his week's
wages over a game of monte.

As Alcalde of Tubac, under the government of New Mexico
[Arizona had not yet been organized as a territory] I was legally
authorized to celebrate the rites of matrimony, baptize children,
grant divorces, execute criminals, declare war, and perform all the
functions of the ancient El Cadi.

Tubac became a sort of Gretna Green for runaway couples
from Sonora, as the priest there charged them twenty-five dollars,
and the Alcalde of Tubac [Poston himself] tied the knot gratis,
and gave them a treat besides.

By so assuming the authority of church and state, Poston
eventually got into trouble with both, but particularly with the
church. Bishop Lane in Santa Fe sent Father Joseph P. Machebeuf
(vicar apostolic) to Tubac to put a stop to this reign of sin. Not too
tactfully, Father Machebeuf declared all of Poston's marriages, divorces, and baptisms null and void. This caused a great hue and
cry among the emotional and childlike Mexicans. After having
thoroughly upset Poston's social, civil, and religious applecart, and
caused much hysterical weeping and wailing on the part of the

people, Father Machebeuf decided that all the ceremonies were
legal in the eyes of God after all. Poston intimates that he was
helped to this conclusion by being paid the sum of $700 by the
Sonora Mining and Exploring Company, and again all was well
and happy and blessed.

Poston's narrative continues:

An idea that it was lonesome at Tubac would be incorrect.
One can never be lonesome who is useful, and it was considered
at the time that the opening of mines which yielded nothing before, the cultivation of land which lay fallow, the employment of
labor which was idle, and the development of a new country, were
meritorious undertakings.

The table at Tubac was generously supplied with the best
the market afforded. Besides venison, antelope, turkeys, bear, quail,
wild ducks, and other game, we obtained through Guaymas [So-
noran port on the Gulf of California] a reasonable supply of
French wines for Sunday dinners and the celebration of feast
days.

It is astonishing how rapidly the development of mines in-
creases commerce. We had scarcely commenced to make silver bars,
when the plaza of Tubac presented a picturesque scene of primitive commerce. Pack trains arrived from Mexico, loaded with all
kinds of provisions. The rule was to purchase everything they
brought, whether we wanted it or not. They were quite willing
to take in exchange silver bars or American merchandise. Whether
they paid duties in Mexico was none of our business. We were
essentially free traders.

The usual routine at Tubac, in addition to the regular business of distributing supplies to the mining camps, was chocolate
or strong coffee the first thing in the morning, breakfast at sunrise,
dinner at noon, and supper at sunset.

Sunday was the day of days at Tubac, as the superintendents
came in from the mining camps to spend the day, and take dinner,

returning in the afternoon. One Sunday we had a fat wild turkey, weighing twenty-five pounds, and one of my engineers asked permission to assist in the cocina [kitchen]. It was done to a charm and stuffed with pine nuts, which gave it a fine flavor.

Poston mentions such diversions as a Sunday canter to the nearby ruin of the Mission San José de Tumacacori, and apparently he had in his heart a certain nostalgia for the old mission days. He was a very practical man coupled with something akin to genius in meeting and solving an unexpected situation, but he had a romantic streak in his nature. In spite of the successes and failures of his subsequent career he looked back at Tubac from a perspective of almost twenty years with pleasant warmth.

In the spring of 1857 a garden containing about two acres was prepared, and irrigated by a canal from the Santa Cruz River. By the industry of a German gardener, with two Mexican assistants, we soon produced all the vegetables, melons, etc., that we required; and many a weary traveler remembers, or ought to remember, the hospitality of Tubac. We were never a week without some company and sometimes had more than we required; but nobody was ever charged anything for entertainment, horse-shoeing, and fresh supplies for the road. Hospitality is a savage virtue, and disappears with civilization.

J. Ross Browne, who visited Tubac some years later—in 1864, to be exact—when it was fast crumbling to a ghost town, gives an interesting sidelight on Pioneer Poston and life in Tubac. The following quotation is from Browne's *Adventures in the Apache Country*:

. . . it may literally be said "the wilderness blossomed as the rose." In 1858, and '60, during which the mines were in progress of development, Tubac might well be regarded as the headquarters of civilization in the Territory. Men of education and refinement connected with the mines were here occasionally assembled, and even the fair sex was well represented. The gardens afforded a pleasant place of retreat in summer, with their shady groves of acacias and peach trees; and deep pools in the river, overhung by willows, were cleared out and made into bathing places, in which all who pleased might refresh themselves with a luxurious bath. Poston used to sit in the water, like the Englishman in Hyperion, and read the newspapers, by which means he kept his temper cool amid the various disturbing influences that surrounded him.

The problem of monetary exchange had to be faced at Tubac. The Mexicans had little or no money when the Sonora Mining and Exploring Company revitalized their community's existence. Silver bullion was a little too heavy for hand-to-hand transactions when Pedro Martinez wished to buy a handful of peppers from Juan Garcia. So the company decided to use paper money. There was none on hand. Therefore, the resourceful Poston had some printed in New York City and sent west. These were called boletas, which can be translated as tickets, but more properly in this instance as notes payable on demand.

The notes were small pieces of pasteboard, "two inches by three, all in small denominations," according to historian Thomas Edwin Farish. Because the majority of the citizens of Tubac were unable to read, the values of the notes were indicated by pictures of animals. A pig on the currency meant that it was worth one bit, 12½ cents. A calf was worth two bits, 25 cents; a rooster was 50 cents; a horse was good for $1; a bull was a $5 bill; and a lion on the currency denoted a value of $10. Historian Farish stated: "With these *boletas* the hands were paid off every Saturday, and they were taken as currency at the stores, and among the merchants in the country and in Mexico. When a run of silver was made, anyone holding tickets could have them redeemed in silver bars, or in exchange on San Francisco. This primitive system of fiat money had an excellent effect. Everybody holding these *boletas* was interested in the success of the mines, and the entire community was dependent for its prosperity upon that of the company. They were all redeemed and retired from circulation."

The Americans used this money as well as the natives, but the Americans were not illiterate. And when people can read it is only a foregone conclusion that they will require reading matter. This demand brought into existence at Tubac in 1859 Arizona's first newspaper. It was called, without any strain on anyone's imagination, the *Weekly Arizonian,* and it reported the news of the area which everyone knew by hearsay and gossip before the week was over, but which everyone who could read wanted to see in print.

The editor was Edward Cross, and his two printers were Jack Sims and George Smithson. The press had come from Philadelphia (some authorities believe it was from Boston and they may be correct) around Cape Horn to California, and then overland to Tubac. A different historical version has the press coming from an unidentified eastern port and being put ashore at Mazatlán, Mexico, and from that port it was presumably transported in separate pieces to Tubac and there assembled. No matter which story is true, Tubac had a newspaper in 1859. Volume I Number 1 appeared in March of that year. It was a sell-out.

Poston spoke highly of this boon to culture and all Tubac was equally proud of the pioneer publication. Without doubt this is the paper that J. Ross Browne referred to when he told how Poston used to sit in the water of the Santa Cruz River and read. When the mining boom was over, the press was taken to Tucson in 1860, and publication was officially suspended in

1861. The paper had never been an economic success, and when it could no longer sustain itself the editor sold the remaining office furniture to help meet his bills. And the only pieces of "furniture" remaining in 1861 were two derringers. Today the old press is still preserved among the treasures of the Pioneers' Historical Society in Tucson.

Poston continued his mining projects with considerable success, not only at Tubac but at other locations in the Gila watershed. There were many handicaps, such as unskilled Mexican labor, problems of transportation of ore so that the cost would not make the mining prohibitive, and the ever-present danger of the nomadic, marauding Apaches.

With the outbreak of the Civil War, Poston became a strong Union man. He volunteered for military service and was commissioned a colonel. While stationed in Washington in 1862, he bent every effort to make it clear to representatives and senators alike that Arizona could not continue to exist as a part of New Mexico but must have a civil government of its own. To Poston, Arizona's future depended upon being made a territory of the United States, and he was certain that someday it might achieve statehood even though that "someday" was obviously far in the future.

But while Poston was in Washington all federal troops—the "boys in blue"—were ordered back east from the half dozen forts that had been established after the Gadsden Purchase. Arizona was of no importance in the midst of the great crisis that might mean the dissolving of the Union. Lincoln and his generals needed troops, and Arizona was abandoned, as far as the War Department was concerned, to the Mexicans, the American pioneers, and the Apache Indians. The Apaches, of course, immediately made the most of their opportunity. They ruled the area and not a white man in Arizona cared to travel from Tucson to

Tubac, or to Yuma, or to any part of the Gila water-shed, alone. From an Apache point of view it was a victory; they reasoned that the white soldiers had given up and retreated to their own country. They became more bold and arrogant. At-tacks became more frequent, numerous massacres occurred, and the white man or woman who was captured was never seen again. To be a pioneer citizen in Arizona was so dangerous that, instead of advancing, the Gila Valley went into a period of retrogression. Walt Whitman's lines, written at this time, were indeed apt.

> *Come, my tan-faced children,*
> *Follow well in order, get your weapons ready;*
> *Have you your pistols? have you your sharp-edged axes?*
> *Pioneers! O Pioneers!*

Meanwhile, as the Civil War's struggles went on and bloody battle followed bloody battle, Poston worked in Washington for Arizona. Up to this time it is probable that not more than four or five senators and a dozen representatives had ever understood the problems, politics, and populace of the Gila Valley and its watershed. But with the same combination of quick know-how, lively imagination, and a practical sense of values, Poston put his project over with Washington, just as he had sold L. J. F. Jae-ger a lot in a nonexistent city for ferry fare, and created a form of fiat money for the illiterates of Tubac. He had no au-thority to create Arizona City in 1854 or to establish a new cur-rency in Tubac in 1858. And he had no authority to press the cause of territorial status for Arizona as a separate political unit from New Mexico in 1862. But he did all three. And all three succeeded. In 1863, on February 24, Congress separated Arizona from New Mexico, and the Territory of Arizona was born. It took her another forty-nine years to reach statehood and Charles D. Poston never lived to see the final achievement in 1912. In

1950 this pioneer, who was once called "the father of Arizona," was all but forgotten. His name occurs rarely in Arizona. No county and no city is named for him. But in 1942 his memory did receive a dubious honor; the government selected a location for a Japanese concentration camp on the Colorado River a hundred miles north of the Gila and called it, generously, "Poston."

After his Washington experiences Poston returned to Arizona and was quite properly elected Arizona's first delegate to Congress. It was a just election, for no man had done more to win recognition for Arizona in Washington, and no man had done more to build up Arizona from within. L. J. F. Jaeger was a sound businessman, an alert and careful shopkeeper, who became rich. Charles D. Poston was a capitalist with a quick wit and the imagination of an empire builder who, incredible as it may seem, very nearly died in poverty.

In spite of his abilities, Poston could do little in Congress. He wrote: "A delegate from a territory is like a tadpole among frogs. His name is not on the roll-call, and he has no vote. Nothing is expected of him but silence, and not much of that."

The *Arizona State Guide,* sponsored by the Arizona State Teachers College at Flagstaff in 1940, gave a succinct and objective account of his later years, which could hardly be presented in better condensation. It follows:

After completing his term in Congress, he traveled extensively in Europe and Asia and returned to Florence [Arizona] in 1878. While in India he became a sun worshiper and upon his return built a road, costing several thousand dollars, to the top of a butte, which he called "Parsee Hill," and where he erected a pyre of continuous fire as a temple to the sun. After burning for several months the fire died and the project became "Poston's Folly." Poston served as consular agent at Nogales, military agent at El

Paso, agent of the Department of Agriculture at Phoenix, and for a number of years was employed by departments in Washington studying and promoting government irrigation on desert lands. In 1899 the legislature voted him a small pension for public services rendered Arizona during its infancy. It was his wish that he be buried on Parsee Hill, but when he died in Phoenix in 1902 he was interred in a Phoenix cemetery.

In 1925, with some state self-consciousness at work, Poston's body was taken to his "Parsee Hill" for reinterment. There his dust was scattered and a monument was erected to his memory.

Parsee Hill is usually known today as Poston's Butte. It is a barren rocky prominence, of little or no interest to the passing tourist, who must drive out of his way to see it. Few do. Those who did in 1950 could look across the desert valley to the Gila River, only a short distance away. And, fittingly, in recent years the Gila at this spot has been as dry as Poston's dust.

A quotation from E. E. Dunbar, who knew Poston well in Arizona, and who was in Washington working for Poston's—and Arizona's—cause, is indicative of the uphill pull to create Arizona:

I escaped out of Arizona, a territory teeming with precious and other metals, and came to Washington, believing in my verdancy that I should be able to excite some interest for that most important but suffering and neglected frontier. I encountered a member of Congress from one of the eastern states. He was puffing a cigar and toasting his feet before a good fire at Willard's Hotel. I approached this member of Congress in my most bland and winning manner, and after begging his pardon, recounted to him in thrilling tones and impressive manner the trials, difficulties, and dangers we were encountering in opening the new territory to civilization. The member of Congress quietly heard what I had to say, and then coolly turning to me, inquired: "What the devil did you go to such a Godforsaken country for?"

"Pioneers! O pioneers!"

18

THE MAIL MUST GET THROUGH

Pioneers are not only people like L. J. F. Jaeger and Charles D. Poston, but sometimes they are projects.

The Gila Valley felt the effects of three pioneering projects between 1857 and 1860, all in the field of transportation. None of them lasted, but all of them were important. And the need for them was at last superseded by the transcontinental Southern Pacific Railroad. The three projects depended upon three means of locomotion: the first used camels, the second mules, and the third horses.

Many stories and legends and not a few lies have been circulated because of the camel experiment in the American Southwest. It was a particularly colorful episode and most of the stories are equally chromatic. Yet there is that undeniable modicum of truth in every one of them.

They run something like this:

A lone prospector has made his camp somewhere in the Arizona desert—near the Gila or miles away from it—but somewhere within the Gila watershed and the Gadsden Purchase. Perhaps the scene is on the slope of the Agua Dulce Mountains near the Mexican border, and in 1860 a good hundred desert miles from the nearest town. The lone prospector has hobbled his burros or mules so that they can graze on the scant desert growth throughout the night, but cannot stray so far away that he will have to search for them in the morning. Weary, after a hard day with his pick and shovel, and to celebrate the fact that he has found gold, or to console himself because he had not, he takes a few good swigs from a pint of whisky. The swigs go down so well, and warm what he calls his heart but is actually his stomach and his liver, that he has two or three more. Soon the pint is a little more than half gone. And as he sits drinking alone and watching a handsome full moon rise over the desert mountains and almost light up the Saguaro cactus and the cholla and the greasewood, he is suddenly startled. For he sees the positive silhouette of an Oriental beast marching across the desert horizon and plainly outlined in the bright moonlight. It is a camel. The prospector stares open-mouthed, and then quickly takes a double drink. Then, as he stares anew, a second, a third, a fourth, and a fifth of the bactrians plod slowly in single file between himself and the rising moon. He is appalled, and he mutters to himself, "I've got 'em! The d.t.'s!" Quickly he pours his remaining whisky into the desert sand, tosses the empty bottle away, and vows, "Never again."

And the point of the story is always the fact that the prospector did indeed see four or five camels or dromedaries, and at that time there were about a hundred or more of them sleeping by day and roaming nocturnally in southern Arizona.

How this came about was due to the lively imagination of Lieutenant Edward F. Beale and the practicality of Secretary of War Jefferson Davis. Even before Beale, and as early as 1836, Major George H. Crossman had suggested the use of camels as beasts of burden in Florida. The idea got nowhere until 1848, when Major Henry C. Wayne suggested that the War Department send a camel-purchasing expedition to the Orient for hardy beasts to use in the far West. Wayne was laughed out of the War Department, and took his plan to Jefferson Davis, then a senator from Mississippi. Davis thought the idea practicable, but the Senate did not. In 1853 Jefferson Davis became secretary of war in the Cabinet of President Franklin Pierce. He firmly believed that if the camel was the "ship of the desert" in the Sahara, the animal could do as well in the American Southwest. He visualized the beasts enjoying long drafts of Mississippi River water and not having to drink again until they reached the Rio Grande, the Gila, or the Colorado. Here was the God-given answer to desert transportation. After tedious debate, an appropriation of $30,000 to purchase camels and deliver them to the Southwest passed both House and Senate on March 3, 1855.

More than a year later, on May 14, 1856, the first shipment of camels arrived at Indianola, Texas. Four of the animals had died during an especially stormy and harrowing Atlantic crossing from Egypt to Texas, but six baby camels were born on shipboard, and the total placed on American soil was thirty-four. Lieutenant David D. Porter, who was in command of the expedition, wrote: "The animals, led by their American and Oriental guides, marched down the gang-plank in a most docile manner. As soon as they hit the solid earth, however, their demeanor suddenly changed. They became excited and uncontrollable. They reared, kicked, cried, broke their halters, tore up picket lines, and engaged in other fantastic tricks such as pawing and biting each other. The Texans, at first amused at these antics, became panic-stricken and fled."

This unpredictability of the camel was indicative of their behavior in Arizona. For days they were the best-behaved beasts that could be desired; and then, on no palpable provocation, they would go berserk and enjoy themselves in any way they jolly well pleased, which included squatting on their knees and refusing to get up, biting each other, running in circles, romping in what seemed to be a game of tag, and finally four of them running off in all four cardinal directions and never even looking back to see if they were pursued.

But in spite of these unaccountable outbreaks of temperament, Lieutenant Edward F. Beale was a strong advocate of camel caravans. He had hit upon the scheme when crossing the Gila Valley on a mule which nearly died for lack of water. When there

was plenty of water the mule didn't care to drink. There was no way to explain to the mule that the next ten days' journey might be a hundred and fifty miles of terrible desert from the Gila's mouth to Warner's Ranch in the California Coast Range. Then, when there was no water, the mule quite naturally wished to drink. A camel, on the contrary, would drink gallons of water at one time, and never suffer from thirst, no matter what the nature of the country, for another ten days or more. Lieutenant Beale led the first camel caravan from Texas to California and he wrote warm and praising letters about the beasts to Jefferson Davis, although he had no love for the Gila and always called the river "that fresh water abomination." Apparently the project was destined for success. And within another year a second shipment brought forty-one more camels to Texas, making seventy-five in all. But the camel is a prolific beast, and by 1858 there were at least a hundred and thirty camels at work (and occasionally at unpredictable play) in the American Southwest.

This project, seemingly off to a successful start, proved more costly than practical. In spite of the fact that one camel could carry as much as twelve hundred pounds, there were other factors that in a short time caused the camel caravans to be abandoned as a failure.

It has been written that they broke down on rocky terrain and needle-sharp lava beds, but this is not a proved fact. It is more than likely that the patient (up to a point) beasts plodded over mountains and desert—rocks, sand and lava—with nonchalant ease. The main trouble lay in inexpert riders who were made seasick by the camel's peculiar rolling gait; soldiers and muleskinners who were ignorant of bactrian temperament and unable to discipline them; and the antipathy and even fear of horses and mules which were stampeded by the mere sight and smell of them.

Ten native drivers had been brought from the Near East, notably Hadji Ali and Georges Xaralampo. The former was known as Hi Jolly and the latter as Greek George, and both these men could handle the camels with ease. But they did it by swearing at them in Syrian, which the camels apparently understood and obeyed; and no American soldiers or muleskinners had time to learn Syrian. Had fifty or more native drivers been imported these men might have been the needed element to swing the project to success. And at the time the scheme appeared to be getting out of hand along came the Civil War. Jefferson Davis, who had been the strongest advocate of government-owned camels for the American Southwest, became the president of another government, and the camel experiment was forgotten in the greater issues involved in the war between the states.

Greek George decided to live in El Monte, near Los Angeles, where he bought a small ranch and lived happily until his death in 1915. Hi Jolly caught the gold fever and got himself a mule, a pick, and a canteen; and turned the welfare of the camels over to Allah while he prospected in Arizona. He died in 1902 and his grave is plainly marked at the small town of Quartzite about eighty miles north of the mouth of the Gila River on U.S. Highway 70.

A few of the animals were sold, some were shot, and the Apache Indians soon learned to eat camel meat and thereby accounted for a number of others. But the majority were turned loose in the desert along the banks of the lower Gila River. They were at home in this desert country and they roamed far and wide within the Gila watershed, usually sleeping by day and foraging by night. And of course they multiplied. Free from being beasts of burden, they soon forgot their Syrian commands, and their subsequent generations became wild instead of domestic, shy as deer, and nimble enough to outdistance the occasional predatory coyote or hungry Indian. But since they were usually and wantonly slain on sight by white men and red, the camel death rate finally passed the birth rate.

The following story appeared in the Prescott, Arizona, *Democrat* of December 30, 1881:

A capture [of camels] has at last been made by Indians in the vicinity of Gila Bend, and last Wednesday a carload passed through on their way to the East. While they stopped at the depot quite a large crowd gathered to see them. The carload consisted of seven large and two small ones and were consigned to a circus menagerie at Kansas City. They were in charge of an Egyptian,

Al Zel, who had been sent out expressly to get them. They do not differ from ordinary camels seen in this country except that they far exceed in size any ever yet exhibited. The price said to have been paid for them is trifling, the Indians being very anxious to get rid of them as their horses and cattle are greatly frightened by them. There are a large number still in that vicinity.

The last apparently authentic report of camels along the Gila was in 1905, forty-five years after they had been turned loose, when several were captured and exhibited as "indigenous" to North America. These animals were native, but their immediate ancestors had not been indigenous.

There have been many reports of camels seen in Arizona since 1905. The Tucson *Star* carried a convincing story dated November 28, 1913, in which John Nelson, employed at Ajo at that time, saw, and pursued on horseback, three camels across the desert but soon was outstripped by them. The fact that Nelson first told his story in a Tucson saloon led some people to scoff at it. It is unlikely that any of the beasts have descendants still living in 1950, although that is not utterly impossible. Numerous legends and lies have persisted as a result of the project. Some have it that a great white male (sometimes a black male and sometimes a red one) still lives and is followed around the desert wastes by a harem of females. Another story tells of a dead rider being lashed to one of the beasts. In the dry air and the hot sun, a slow decomposition went on until the rider became a grinning skeleton, still strapped on the back of the roving animal. Finally the skeleton fell apart and only the legs were left, still strapped to the sides of the beast. It is a tale that might have been told by Edgar Allan Poe, out of *The Flying Dutchman*. Don't believe it, but it is a fitting punctuation to the whole camel episode.

The second transportation project, which used the mule instead of the camel, began almost simultaneously but had even less success. This was called the San Antonio and San Diego Stage Company. While the original plans called for the stages to be pulled by horses, it was soon discovered that the horse could not stand the trip. The mule was the animal that saved the day for the company, short as that day may have been. This was called the Jackass Mail, but should not be confused with the first so-called Jackass Mail that attempted overland mail service by mules between Hangtown in California's High Sierras and Salt Lake City.

The San Antonio and San Diego Stage Company sent its carriers through twice a month. The stages followed the general route of Colonel P. St. George Cooke's Mormon Battalion, and the journey from one terminal to the other took from twenty-one to twenty-five days—with luck.

Six mules were used to pull a stagecoach. But for more than a hundred miles of sand dunes and wind-swept desert west of Fort Yuma the intrepid traveler had to abandon the stagecoach and continue by muleback. And throughout the eastern portion of the Gila watershed, the heart of the Apache country, each stagecoach had to be accompanied by a heavily armed escort. Travel under these conditions could hardly be called pleasant.

Moreover, the operation of such a line was a great risk involving a considerable amount of capital. A contract from the government to carry mail for the sum of $149,000 a year made such a stage service possible, and it cost the government about $60 a letter! The passenger paid $200 for his fare from San Antonio to San Diego, and if he couldn't stay on a mule for more than one hundred of the worst miles he'd better not start.

But the San Antonio and San Diego Stage Company had blazed the trail for a far more ambitious project—the Butterfield Overland Mail, which came into existence in 1858.

California had been a state for eight years, and her citizens were demanding a mail and express service that would connect San Francisco with eastern cities in the shortest possible time. In 1857 Congress passed the Post Office Appropriation Act which ordered the postmaster general, Aaron V. Brown, to advertise for bids to carry mail to California in twenty-five days or less from the Mississippi River. The contract went to John Butterfield of Utica, New York, and he had one year in which to get his coaches ready. He was to receive $600,000 a year for three years. His projected route made a great oxbow across the map of the West from St. Louis to San Francisco by way of Missouri, Arkansas, Oklahoma (then Indian Territory), Texas, southern New Mexico, and then following, with a few cutoffs, the route of Cooke and the Mormon Battalion through Tucson and down the Santa Cruz to the Pima villages on the Gila, west to Fort Yuma, across the desert of southeastern California to Warner's Ranch, and thence north to Los Angeles and eventually to San Francisco. It was a trip of 2,785 miles and it had to be made in twenty-five days or less.

A project of this magnitude could not be done by halves. That it was functioning successfully as far as operations were concerned within one year was the result of careful planning and the pioneering efforts of the Mormon Battalion of 1846 and the San Antonio and San Diego Stage Company of 1857. This latter, of course, went out of business when the new government contract went to Butterfield.

Stage stations, mostly one-story adobe buildings, were established at irregular intervals along the route. In the Indian country three or four armed men were constantly on duty at each station. The running overhead was extremely high. Supplies, and even water, often had to be transported for miles to the company's long strung-out line of stations and personnel. The company bought one hundred stagecoaches of a make known as the Abbott-Downing coach manufactured in Concord, New Hampshire. The coach could carry fourteen passengers, nine of whom could be seated inside, and five of whom, including the driver, were on the roof and the "box." At the rear was the "boot" on which mail sacks were packed. If more space for mail was needed, it was packed into the coach proper to the exclusion of a passenger or two. Mail had priority and it had to get through. An individual was allowed twenty-five pounds of personal luggage and no more. Speed, of course—breakneck speed—was essential to the 25-day schedule. With wheels almost as heavy as those of a prairie schooner, it took six husky horses to make up the team. There were only 10-minute stops at many of the stations—just enough to change horses while the cramped and weary passengers stretched their legs. It was very much like

spending twenty-five days in a careening ambulance. The journey was pithily described by one of the early passengers in one word, "Hell."

There were times when speed was impossible. Streams and rivers had to be forded; there was plenty of mud during rainy weather in Texas and Oklahoma; and speed over sharp lava beds or through deep sand was utterly impossible. But the wheels must keep turning regardless of road conditions, and turn they did.

About every fifth station was a supply base, or so-called "home" station. At these stations there would be food of some kind available, and a blacksmith and a wheelwright on hand. The Gila Valley played hob with the tires and fellies. At times a coach would have to stop and wait for a driver to repair fellies and spokes shrunken by desert heat, or wait while the wheels were allowed to soak in the Gila so that the wood could swell sufficiently to hold the tires in place. And there was nothing pneumatic about a stagecoach tire!

Service was opened to the public on September 15, 1858, and Butterfield started two stages simultaneously, one leaving from San Francisco eastbound and one from Tipton, Missouri, westbound. Tipton, about thirty-five miles west of Jefferson City, was the end of the railroad. The coaches passed near El Paso, Texas, and the eastbound coach, carrying a post office inspector, pulled into Tipton from San Francisco in exactly 24 days, 14 hours, and 35 minutes. Six hours later the mail arrived in St. Louis. President James Buchanan was so delighted with this news that he sent John Butterfield the following telegram:

I cordially congratulate you upon the result. It is a glorious triumph for civilization and the Union. Settlements will soon follow the course of the road, and the East and the West will be bound together by a chain of living Americans which can never be broken.

And later came the news that the westbound coach had clattered to a halt at the Federal Building in San Francisco amid a cheering crowd in exactly 23 days, 23 hours, and 32 minutes out of Tipton, Missouri. American transportation by utilizing the Gila Valley had conquered a continent.

On board, enclosed, ensconced, incarcerated in—or whatever the word should be—the first westbound Butterfield stagecoach was a special correspondent for the alert New York *Herald*. He was Mr. W. L. Ormsby, and he made the trip from Tipton to San Francisco. His plan was to make notes and write his articles during the journey. Obviously Mr. Ormsby had never ridden in a record-seeking stagecoach before or he would have grasped the utter impracticality of writing a news story in a bouncing, jolting, careening conveyance over ground that could be called a road only by the most happy optimist.

Nevertheless, Ormsby left his dispatches at various stops to be picked up by eastbound coaches, and the *Herald* received a lively and often chirographically puzzling account which it printed to the satisfaction of many interested readers. Mr. Ormsby's descriptions of life in the Gila Valley as seen from its "fast mail" stagecoach in 1858 are vivid and accurate and should not be lost to posterity. On October 2, 1858, this New York reporter wrote: "I find myself in Tucson." There is a full stop. No comment. This silence in print is provocative. One can almost sense a sigh. But at last Mr. Ormsby continued:

Tucson is a small place, consisting of a few adobe houses. The inhabitants are mainly Mexicans. There are but few Americans, though they keep the two or three stores, and are elected to

the town offices. The town has considerably improved since acquisition by the United States. The Apache Indians are somewhat
troublesome in the vicinity. We left the town on Saturday, October 2, having to drive forty miles to the next station in the
Picacho Pass, before we came to desirable water . . .

Forty miles beyond the pass the company have a station,
where I saw the first Indians in their wild native costume. They
were a band of fifteen Pimos, engaged in dressing a beeve which
they had just sold to the station keeper. The dexterity with which
they separated the various parts and sliced up the animal into
strings of meat to be dried was remarkable. The men were generally in the costume of Adam, with a dirty cloth in the place of
the fig leaf. The women, of which there were three, had cloths
slightly larger, and a little cleaner, but down to the middle of the
body wore beads on their necks and arms, and DIDN'T WEAR
ANYTHING ELSE. They all of them had fine muscular developments and were the very picture of health. . . .

Some of the band lounged about and looked on with curi-
osity as we changed our horses and partook of our breakfast. This
station was located on the Gila River, near the chain of mountains known as the Casa Grande. A few miles beyond we came to
the Pimos villages, scattered along the Gila. The land here is rich,
and, with irrigation, produces bountiful crops. The Pimos number
in all about 22,000. They raise corn and wheat in very large
quantities, which they sell to the whites. Their houses are miserable huts, built of mesquite bushes or hoops covered with straw.
The Indians are hideous looking objects in their filthy scraps of
clothing and naked brown bodies. The men are lazy and take
good care to make the women do all the work. We saw numbers
of sovereign lords walking along or riding, and making their
squaws carry the loads—a spectacle which would give one of our
women's rights women fits instanter. The women are, however,
lazy, too, and the men have about as much work to drive them as
they would to do the work themselves.

Such was life in the Gila Valley in 1858 as seen from the windows of the Butterfield Overland Mail. A little farther down the Gila the New Yorker had his first meeting with the Maricopa Indians. A difference in economic values was thereby reported at the next stop, called Maricopa Wells.

Here the water is very good. We found a number of Indians and one of them had the audacity to ask me three bits (37½ cents) for a small melon which he wished to sell. I showed him two three cent pieces, and the look of insufferable contempt which he gave me would be worth a fortune to an actor if put in the right place. I am sure his melon would rot before he could get another chance to sell it.

Mr. Ormbsby continued his description of the lower Gila Valley in much the same vein as had his trapper and military predecessors. He reported the tragic Oatman case as he passed Oatman Flat, adding to the well-known account:

The graves of the father and the mother are directly in the road, and the teams often pass over them. They lie some distance from the scene of the murder, which took place on a hill half a mile off. Mr. Jacobs, the road agent on this section of the line, intends having the graves enclosed with a fence, so as to turn the road aside.

I had expected to get supper at the next station, but it not being ready, and Mr. Warren Hall, the road agent, being anxious to get the mail along in time, I had to content myself with a pipe and a glass of water, although I had had nothing to eat since breakfast.

Continuing down the Gila Valley at the rate of five to six miles an hour the stagecoach finally reached the Gila's mouth. Across the Colorado was California, and Fort Yuma.

Fort Yuma is now in command of Colonel Flourney, with fifteen men. It is situated on the Colorado's west bank near its junction with the Gila. Most of the buildings belong to the government. On the Arizona side of the Colorado is Arizona City, consisting of a few adobe houses. We crossed the river at this point on the ferry kept by Mr. Yager [L. J. F. Jaeger], who charges *FIVE DOLLARS* for carrying an ordinary four horse team. The boat is a sort of flat boat, and is propelled by the rapid current, being kept in its course partly by pulleys running on a rope stretched across the river. We crossed just at daybreak, and found the few Americans ready to receive us. After a hasty breakfast we changed our horses and were off again.

Some days later Mr. W. L. Ormsby decoached at San Francisco. He had the distinction of being the first transcontinental passenger to ride in public carriers—railroad and stagecoach— from New York to San Francisco. And Mr. Ormsby was jolly well glad it was over.

Postmaster General Aaron V. Brown declared the project "a conclusive and triumphant success." Passenger fare was as low as $200 from Tipton to San Francisco, and first-class mail was only 20 cents an ounce. The company operated on a regular, even strict, schedule—two stagecoaches left Tipton each week westbound, and two eastbound coaches departed each week from San Francisco—and the slowest time was twenty-five days and the fastest was twenty-one.

Nevertheless, the project had its critics. They were largely the eight bidders who had lost out to John Butterfield. The other eight had all bid on the basis of a route across Nebraska or Kansas, then Wyoming, Utah, Nevada, and California. This route, of course, was made impassable by heavy snows in the winter months. Only John Butterfield had suggested the southern route, utilizing the southwestern deserts and the Gila Valley.

But at the end of the first fiscal year of operation even optimist Aaron V. Brown received a shock. The cost to the government had been $600,000, and the income to the Post Office De-
partment was $27,229.94—or a total loss of $572,770.06 for
one year! The critics leaped upon this with delight. They demanded to know just what margin of profit Mr. Butterfield had
made. Mr. Butterfield saw no official reason for revealing such
information. A contract was a contract, the line was functioning
on schedule, and President Buchanan and Postmaster General
Brown were more than satisfied. As for the government, the service was amply justified upon the grounds of national solidarity.
To the critics of the Overland Mail Mr. Butterfield added "sour
grapes."

But as time went on even Postmaster General Brown had to
admit that the deficit was staggering. His answer was a railroad.
Put rails across the continent along the Butterfield oxbow route,
and the heavy deficit might be moved out of the red into a
neat profit on the black side of the government's ledger.

But this was 1858–59 and a crisis between northern and
southern economies was looming faster every day. Both Brown
and Buchanan were accused of southern partisanship in accepting
a bid which traversed the southern states and the Gila Valley. In
1860 Jefferson Davis made a speech in defense of the route, and
it continued to operate in spite of the tremendous losses.

Then, less than eighteen months later, on April 12, 1861,
Fort Sumter was fired on and the terrible and lamentable Civil
War was on. The Union could not and would not permit gov-
ernment and private mail to be transported from coast to coast
through southern states. Early in 1861 the Butterfield Overland
Mail was stopped, and it was never permitted to operate again.
During the four years of the Civil War a new route was opened
and a new contract was allotted. This route followed the Platte

River in Nebraska, and South Pass in Wyoming, Salt Lake City, the Humboldt River in Nevada, and across the forbidding Sierra Nevada Mountains to the Pacific slope. Stage stations in the Gila Valley were abandoned. The sun of transportation had sunk in the Southwest. All Union soldiers were removed; again the Apaches dominated the country; and all the economy of the Gila watershed felt the pinch of recession due to the bitter struggle in the East between the Blue and the Gray.

A number of the stagecoach drivers returned to the East, others went to California, and one of them decided to settle in Tucson. This man, whose run had been through the most dangerous part of the Apache country in southeastern Arizona, had the exceptional luck never to have his stagecoach suffer an Indian attack. And he himself always wore a bright red shirt. When asked about his good fortune, the driver explained that he had a system with the Apaches. He wore the red shirt so that they would be sure to see him.

"But wouldn't it be better," asked his interviewer, "if they *didn't* see you?"

"Nope."

"Well, why not?"

"Best if they see me. Then they won't bother me. It's a system."

"How does it work?"

"Like this: I have an agreement with a certain Apache chief. I always wear a bright red shirt, and my stagecoach will never be attacked."

"You mean, the Apaches are afraid to attack red?"

"Nope."

"Then how do you account for it?"

"There's a certain big greasewood bush at the foot of Apache Pass near what was old Fort Bowie—now abandoned."

"Yes?"

"I always made one stop—of just one minute—at that big greasewood bush. And under it I always put one jug full of whisky. That was a kind of insurance. The chief liked his liquor. None of his braves were allowed to attack the driver who wore the red shirt. If they should kill that driver in the red shirt, the chief wouldn't get any more whisky. You can always make a deal with an Apache if you're honest. I never failed to leave the whisky; I never failed to get the mail through."

It would be pleasant to believe this yarn, but more than likely it belongs to the imaginative folklore of Arizona. Nevertheless— and there is no denying it—over this most dangerous stretch of the Butterfield route the mail always got through.

19

THE BLUE, THE GRAY, AND THE OLD PUEBLO

For the numerous radio quiz programs a question might well be, "What battle in the Civil War, or the War Between the States, was fought farther west than any other?"

And the unseen audience from Maine to California would learn that it was the Battle of Picacho Pass, fought forty-two miles northwest of Tucson, Arizona, on April 15, 1862.

For its size, Tucson had been under a surprising number of governments since its official founding in 1776, but ironically, in spite of these numerous "governments," the town seldom had any law worthy of the name until after the Civil War. Following the pre-Columbian people—Hohokam and Pima Indians—who lived in the area, Tucson was first a Spanish town with ultimate authority in Madrid. Then it was governed, if such a word can be applied at all, by the short-lived Mexican Empire. Following that fiasco the town came under the government of the Republic of Mexico. The Mexican garrison fled before the oncoming Mormon Battalion, and for a few days in 1846 the American flag flew over the town. After Colonel P. St. George Cooke and his men moved on west, the Mexican comandante returned and "retook" the town. It was Mexican until the Gadsden Purchase of 1853 made it American again, although American troops did not officially occupy it until 1856. From then until 1862 the Stars and Stripes flew over the town. In 1862 a troop of Confederate cavalry commanded by Captain Sherod Hunter occupied the town (all Union soldiers had been withdrawn from Arizona) and for the first time Tucson was governed by the Stars and Bars of the Confederate States of America. After the Battle of Picacho Pass, the only engagement between the Blue and the Gray in Arizona, the Confederates abandoned the town. Tucson was next occupied by Colonel James H. Carleton commanding the California Volunteers and again the Stars and Stripes went up. That was on May 20, 1862, and the red, white, and blue has flown over Tucson ever since.

All this was both interesting and amusing to the Apache Indians, who continued to attack Union and Confederate forces indiscriminately, as well as all Mexicans and other Indians. If it was fighting that the white men wanted so badly that they shot each other because some wore blue and some wore gray, the Apaches were happy to accommodate them by shooting anybody who wasn't an Apache—regardless of blue, gray, or any other color.

When Captain Sherod Hunter and his Confederate cavalry,

consisting of about three hundred men, occupied Tucson in February of 1862 the town greeted the Southerners warmly. Most of the soldiers in gray were from Texas, and most of the American citizens of Tucson were strongly pro-South. The military objective of the Confederacy was to establish a "life line" to California. Los Angeles was largely pro-South while San Francisco was stanchly for the Union. The military intelligence of the South wished to solidify Texas with New Mexico, Arizona, and the Pacific coast. And should the South win the war (and that was a foregone conclusion or the men in gray would never have fired on Fort Sumter and thus precipitated the four-year struggle) there would be a concerted effort to wrest southern California from the state government at Sacramento and set up three new Confederate states—New Mexico, Arizona, and Southern California, which would probably have its name changed to Davis or Lee.

Only one avenue could lead to California from the South and that was the Gila Valley. Only one city of any consequence lay between Texas and California, and that was Tucson. So the Confederates made haste to take it, and the citizens of Tucson who could speak English were delighted.

Captain Sherod Hunter's next objective was Yuma (still officially Poston's Arizona City) but, before he could move west from Tucson, Union forces in California had been organized and the California Volunteers (more popular in the northern part of the state than the southern) marched east and seized Fort Yuma, Arizona City, and the strategic mouth of the Gila and L. J. F. Jaeger's all-important ferry.

The California Volunteers were almost ten to one in strength over the Confederates. The army consisted of the 1st and 5th Regiments of California infantry, the 1st Battalion of California cavalry, an additional company of California cavalry, and one battery of the 3rd United States Artillery. To match that force

totaling more than twenty-five hundred men, Captain Sherod
Hunter with his three hundred C.S.A.Texas Cavalry was virtually
faced with defeat before a shot was fired. But that didn't deter
Captain Hunter.

Both forces sent reconnoitering squads into the field, and
Hunter's men captured a few Union scouts. It was still a gentlemen's war, and Hunter graciously allowed the Union men to return to their lines. Contact between the two opposing forces had
been made. From there on it was to be a shooting war. But while
the Union men were missing, Colonel Carleton sent Captain Mc-
Cleave with ten or a dozen men to find them. The Confederates promptly captured McCleave at the Pima villages at the
juncture of the Salt River with the Gila.

With his advance men disappearing into the desert limbo,
Colonel Carleton sent a company of infantry east to find out
what under the Arizona sun was going on. Part of this company,
under command of Lieutenant J. J. Barrett, ran head on into a
group of Captain Hunter's Confederates at Picacho Pass, and the
war in Arizona was on.

The result was the Battle of Picacho Pass. It could be called
nothing more than a minor skirmish today, but it was the de-
cisive engagement that determined the South's greatest westward
advance toward its objective, the Pacific coast.

The battle was a draw. Lieutenant Barrett and two Union
privates were killed; on the Confederate side, although it cannot
be substantiated, it is generally accepted that two men were killed
and two captured. Such a battle would not even make a news
story in the scale of twentieth-century methods of war. But all
of Tucson, on the one hand, and all of Fort Yuma and Arizona
City, on the other, were eager to learn the outcome.

The Confederates fell back on Tucson and the Union forces
continued to hold the Pima villages.

THE U.S.A. PRODUCES THE SHOW

The next engagement would, of course, be the knockout punch—the Battle of Tucson—and Colonel Carleton began moving up his infantry and his artillery for this all-out battle to determine whether Arizona was to be held by the Blue or the Gray.

Somewhat surprisingly, Captain Sherod Hunter received new orders from General Robert E. Lee away back in Virginia. Arizona was to be abandoned for the time being. The South needed all its strength in the East. Win the war on the Potomac, take Washington, and then there would be plenty of time for western expansion. In truth, if the South won on the Atlantic seaboard, the Southwest would probably fall into the Confederate sphere of influence without a shot. Captain Hunter and his Texas cavalry were called east for more important and crucial service instead of holding an adobe town in sunny Arizona. The men in gray reluctantly left Tucson to its fate. And on their march east they ran into a major battle, as they were attacked by several hundred Apache Indians. But they held their own, fired a round of howitzers, lost some men and valuable supplies, and finally forced their way back through the Apache country, across New Mexico to El Paso in Texas, and on to the Mississippi to serve the Confederacy as General Lee might command.

On May 20, 1862, Colonel James H. Carleton's officers led the men in blue to Tucson. The Union forces deployed in the hills west of the town, and sent occupation troops into the heart of the city. Not a shot was fired. The war in Arizona was over.

Tucson, at this time, was still intrinsically an "old Spanish town" and was still protected by walls against the ever-ominous Apaches. Men working in fields along the Santa Cruz River no more than a mile or so from the town would be stealthily and silently murdered. The Apaches were that close, and no one

knew when they might attack. With the arrival of the California
Volunteers the Apache threat was greatly reduced. Most of the
citizens of Tucson spoke no English and couldn't tell a Union
man from a Southerner. The Mason-Dixon Line was unheard of
and the issues of the Civil War were never very clear. After
Colonel Carleton's men had been in Tucson for a few weeks,
the Spanish-speaking citizens began to like them just as much as
they had liked Captain Hunter and his Confederates. While the
name Tucson was in constant use, most of the natives referred to
their community as the Old Pueblo—Pueblo Viejo—and the name
continues to this day.

But in spite of the sunshine, the clear air, the warm days,
and the cool evenings (the elevation of this desert city is about
2,400 feet) and the general easy-come easy-go, if-not-today-why-
then-tomorrow, attitude of the Spanish populace, a new element
had come to Tucson with the Gadsden Purchase. These were
Americans; they were rough and they were tough; and a good
many of them were outlaws or fugitives from justice of some
sort. Tucson was a kind of no man's land legally, and jurispru-
dence was unknown. By 1864 it was said that there were two
extraterritorial "travel bureaus" that sent a great number of sight-
seers to Tucson. And if they didn't go to Tucson, they'd find
themselves hanging by their necks in California or Texas. These
two institutions which ran criminals out of the two states were
the California Vigilance Committee and the Texas Rangers. If
a horsethief, petty crook, crooked gambler, confidence man, high-
wayman, burglar, rapist, or common drunkard was wanted by the
California Vigilantes, he made tracks for Arizona. And if one of
the same kidney was about to be strung up by the Texas Rangers,
he "hit the road" for Arizona. The largest town was Tucson—
and to this Old Pueblo came the scum and riffraff of both East
and West. All the Americans were not undesirables, but for every

Charles D. Poston or L. J. F. Jaeger there was also the "Bowery bum" or the current "Skid Row" type of social parasite.

J. Ross Browne, whose *Adventures in the Apache Country* has been quoted previously, took a good look at Tucson in 1864, and this is what he saw:

I had no idea before my visit to Arizona that there existed within the territorial limits of the United States a city more remarkable in many respects than Jericho—the walls of which were blown down by horns; for, in this case, the walls were chiefly built up by horns—a city realizing, to some extent, my impressions of what Sodom and Gomorrah must have been before they were destroyed by the vengeance of the Lord. It is gratifying to find that travel in many lands has not yet fatally impaired my capacity for receiving new sensations . . . It was reserved for the city of Tucson to prove that the world is not yet exhausted of its wonders.

Tucson is a city of mud-boxes, dingy and dilapidated, cracked and baked into a composite of dust and filth; littered about with broken corrals, sheds, bake-ovens, carcasses of dead animals, and broken pottery; barren of verdure, parched, naked, and grimly desolate in the glare of a southern sun. Adobe walls without whitewash inside or out, hard earth-floors, baked and dried Mexicans, sore-backed burros, coyote dogs, and terra-cotta children; soldiers, teamsters, and honest miners lounging about the mescal-shops, soaked with the fiery poison; a noisy band of Sonoran buffoons, dressed in theatrical costume, cutting their antics in the public places to the most diabolical din of fiddles and guitars ever heard; a long train of government wagons preparing to start for Fort Yuma or the Rio Grande—these are what the traveler sees, and a great many things more, but in vain he looks for a hotel or a lodging-house. The best accommodations he can possibly expect are the dried mud walls of some unoccupied outhouse, with a mud floor for his bed . . . and lucky he is to possess such luxuries as these.

I heard of a blacksmith named Burke, who invited a friend to stop awhile with him in Tucson. Both parties drank whisky all day for occupation and pleasure. When bedtime came, Burke said, "Let's go home and turn in." He led the way to the Plaza and began to hand off his clothes. "What are you doing?" inquired his guest. "Going to bed," said Burke. "This is where I gen'rally sleep." And they both turned in on the Plaza, which if hard was at least well-aired and roomy.

J. Ross Browne would never have been interested in settling down in Tucson, but his report of almost a hundred years ago is not resented at all by the present-day Tucson Chamber of Commerce. That body points out that Tucson was unique in 1864. And while those particular characteristics have changed with the years, the city still has its claims to distinction; for today it is one of the most attractive communities in the United States. But as of 1864, Mr. Browne continued:

As the center of trade with the neighboring State of Sonora, and lying on the high-road from the Rio Grande to Fort Yuma, it became quite a place of resort for traders, speculators, gamblers, horse-thieves, murderers, and vagrant politicians. Men who were no longer permitted to live in California found the climate of Tucson congenial to their health. If the world were searched over I suppose there could not be found so degraded a set of villains as formed the principal society of Tucson. Every man went armed to the teeth, and street fights and bloody affrays were of daily occurrence. It was literally a paradise of devils.

But after a little more careful observation Mr. Browne decided that the first impact was the worst and that things were not quite so bad as they had been when the California Volunteers arrived and helped clean up and discipline the town.

"Since the coming of the California Volunteers two years ago, the state of things in this delightful metropolis has materially changed," he wrote. But he does not imply that it had changed for better or for worse, and his further description, while indubitably accurate, is still trenchant and critical. The changes that took place were not for the benefit of the Tucsonians, but for the benefit of the California Volunteers. Mr. Browne's irony continues:

The citizens who are permitted to live here are still very much in the Greaser style—the tenantable houses having been taken away from them for the use of the officers and soldiers who are protecting them from the Apaches . . . Formerly they were troubled a good deal about the care of their cattle and sheep; now they have no trouble at all; the cattle and sheep have fallen into the hands of the Apaches, who have become unusually bold in their depredations; and the pigs which formerly roamed unmolested about the streets during the day, have become a military necessity. Eggs are scarce because the hens that used to lay them cackle no more in hen form. Drunkenness has been effectually prohibited by a written order limiting the sale of spirituous liquors to three specific establishments . . . Gambling is also much discountenanced; and nobody gambles when he is out of money, or can't borrow from any other sources. . . . Volunteer soldiers are stationed all over the town—at the mescal-shops, the monte-tables, and houses of ill-fame—for the preservation of public order, or go there of their own accord for that purpose.

Although there are two companies of able-bodied men well armed and equipped at Tucson, and although the Apaches range within three miles of the place, there is no apprehension felt for the public safety. Citizens in small parties of five or six go out whenever occasion requires, and afford aid and comfort to unfortunate travellers who happen to be waylaid in pursuit of legitimate business . . .

From which it will be seen that Tucson has greatly improved within the past two years, and offers at the present time rare attractions for visitors from all parts of the world, including artists, who can always find its subject worthy of their genius. The views of life, the varied attitudes of humanity that I, a mere sketcher, found in the purlieus of the town as well as in public places, will be valuable to posterity; but, as Dr. Johnson said when looking from an eminence over the road that led out of Scotland into England, it was the finest view that he had seen in the country, so I must be permitted to say the best view of Tucson is the rear view on the road to Fort Yuma.

Apparently Mr. Browne never met any of Tucson's more important pillars of society during his brief stay, or if he did, he did not recognize them. There were far better elements in young and sprawling Tucson than the peripatetic author discovered.

A condition of unbearable and needless crime usually brings its just wrath down upon its own head. Since there was no law, society demanded justice of some sort—no matter how formal or informal—and Dr. Charles H. Meyer, a German druggist, served as a justice of the peace for no better reason than that he was a man of education and owned two books. They may have been the only two books in Tucson. One was a publication on the technique of setting broken bones and the other was *Materia Medica* and both were printed in German.

Charles Meyer was prevailed upon from time to time, after his arrival in 1858, to settle an altercation or a dispute or even to referee a fight. This position of "judge" was soon socially accepted and Meyer's drugstore became an impromptu court. When in doubt about a decision, and in order to stall for time and to weigh the problem in his mind, Meyer would frown, ponder, and finally consult *Materia Medica*. After studying this "legal code" for a few minutes he would look up, and keeping a finger on the printed page, say something like, "In the case of Heffelfinger versus Danziger, an identical case as the one with which we are now faced, it says here, in legal phraseology, that the plaintiff is correct, and that the defendant is guilty. I fine the defendant ten dollars. Case dismissed." Nobody had the effrontery to question the decision. And how many citizens of Tucson could read a German *Materia Medica*?

Numerous are the tales in the legendry of Tucson about "Judge" Meyer. And in 1863 when Charles D. Poston's efforts in Washington were instrumental in the creation of the Territory of Arizona, Meyer was legally appointed justice of the peace, a position he had been unintentionally holding for six years.

Perhaps the best story, doubtless enhanced in the years of telling but certainly holding some kernel of truth, is the one about his being awakened about midnight. A man was rapping on his door and Meyer finally got out of bed and called out a window, "Who is there?"

"I want to give myself up," said a voice in the darkness. "I just killed a man in the Cactus Saloon."

Now, the Cactus Saloon was the toughest in town, and served not only bad whisky and worse tequila, but was the stamping ground of gamblers, pimps, and prostitutes.

"In the Cactus Saloon, you say?"

"Yes, Judge."

"Are you sure it wasn't the Shoo Fly restaurant?"

"No, your Honor."

"Because I own part of the Shoo Fly and I won't have any trouble there."

"Your Honor—I killed him in the Cactus Saloon."

"For why did you kill him?"

"He pulled a knife on me and I shot him in self-defense."

"Well—" said Meyer. "It is pretty late to do anything about it tonight. My friend, you go back there and kill another one and then get out of town before morning. Case dismissed."

Meyer went back to bed and the killer disappeared in the darkness. In the morning the body of the victim was buried by the city, but the murderer never was found.

Judge Meyer's chief contribution to penal progress in Tucson (there being no jail worthy of the name) was the chain gang. The thieves, crooked gamblers, drunks, and general undesirables were put to work in chained groups at cleaning the city streets and removing the garbage and sewage, although there were no sewers but only outhouses. This was not a popular occupation, and once released from durance vile the miscreants quickly headed westerly for Yuma or easterly for El Paso. They had no more interest in remaining in Tucson as "guests of the city."

Men such as Charles H. Meyer were slowly bringing civilization to a raw frontier town. Later, in his sunset years, Meyer became the city recorder. He died in 1903 at the age of seventy-four and his name has been passed on to posterity in modern downtown Tucson's Meyer Street.

Throughout Tucson's long adolescence no American woman was a permanent resident of the town until 1870. Most of the American men married Mexican girls, some of them as young as thirteen, and the majority of these marriages were happy and usually resulted in two to seven children, and sometimes as many as fifteen. Atanacia Santa Cruz, a Tucson maid, born in 1850 in the Old Pueblo, is an example. She became Mrs. Samuel Hughes in 1863. Sam Hughes, a native of Wales, was then thirty-four. He had been brought to America as a child, lived in Pennsylvania, and finally went west in the gold rush. Suffering a severe chest injury on a hunting trip in California, he was told by a San Francisco doctor that he would surely die if he did not immediately move to a warm dry climate. Hughes left for Texas and got as far as Tucson in 1858. Contrary to the reaction of J. Ross Browne, he was charmed with the mild warm climate and friendly Spanish people. He decided that Tucson was meant for him. Atanacia Santa Cruz was then eight years old. Because of the death of her parents she lived with an American family, Hiram Stevens and his wife. Stevens was from Vermont. But Mrs. Stevens, a Tucson girl, was Atanacia's elder sister, and the little 8-year-old Mexican child was happy in her sister and brother-in-law's home. Sam Hughes moved into the house next door. That five years later he would marry the child who played in the adjacent yard was farthest from his thoughts.

Hughes had a little money and he invested it in a butcher-shop; and in horses, cattle, sheep, mining ventures, and real estate. His politics were first Whig (as a cabin boy on a Mississippi River steamboat he had once met Henry Clay and had been tipped $5 by the great man), and when the Civil War broke out Hughes became a Republican and was strongly pro-Union. When the Confederates under Captain Sherod Hunter took the town, William Oury, a stanch Southerner, warned Hughes that he had better leave Tucson. If there was trouble, he might be shot. Hughes thought it over, decided that common sense was the better part of valor, and left for California. He entrusted all his interests in Tucson to his neighbor and partner, Hiram Stevens.

In 1862, when the California Volunteers took Tucson, Hughes was with them as a civilian employee hired to drive cattle. In this guise he returned to the town of his choice and again went into business. He was kind, generous, but always shrewd enough to make every dollar in his possession work for him.

In 1863 the Stevens family gave a baile (a dancing-party,) and of course Hughes attended. He was amazed to see Atanacia Santa Cruz. The child he had seen playing games in the next yard only a few years before was now a lovely young girl, having at the age of thirteen reached a maturity that the average

American girl achieved at seventeen. For the first time in his life Sam Hughes fell in love. And within six months Atanacia became his bride. The marriage service was performed at Mission San Xavier del Bac. But there was no time for a honeymoon. Sam Hughes was too busy in Tucson to be able to afford such a luxury. But he promised Atanacia that within a few years they would take a belated wedding trip. Meanwhile Atanacia became a good wife, spoke perfect English as well as Spanish, and learned to be a perfectionist with her sewing needle.

Then, in 1866, Sam Hughes decided that his security in Tucson was assured and the delayed wedding journey might be made. The couple went by wagon to Guaymas in Sonora, Mexico, and there they took a ship to San Francisco. The journey took six months, and such sights as Guaymas, the Gulf of California, and the Pacific Ocean, not to mention San Diego, Monterey, and gay San Francisco, were a new world to the little lady from Tucson. When at last the couple returned home from this cosmopolitan travel, Atanacia brought with her, by way of Fort Yuma and the Gila Valley, something she had asked her husband to buy for her in San Francisco. It was an object never before seen in Arizona, and all the wives of Tucson came to the Hughes home to admire this miraculous invention. It was a Singer sewing machine.

For all his business ability and his many interests, Sam Hughes never became a millionaire. But he was an intelligent and civic-minded citizen, anxious to see Tucson grow and prosper just as much as his own bank account. He did a great deal to foster churches and schools, and he contributed money to both Catholic and Protestant causes. He himself was a Mason and he liked to brag about the fact that he was the first Mason in the Gadsden Purchase—or he might have said the Gila Valley. During his long career he served as an alderman, sheriff, county treasurer, and finally adjutant general of Arizona. Apart from Charles D.

Poston, Sam Hughes was one of the best known men in the Gila watershed. He died at the age of eighty-eight in 1917 and was the last surviving pioneer of the men who settled in Arizona previous to the Gadsden Purchase. All Tucson paid him a silent tribute.

And Atanacia Santa Cruz Hughes lived until 1934. She died at the age of eighty-four, and left seven children, sixteen grandchildren, and thirteen great-grandchildren. This pretty, gentle, and gracious Mexican girl who had been married at thirteen had become a kind of matriarch of the Old Pueblo. At her death a city of forty thousand people paid its respects to a woman who had become an epitomization of the blending of Spanish and American cultures.

Charles Meyer, Sam Hughes, Hiram Stevens, Atanacia Santa Cruz—these were a few of the people of Tucson whom J. Ross Browne failed to meet in 1864. And the loss was his.

Space precludes the mention of many other prominent pioneering Tucsonians, but the names of most of them figure somewhere within the Gila watershed and in other chapters of this book. This is the story of Tucson itself as it grew from a walled Spanish town to an American city.

When the Civil War was officially over, and Arizona was at the same time officially a territory of the United States, it would have been logical to take for granted that Tucson would become the capital. But it did not.

That honor went to the tiny hamlet of Prescott. The reason for this was the fact that the citizens of Tucson had been too cordial to Captain Sherod Hunter and his Confederate cavalry, and the political powers in Washington punished the community by depriving it of its obvious right, as the largest town in the territory, to become the capital. And those who lived in Prescott (named for the famous historian William H. Prescott, who wrote *The Conquest of Mexico* and *The Conquest of Peru,* and who never saw Mexico or Peru or Arizona's first capital) were none too happy about it and called the outpost Fort Misery.

Nevertheless, Tucson did become the capital in 1867. There was no denying the justice of it due to the town's location and size over Prescott. But the honor went back to Prescott in 1877, and in 1879 was transferred to Phoenix (nonexistent in 1867), and there it has remained.

There was one incontestable factor about Tucson that was inherently healthy. And that was the fact that it had never been a "boom" town based on the quick riches of a gold or silver or copper strike. It had a more fundamental reason for existence than being a mining town devoted only to quick wealth and then abandonment. And that reason was its location on one of the major trade routes between the Mississippi Valley and California. Therefore the town had a slow—painfully slow—but consistently steady growth.

In 1870 it had its first newspaper and its first bathtub. Many of the citizens could not read the newspaper, and equally as many did not know how to use the bathtub. The paper reported mostly the street fights, the Indian depredations, and the routine run of robberies and a few lynchings. The bathtub was owned by a barber who was a Negro. From time to time a few of the more curious citizens tried it. Others used the Santa Cruz River or the family washcloth.

In 1871 the first school was opened. The solitary teacher was John Spring, who had come to the Old Pueblo as a soldier with the California Volunteers. His classes consisted of about one hundred and thirty Mexican children and a few who were half Mexican and half American. Spring was both overworked and underpaid, and it is said that this altruist in education not only instructed his pupils in reading, writing, and arithmetic, but also washed and scrubbed them, taught them deportment, and even repaired their clothes. If modern Tucson ever dedicates a new high school, it might well call it the John Spring.

Also, in 1871, Tucson was formally incorporated as a municipality. The population at that time was about thirty-five hundred. As the historian Frank C. Lockwood describes it:

The town was almost as foreign as any community of like size in Spain, Italy, or France. The language, food, dress, amusements, holidays, ceremonials, and religious exercises were wholly different from what one would find in any Western village founded by Americans. As yet there was no Protestant church and there were only three or four women of American birth.

And in 1871 the demand for goods and commodities so far exceeded supply that prices were fantastic. Coal oil was $8 a gallon; brandy was $40 a gallon; sugar was $1 a pound; coffee was $4 a pound; soap was 50 cents a bar; flour was $18 a hundred pounds; a broom cost $6; and a pair of boots was cheap at $25. Twenty-five cents was the smallest coin in use simply because a dime or a nickel or a penny had no purchasing power whatever.

On the other hand, chili peppers cost but little and mescal was a cheap drink. A pair of pants made in Massachusetts might fetch $30 but a beautifully handmade shawl and mantilla (worth $100 in Massachusetts) would sell for about $5.

But in spite of these economic incongruities, Americanization was beginning to stabilize the town. In 1872 the 5th Cavalry gave the Old Pueblo its first brass band concert. The sponsors of the guitar and the violin were amazed. And in the same year J. S. Mansfield announced the opening to the public of Tucson's first circulating library. Those who could not read were amazed; who would walk out of his way to get a book? An

Irishman named Martin Toughey, who sold "agua fresca" from the Santa Cruz River (he always called it "fresh water as sweet as Erin's Shannon"), decided to freeze some of it, and the citizens of Tucson had their first ice. They were a bit baffled; what could one do with ice? Let it melt and all you had was water again. About the same time Hiram Stevens built the first windmill ever seen in the Gila watershed, and Sam Hughes was so extravagant as to sow grass seed for no other purpose than to make a lawn. What was Tucson coming to?

But even more strange events were in order. In 1873 a "Young Men's Literary Society" was organized. In 1877 the struggling weekly newspaper was superseded by a paper called the *Arizona Star*. It has not yet ceased publication and is a metropolitan daily in 1950.

In 1878 St. Paul the Apostle came to town. In reality he had been a peddler in Texas, but having no goods left to peddle he decided to try a commodity that required no running overhead—namely, religion. He served salvation to those who cared to listen (and to those who wished to pay for the privilege by a donation no matter how large or how small) because those who came must obviously need it or they would not have remained to listen. He lasted for six months and then moved west to California, there being no community along the lower Gila—not even Yuma—as attractive to St. Paul the Apostle as the promise of Los Angeles.

In 1879 two doctors of medicine arrived in Tucson. Some of the citizens were skeptical and even sympathetic about their possibilities of making a living. After all, the town had survived very well for over a hundred years without a medical doctor. It was to be hoped that among the thirty-five hundred citizens these two ambitious young Americans (one was from the University of

Pennsylvania and the other was from Harvard University) could find a means of making a living. Before their arrival everyone cured himself or, in a pinch, bought some medicine from Judge (and druggist) Charles Meyer. It was agreeable to Tucsonians to have two medical doctors in town, but where could the two of them ever find enough sick people among thirty-five hundred healthy citizens?

But to top all of these new and startling innovations, the greatest of them came in 1880. On March 20 of that year the railroad was completed to the Old Pueblo. Not from the East did it come, but from California. This link of the future Southern Pacific System connected Tucson with Los Angeles, San Francisco, and thence overland to the Atlantic seaboard. Tucson—at last—was on the map of the world that thrilling day in 1880 when the first steam engine came puffing into the brand-new, spick-and-span depot.

After one hundred years of adolescence the Old Pueblo had come of age. Such an event demanded a glorious celebration. In a previous book, *Desert Country,* I have described the final prank just before Tucson put away its childish things forever:

Bands blared and cannon boomed, and many citizens of the Old Pueblo enjoyed one final spree. They telegraphed the President of the United States, and sent wires to the mayors of Los Angeles, San Francisco, and New York, informing them of Tucson's coming of age. With a little more alcoholic encouragement the mayor of Tucson decided to wire His Holiness the Pope. Why not? Hadn't the Catholic Church been responsible for the birth of Tucson (the mayor had forgotten the Hohokam or doubtless he would have tried to telegraph them), and shouldn't the Pope hear about this triumphant day? With some labor and a few more drinks the great message was composed. It read:

Tucson, Arizona,
March 20, 1880

To His Holiness the Pope of Rome, Italy:

The Mayor of Tucson begs the honor of reminding Your Holiness
that this ancient and honorable pueblo was founded by the Spaniards under the sanction of the Church more than three (3)
centuries ago, and to inform Your Holiness that a railroad from
San Francisco, California, now connects us with the entire Christian world.

R. N. Leatherwood, Mayor

Asking your benediction:

J. B. Salpointe, Vic. ap.

This effusive message was handed to the telegraph operator, and
he was told to send it pronto. Other citizens of Tucson, however,
feeling in a less expansive and more conservative frame of mind
over this gala day, succeeded in intervening between the telegraph operator and the outside world. He was bribed to take it
all as a joke and forget it.

As the day wore on, the celebration continued, and the telegraph operator stared at the unsent message before him. His conscience bothered him terribly. When he was ordered to send a
message it was his sacred duty to send it, and he felt guilty indeed
in shirking the obligations of his post. For hours he racked his
brains to find some way to please both parties—those who thought
they had sent the message and those who had prevented its leaving
Tucson. By nightfall he had hit upon a compromise. He would
not send the message, but in order to please the mayor and other
city officers he would send them a false answer. Thus all parties
would be satisfied. He congratulated himself upon his diplomacy.
He would go far indeed.

At a very exuberant banquet that evening the city fathers
were in fine fettle. The mayor was on his feet proposing the
health of Tucson for the twentieth or thirtieth time when a mes-

senger boy touched his elbow. A telegram for Mayor Leather-wood. With a grandiloquent gesture and a pat on the head for the messenger boy, the mayor opened the telegram and looked first at the signature and beamed. Then he read the message aloud, slowly, for all to hear.

His Holiness the Pope acknowledges with appreciation re-ceipt of your telegram informing him that the ancient city of Tucson at last has been connected by rail with the outside world and sends his benediction, but for his own satisfaction would ask, where in hell is Tucson anyway?

                                                        Antonelli

No Western Union operator has ever performed his duty more faithfully.

And as for Tucson, although she may have been put in her place, there was no gainsaying the fact that the Old Pueblo had grown up.

20

OF MINES AND MINING MEN

A very long book could be written about the mines and mining men of the Gila watershed. To bring the great mining industry of Arizona down to a chapter means a condensation un-fair to the scope of the subject and an omission of many strong and colorful personalities and the dramatic stories of the discov-ering and operating of many mines. But there are certain indispensable stories, and the best of them give a good indication of the general run of the others.

Within the area drained by the Gila and its tributaries there have been some of the richest and most sensational mines in the United States. Their names are as colorful as their history: the Vulture, the Gunsight, the Old Dominion, the Irish Mag, the Big Bug, the Wandering Jew, the Honeymoon, the North Star, the Christmas, the Toughnut, the Lucky Cuss, and the ever-famous Lost Dutchman. Some of these, and a number of others, will be mentioned in a chapter on the character of the towns they caused to develop. But to bring the lot down to a least common denominator of two, perhaps the stories of Mr. Wickenburg and the Vulture, and the fabulous Lost Dutchman, will be enough to lead anyone who is sufficiently interested far deeper into the labyrinths of Arizona's dramatic mining history.

Both the Vulture and the Lost Dutchman were gold strikes. In spite of such magnificent copper mines as Ajo, Morenci, and the Copper Queen at Bisbee, silver has always been more alluring to the mass imagination than copper, and gold has always outshone them both.

Heinrich Heinsel was born in Essen, Germany, in 1817, and for more than forty years he never knew the Gila River existed. He was a good student, a devoted mineralogist, and up to the age of forty-four apparently destined to live in Germany all his life. But in 1861 something happened in Essen, and history cannot say what, that made it imperative for Heinsel to get out of Germany in a hurry. He came to America on a sailing vessel around Cape Horn and arrived at San Francisco in 1862. Once he set foot on American soil Heinrich Heinsel disappeared forever, and a man named Henry Wickenburg came into existence.

By 1862 the illusion of quick wealth in the California gold fields had been pretty well dissipated. More men were returning from the "diggings" bitter and frustrated than there were successful miners happily panning gold. Heinsel-turned-Wickenburg decided that what he needed most to utilize his mineralogical education was a virgin field. At this time gold had been found on the Gila and the short-lived Gila City had sprung up in 1858 and was a ghost town four years later. Other rich strikes in Arizona, however, were reported in San Francisco. The rumors were wonderful. With hope in his heart the newly created Henry Wickenburg set off for the Gila Valley. There he met Pauline Weaver, the scout, trapper, and prospector, who knew Arizona as well as he did the palm of his hand. The two prospected without any luck and soon dissolved their partnership. Weaver moved north to the area around Prescott and Wickenburg followed the Hassayampa River south toward the Gila.

On the banks of the Hassayampa Wickenburg fell in with a party of gold seekers. All were discouraged. There was plenty of desert but there was no gold. The group of men camped beside the pleasant stream and debated the subject of where to look next. But Wickenburg, new to Arizona and his first enthusiasm as yet undimmed, left the men to their talk and walked off to explore by himself. Within a few miles of the west bank of the Hassayampa he found unmistakable evidence of gold outcroppings. And a few steps farther he picked up nuggets of free gold. First one. Then two. Then three. And then a dozen.

Here it was: the real thing; the great objective. His life's ambition was suddenly realized and fulfilled. For a minute or two, or perhaps for only a fleeting instant, taciturn, phlegmatic Henry Wickenburg enjoyed the experience of concentrated, intrinsic happiness. It was almost unbearable. He was aghast at the victory symbolized by the gold he held in his hand. It was unquestionably the climax of his life. Nothing before had ever equaled it, and nothing in the future could even approach it.

Gold!

And no end of it.

And then came the vulture.

As Henry Wickenburg stooped to pick up nugget after nugget, a shadow passed over him. Looking up he saw a vulture banking slowly and gracefully against the bright blue sky. It made an effortless arc above him and then began to drop nearer in smaller and smaller concentric circles.

Wickenburg looked at the bird and the bird looked at him —the Ancient Mariner and the albatross—and as it floated nearer in an easy graceful curve, he said to it, "Gold." Whereupon the vulture landed on a ledge some distance away and said nothing. But the Vulture Mine was born, and mining history was about to be made.

Henry Wickenburg, with free gold in his hands, never gave a thought to the shadow of the vulture, or that the gold and the shadow came into his life almost simultaneously. He hurried back to his companion gold seekers who were lounging on the banks of the Hassayampa. He had great news for them.

And incredible as it may seem, not one of this party of fortune hunters was even mildly interested in Henry Wickenburg's discovery. They laughed at him. That stuff gold? Of course not—fool's gold maybe. Hadn't they prospected the Hassayampa area? If there had been gold here wouldn't they have found it long before this newly arrived German? Better throw that stuff in the river and pack up and strike on south down to the Gila itself. There was gold on the Gila. That had been assured. But this tributary, the Hassayampa, wasn't worth the prospecting.

Wickenburg knew better. He said "auf Wiedersehen" to his friends. They went on their way downstream, and he returned to the place where he had found the gold. The vulture had flown away.

Later a number of the men who had scoffed at the very idea of gold on the Hassayampa sued Henry Wickenburg for an accounting and division of the profits, claiming that they were all equal partners. They never got a cent. And in justice they didn't deserve any. While the case was dragging through the courts the Vulture Mine was producing $3,000 a day. There could be no other words for it but gold mine—and one of the greatest in the history not only of the Gila watershed, but of the American West.

The Hassayampa River has a curious bit of legendry unlike any other of the Gila's tributaries. It is said that if once you drink from the stream you will never tell the truth again. This apocrypha even entered the lawsuit against Wickenburg, and one of the plaintiffs claimed that he hadn't believed Wickenburg and hadn't investigated his claim simply because he knew Wickenburg had drunk water from the Hassayampa and was therefore lying. For useless testimony it was close to an all-time low.

But the "Lying Waters of the Hassayampa" is a legend that cannot be traced to its source and a legend that persists to the present day. The legend also has variations upon its theme. One is this: if you approach the river and reach its bank, turn upstream and drink and you'll always be truthful; but turn downstream and drink and you'll never speak anything but lies. Why this should be so is, of course, never explained.

The origin of the word "Hassayampa" is debatable. Some say the name was given by Pauline Weaver from a Mojave Indian word meaning "beautiful water." Other historians believe the word is from the Yuma language and means "hidden water." Be that as it may, Orick Jackson wrote a poem about it:

> You've heard about the wondrous stream
> They call the Hassyamp.

> They say it turns a truthful guy
> Into a lying scamp.
> And if you quaff its waters once
> It's sure to prove your bane.
> You'll ne'er forsake the blasted stream
> Or tell the truth again.

This legend of mendacity is further substantiated by another jingle, the authorship of which is unknown. It may have come from Charles D. Poston, who occasionally wrote doggerel verse about Arizona for his own amusement.

> Those who drink its waters bright,
> Red man, white man, boor, or knight,
> Girls or women, boys or men,
> Never can tell the truth again.

And if one Arizonan today calls another a "Hassayamp," it is fighting talk; for one man has simply called another a liar.

But placid, calm, easygoing Henry Wickenburg had been no Hassayamp when he first told of his gold to the skeptics. If they would have none of it, that was satisfactory to him. At first he worked alone, and laboriously hauled ore from the mine to the Hassayampa. When he had accumulated a ton he built an arrastre for crushing ore. The arrastre is of Spanish invention, a mill with a vat and with crude heavy rollers worked by a horizontal beam. The yield was so sensational to an occasional passing prospector that the news got abroad, and a gold rush to the banks of the Hassayampa was soon on. It was far too big a project for Wickenburg to handle alone. He set up a novel policy of selling his ore at the scene of the strike, to anybody who wanted to buy it, for $15 a ton. Then the buyer had to pack it by mule or burro to the Hassayampa and *rent* Henry Wickenburg's mill. Of course others could build arrastres up and down the Hassayampa and they did so. But all had to buy from Wickenburg the rich ore to feed to their mills. Within a year there were more than forty arrastres along the river, while the mine itself lay about six miles to the west in the low, rolling, cactus-studded desert hills. And on the river the town of Wickenburg sprang up almost over-night.

By 1866 there was a 20-stamp mill on the Hassayampa, and in 1870 Wickenburg leased the Vulture to an eastern corpora-tion, but retained a fifth of the property for himself. And this new organization built an 80-stamp mill at the mine. By 1879 this greatest of gold mines reached a production gross of $21,000 a week. And there seemed to be no end to it. But with all that, there was no happiness to it either. The following summary of what happened to Henry Wickenburg and the Vulture is from *Desert Country*:

Of course, where there are riches as great as this, the greed of men is bound to follow, and the shadow of the vulture that flew over Henry Wickenburg as he held the gold in his hands and knew he had achieved his objective marked a line of demarcation between the two halves of his career. Up to the moment of that passing shadow Henry Wickenburg had been searching and hop-ing, and from that moment on he was on the defensive—guarding, protecting, defending, trying to possess the very real property dur-ing the last half of his life which the first half had been devoted to bringing into being. There is no doubt that Henry Wicken-burg spent his happiest years without the gold he thought he wanted.

There is little point in following the Vulture Mine through the labyrinths of litigation. Complaint and cross-complaint became a maze of charges and counter-charges worthy of the service of the firm of Dodson and Fogg who so ably entwined Mr. Pick-wick. The trials of the Vulture reached national significance, for after the Civil War, when the government was in need of gold for the reconstruction period, Henry Wickenburg's mine supplied a goodly share of the metal. Mr. Wickenburg was happy to get out from under the burden, and he sold four-fifths of the Vulture [that portion which he had formerly leased] to a New York capitalist for $85,000. [And at this time the Vulture was producing a million dollars a year!] So much litigation followed this deal that even a firm such as Dodson and Fogg would have been unable to untangle the complications, and the transaction was never legally consummated. Who owns what is still debatable today.

And not only did the shadow of the original vulture bring unceasing legal bickering, but it marked a boom in murder and rapine throughout western Arizona. It is estimated that more than four hundred men were killed by Indians, bandits, and the general lawless populace of the town of Wickenburg during the fifteen years between 1865 and 1880. Wells Fargo drivers were shot from ambush, and bullion carriers and guards were murdered for the gold they protected. Then there was hijacking within the banditry itself—and the chief product of Henry Wickenburg's Vulture became a mass of shootings, stabbings, holdups, bribes, thefts, blackmailings, stock swindlings, mismanagement, and general fraud. Mankind had arrived on the banks of the Hassayampa and had brought civilization along.

This went on until 1890, when the forces of nature stepped in and brought a flood to the land. The raging Hassayampa broke loose, during a terrific rainstorm, over, around, and through a weakly constructed dam some eighteen miles north of the town of Wickenburg and purged the land of the greed and stench of man. It was one of Arizona's greatest disasters, some eighty lives being lost, and ranches and mills and mines and towns ruined. After that there were plenty of vultures in the sky for days to come.

Simultaneous with this cataclysm the Vulture Mine received its first setback. A major fault was found in the vein, and the body of rich ore could not be found again. Specialists and authorities in mineralogy and geology have tried time and again, but the

Vulture cut off its supply of wealth as cleanly as you or I might slice a sausage with a knife. Somewhere in the vicinity the rich vein continues—but up to the present writing it has never been located again. The Vulture gave men more than $15,000,000 and then said, "That's enough."

Henry Wickenburg, tired by the unceasing litigation, his ranch ruined by the floods, the town which bore his name a shambles, and his beloved Vulture dead, retired to a small house on his property, a beaten, disillusioned, and exhausted man. What was it all about and what was it all worth? He had accomplished all that his youthful ambitions had desired. And now, as an old man, what did it all mean? Life baffled him—he couldn't find any answer. Somehow it was all a failure.

But he hung on, following the line of least resistance, which meant living through day after day, with no real solution as to what it all meant, until his eighty-eighth birthday in 1905. Many times he had been heard to remark that he was very, very tired of this meaningless experience called living. And at sunset on his eighty-eighth birthday, at the same spot on which he had first camped when he came to the banks of the Hassayampa, Henry Wickenburg was found dead, a pistol in his hand and a bullet in his brain. . . .

But not so the Vulture.

Men refused to give it up. In 1908 a new vein was found, and the bird spread its wings again. And while it was never the Vulture of old, it did produce close to $2,000,000 between 1908 and 1915. Even the old rock buildings which housed the first miners were torn down and run through the stamp mill. And these buildings had in them sufficient gold to be worth $20 a ton. Then the vein ran out, and water seeped into the lower levels, and the Vulture went to sleep again. Parts of its complicated machinery were sold for junk in 1917 and 1918.

It slept until 1931, when the pinch of depression made men try again. And there was still life in the old bird. During the

1930's a considerable amount of low-grade ore was mined, and in 1940 a 200-ton mill was still crushing ore. There are many old-timers who are confident that some day, somewhere, somebody will discover the original vein and the old mine will again approximate its boom days . . . That vein is there, they argue; and of course they are right.

The terrain about the mine looks today very much as it must have looked when Henry Wickenburg first explored it. It is stark, raw, uncompromising country. If you care to leave the highway and strike out into the desert adjacent to the mine, you will see just about what Henry Wickenburg saw in 1863. And if you sit quietly beside the desert rocks and look casually up at the light blue sky, if you will but be patient, eventually, banking slowly in a graceful arc against the blue, a vulture is sure to come.

In 1950 a limited amount of work was still being done at the Vulture Mine. It is improbable that the old bird will ever relive the days of its glory; but as always, there is that gamble in the game called mining. Wickenburg's first companions laughed away something approaching a twenty-million dollar gold mine. Who dares to laugh at the Vulture today?

If the story of Mr. Wickenburg and the Vulture comes to a wistful and sad ending, the story of the Lost Dutchman is a case of "the lady or the tiger." It is a dilemma unsolved, a riddle unanswerable. And, like the Vulture, the Lost Dutchman has outlived the little men who gave it fame.

Mining is something like fishing. In other words, "you should have seen the one that got away." The "lost" mines of the West, and of the Gila watershed, are always the big ones. No "lost" mine was ever trivial. Had it not been lost it might have turned out to be trivial. But once lost, imagination, hope, lies, wishful thinking—all make it the big one that got away.

The Lost Dutchman, obviously, is one of those. That

the wealth is there is pretty close to incontestable, but after almost a century the mine has not been found. But again, in mining there is that omnipresent lure—it might be found tomorrow.

But one fact is a certainty, and that is that the Lost Dutchman is located somewhere in the Superstition Mountains between the Gila River and its parallel tributary, the Salt.

The story of the mine begins in a haze of history. Some maintain that the Apache Indians were the first discoverers. If so, they had little use for it. Gold was not a medium of aboriginal exchange. Other legends tell of the discovery of the mine by Spanish pioneers. This version is rife with Indian attacks, cryptic maps, and the passing on of information by word of mouth and sworn secrecy from generation to generation. Most or all of this can be codified as the folklore behind the Lost Dutchman.

The factual story emerges from the fog of legendry with the arrival on the scene of the Dutchman himself. This was in 1870. His name was Jacob Walz, and like most "Dutchmen" of the frontier, he was actually a German.

Walz, along with countless other gold seekers, had been attracted to Arizona by the news of Henry Wickenburg's great Vulture Mine. For a brief time he was employed at the Vulture but was caught "high-grading." This is a miner's term for stealing nuggets of free gold, or pieces and chunks of rich ore. A crafty high-grader could slip a few choice bits of ore in his clothing, and thus collect for himself ten times more per day than his wages. Walz did just this, concealing rich ore on his person, stealing from the company that employed him, until he was apprehended and promptly fired. He roamed on, searching for gold on his own, having no luck, and finally met another German with a first name the same as his own—Jacob Wiser.

Little is known of Wiser's past. By trade he was a carpenter,

but by choice he was a prospector. Where the two Germans met
is not known, but it is usually attributed to the then new and
tiny settlement on the Mexican border called Nogales. At any
rate, they became partners and arrived in another new settlement,
the town of Florence, on the Gila River. Florence is the site of
Arizona's state penitentiary today, and the prison would make a
fitting home for the team of Walz and Wiser were they alive.

The two Germans had heard rumors of great wealth in the
Superstition Mountains. Probably some of this was the legendry
back of the story—Indian caches and bonanzas kept secret by
Spanish pioneers. At Florence, the nearest settlement to the Superstitions, they procured supplies. It was the spring of 1871 when
they packed into the grim cactus-studded rocky fastness of the
Superstition Mountains. In this combination of mountain and
desert wilderness the outstanding landmark is Weaver's Needle,
a sharp rocky peak that may be seen for miles in all directions.
The great mine is somewhere in the general vicinity of this peak.
It was there in 1871 and it is there today. Hundreds of men
have tried to find the Lost Dutchman, but only Walz and Wiser

knew where it was, and they died without ever quite revealing the great secret. As they faced death, each tried to pass the information on, but neither was sufficiently coherent to make sense.

In 1871, as prospectors, they had no comprehension of what lay ahead of them as they made camp in Needle Canyon in the heart of the Superstitions. They cooked an early supper, and as they sat eating they heard a strange noise. They listened and stared at each other. It was the unmistakable sound of a miner's hammer, the chink-chink of steel on rock. Somebody was ahead of them, and that somebody was looking for gold. Back to their minds came the legends of fabulous riches—the story behind the mine—Apache gold and Spanish bonanzas.

Incredible as it may seem, Walz and Wiser made no effort to approach their predecessor peacefully. They both picked up their rifles and began a stealthy reconnoitering toward the sound of the blows. Creeping up a canyon, using boulders and cactus for cover, they slowly came upon the scene of the pounding. In the growing dusk two men were working eagerly, almost frantically, part way up the canyon wall. They had dug out a part of the cliff, making a combination pit and cave. They were plainly visible, and so concentrated on their work that they were unaware that they were being watched.

Walz looked at Wiser and nodded his head and leveled his rifle at the miner on the right. Wiser nodded back and aimed his rifle at the man on the left. Then both Germans fired at once and the canyons of the Superstitions echoed with the roar.

Both victims fell, shot through, and Walz and Wiser moved forward, still cautious, prepared to kill again should other men appear. By this time it was fast growing dark. With no thought for the men they had murdered, the two villains quickly examined the ore. It was gold-bearing quartz, they were sure. But in the fading light it was impossible to tell more. They ignored their victims and groped their way down the rocky slope and down the canyon to their camp and jubilantly finished their supper. Success was theirs!

With the first streak of dawn Walz and Wiser returned to the scene of their villainy. And then they received their first shock. The bodies of the two miners were gone!

The Germans stood aghast for a moment and then shrugged it off and fell to examining the ore. It surpassed all their expectations—a huge vein of quartz that was almost one-third gold. Wiser became hysterical. He danced in glee and tossed ore in the air. He was both laughing and crying.

Not so Walz.

This greater of the two criminals had a passing thought. Two bodies had disappeared. Wiser knew too much. Why divide this gold with the ecstatic lunatic who was no longer a desirable partner? As calmly as if he were reaching for his handkerchief, Walz reached for his rifle. A second or two later he shot his ecstatic partner through the back. Wiser's cries of glee became screams and then groans of agony. He lay writhing on the ground, a pool of blood slowly forming around him. Walz didn't even look at him. Taking one sample of ore for luck, he struck off down the canyon to the camp. Here he collected all of Wiser's property—cooking utensils, a box of shells, a pick, a canteen, a hammer, a saw, a box of nails—and carefully buried all the items and leveled off the ground. Jacob Wiser? Walz had never heard of him. He smiled while he worked. Why not? One of the greatest mines in the world was now his, and his alone. He was rich!

Three men were dead—or at least one was dead and two bodies were missing. To Walz's emotionless and brutish mind that meant little. He was on his own and nobody could prove anything against him, for there were no witnesses.

The story of the two missing bodies was simply this: both men, mortally wounded and left for dead, had tried to crawl to help. One of them died during the night and his remains were found weeks later. The other, a man named Jacobs (same last name as the first of Walz and Wiser), finally emerged from the Superstitions and stumbled to the cabin of a settler named Andy Starr. Here he collapsed and died in Starr's arms, ranting and moaning and trying to tell of infinite riches and a murderous ambush. Starr could make but little sense of any of it.

Oddly enough, Wiser too survived for some time, and he too managed to crawl toward help. He was found near death in the desert area just south of the Superstitions and was taken to a nearby ranch by Pima Indians. The ranch owner was John D. Walker. He listened to Wiser's dying babblings. Still frantic over the wealth he had seen, and knowing that he was dying, Wiser even tried to draw Walker a map, but became too delirious to co-ordinate, and died screaming for the gold he would never see again.

That left only Walz—the "Dutchman."

Conscience, remorse, emotions—none of these bothered Jacob Walz. Human sympathy was not in his soul; nevertheless, he was not completely happy in his stupid animal way. He had the gold and it was all his. But there is no fun in having hunks and gobs of gold deep in the Superstition Mountains. Gold was to spend and enjoy. So Walz made a trip back to the town of Florence. And there, and up and down the Gila, for many miles, ran the story of the great strike. For Walz had not come to town with ore to be milled; he had come to town with a sackful of nuggets that were merely the surface scrapings of a great mine to be.

"And where is your mine?" he was asked a hundred times.

"In the Superstitions," was his only answer.

"And where is your partner, Wiser?" somebody asked.

"Killed by the Apache Indians," explained Walz. "Died brave. With his boots on."

"What's the name of your mine?"

"Oh, just say it belongs to the Dutchman."

And so the strike became known as the Dutchman Mine.

But John D. Walker came into the town of Florence one day and heard all about the great new strike. Then he recalled the wounded, crazed, and dying Wiser who was buried on his ranch and who had drawn for him an unintelligible map showing the location of great riches. For the first time he gave Wiser's story credence. But when he looked for Walz the "Dutchman" had left Florence and gone back into the Superstitions. Walker had ranching and mining interests of his own sufficient to keep him busy; but he kept the Wiser story in mind.

It may seem incredible in view of modern times that men could come and go, appear and disappear, murder and be murdered, without any formal investigation at all. But it must be remembered that this was still the frontier, that Arizona Territory had only recently been organized, and that every man's business was his own. A man who called himself Smith in one part of the Gila Valley might prefer to present himself as Jones in another, and no questions were asked. It was a land of individuals and what happened or did not happen to you was your individual concern and not society's.

About a month after the news of a great strike in the Superstitions had been bruited up and down the Gila, Jacob Walz turned up in the newly formed community of Phoenix on the lower Salt River near its junction with the Gila.

Nobody in Phoenix had ever heard of Walz or Wiser, but

they soon heard of the Dutchman Mine, for Jacob Walz had enough free gold on his person to amount to four or five thousand dollars. These riches amazed the small community called Phoenix, which had a population of several hundred, and which, eighteen years later in 1889, was destined to be the capital city of the territory. Walz went on a drunken orgy and boasted and bragged about his great mine. Every man was convinced of the truth of these drunken statements because Walz had the gold to prove it. But even in his cups the crafty German would not reveal the location of his ill-gotten gold mine. When sufficiently sober he disappeared from Phoenix one night and nobody knew just when he had left. Thus there was nobody to follow him into the lonely terrain of the Superstitions.

It all made good gossip for a month or more, and then Walz returned to Phoenix. This time he had a burroload of selected ore, and it assayed at $10,000 a ton! All Phoenix was stunned. Where was this wealth coming from?

"Just call it the Dutchman Mine," said Walz, and he proceeded to go on a 5-day drunk. When he left Phoenix this time there were plenty of men prepared to follow him, and a number of others had camped between Phoenix and the Superstitions forty or more miles to the east, hoping to intercept and follow his trail.

But he shifted his course, doubled on his own tracks, dragged a blanket behind his burro to conceal the trail, finally abandoned the burro, and completely disappeared deep in the Superstitions somewhere near the outstanding peak, Weaver's Needle. All trackers and scouts had to give up and return to Phoenix. Numerous prospectors went into the Superstitions on their own, searching not for Walz in particular but for quartz outcroppings and any other possible indications of gold. They found none and they saw no trace of Walz. Some of them never came back, and it was generally believed that the desperate and gold-crazed German had shot them from ambush. Other men camped around Weaver's Needle for days without seeing a living soul. And for a month or more Walz seemed to have been swallowed up by the earth. The discouraged returned to Phoenix only to learn that Walz had turned up in Tucson with a sack of ore that he sold to Charles Meyer for $2,400.

And again the same thing happened: men who attempted to trail him back to the Superstitions from Tucson followed him with ease to the south bank of the Gila. Once north of the Gila and in the foothills of the Superstitions, the canny German became a will-o'-the-wisp.

Barry Storm, whose book *Thunder Gods Gold* tells the dramatic story of many Arizona mines, and who has covered on foot most of the Superstition range, and who has analyzed the mystery of Walz, is reasonably certain that the German had a secret cave which he had supplied with food and water and in which he could live for days or weeks. The entrance to this cave was very small and completely concealed by an overhanging ledge and dense brush. In his book Mr. Storm states:

Everyone in Arizona Territory was thoroughly convinced that the Dutchman was secretly working a hidden bonanza. In fact, there could have been no doubt of it in the face of his well-witnessed ore sales and continuous production of the same type of fabulous ore for more than six years. Yet he seemed satisfied with merely bringing out enough of his bonanza ore at one time to "have a spree." Perhaps he also had a secret cache somewhere in the Superstitions where he was accumulating a fantastic fortune against a time of need. More than once Walz himself hinted at such a possibility. And anyway the small frontier villages hardly offered opportunity for undue extravagance.

For years then this game of hide and seek continued with

Walz always proving the more canny outdoorsman. But in 1877, in advancing age—Walz was now sixty-nine—and with the ever increasing persistence of followers as his golden fame spread, he decided to abandon his bonanza and retire. And he rented a plot of ground and an adobe hut, located near the present intersection of Henshaw Road and Sixteenth Street in Phoenix, from the pioneer Henshaw family and settled down at last to a life of ease and the prosaic pastime of raising chickens and wine grapes. There he guarded his secret with all the delighted perversity of a child who knows something but won't quite tell it.

But at this time, at the age of sixty-nine, this conscience-free, remorseless, extroverted murderer fell in love. The object of his attentions was Julia Thomas, a woman who was one-quarter Negress and whose mother had been a servant in a German family. Julia Thomas spoke German and ran an ice-cream parlor in downtown Phoenix. Jacob Walz often took her presents (mostly wine) and the two became close friends. Gossips had the relationship even closer.

The story goes that Julia wanted money to install a new ice-cream fountain. Walz was ill, but told her to dig at a certain spot in his yard. She did so, and unearthed a tin can containing $2,000 in gold. So Julia got her new fountain.

Numerous other stories of Walz and his inamorata have been told and many of them have doubtless gained in the telling but have lost in veracity with the years. More important in the history of the mine than Julia Thomas was the earthquake of 1887. It shook all of central Arizona, especially rocking the land following the great geological fault that runs from the Superstition Mountains to the Santa Catalinas north of Tucson. This earthquake may have altered many of Walz's landmarks (of course it could not change Weaver's Needle) and might conceivably have sealed his cave (if he had a cave) and further concealed his cache of gold—if he had a cache. It had been ten years since Walz had been to the Superstitions when the quake occurred. He was cramped with arthritis and had great difficulty in getting about.

Julia Thomas knew that the German could not last much longer. And once he was gone, who could find his mine? During his residence in Phoenix, hundreds of gold seekers had combed the Superstitions—all to no avail. In 1891, when Walz was eighty-three years old, Julia had a long talk with him. Nobody could live forever, she pointed out. If he should die suddenly, the great mine would be lost forever. Julia was in her middle forties. Wouldn't it be reasonable for him to tell her—or, even better, *show* her—the exact location of the mine?

Walz agreed. They planned to take a trip to Florence. At least that is what they would say. But between Phoenix and Florence they would turn into the Superstitions, head toward Weaver's Needle, and if not that night, why, then sometime the next day, Julia Thomas would be the first person to see the great Dutchman Mine, apart from Walz himself, in the last twenty years. They would bring back fifty or sixty thousand dollars in gold which Julia could have if anything happened to Walz. Then, knowing where the mine lay, Julia could file on it the day Walz died. For this great mine was still nobody's legal property. Walz had never filed a claim. He hadn't dared to do so, for that would have made it necessary to reveal its location.

Walz went to bed early that night, and Julia closed her ice-cream parlor and smiled expectantly at what the next day might mean to her. Walz slept in his little adobe house, and a few blocks away in her own home Julia lay awake, unable to sleep, but none the less happy.

Then destiny stepped in.

Pouring down from the mountains came a tremendous torrent,

the result of a great storm, flooding the Gila, flooding the Salt, and wiping out towns and ranches, dikes, ditches, and farms.

At two in the morning the house of Jacob Walz was completely washed away, and the roaring waters of the Salt River carried a good third of the town of Phoenix along with it.

Somehow the aged German managed to survive. With the dawn rescuers found him perched in a cottonwood tree, half dead from exposure. Julia rushed to help him. It was obvious that the end was near. He was carried to her house and put to bed.

A friend of them both, another German, Reinhart Petrasch, who was a baker in Phoenix and had been partially financed in his business by Walz, remained at the bedside of the dying man. Petrasch and Julia listened attentively as Walz told them exactly how to find the mine. He said it was composed of an 18-inch vein of rose quartz impregnated with golden nuggets. Apart from that there was a second vein of hematite quartz that was in itself one-third pure gold. He had worked these veins repeatedly and when he last saw them he had come nowhere near the end of either of them. A hundred million dollars might still be there. Maybe more.

Then Walz gave the two listeners the directions for finding this spot in the midst of the vastness of the Superstitions. He explained his cave. That was merely a hideout. About a mile north from the cave there was a rock that formed a natural face looking east. To the southward was Weaver's Needle. Follow the right of two canyons—not far. The mine faced west because the setting sun, at certain times of the year, would shine through a pass between two high ridges and the gold would actually glitter.

Julia Thomas and Reinhart Petrasch were hanging on every word, and Julia was feverishly jotting them down. But Jacob Walz had only one more sentence to utter.

"I killed eight men," he whispered.

And with that, he died.

It was February 22, 1891.

And to this day the Lost Dutchman Mine has never been found.

In the spring and summer of 1891 Julia Thomas sold her ice-cream parlor and formed a partnership with the Petrasch family to find the Lost Dutchman. Three months of diligent search proved utterly fruitless. They couldn't even find the cave that was the starting point. Perhaps a combination of earthquake, flash flood, and the faulty memory of a dying man recalling landmarks of fourteen years before contrived to put them on a consistently cold trail. And the hundreds of fortune hunters who have searched the area for the Lost Dutchman during the past sixty years have had no better luck. But the gold is still there, somewhere in the Superstitions.

The legend of the Lost Dutchman will probably endure as long as Arizona's mining industry. In recent years the whole business has taken on a dude aspect and has become a commercial picnic for tourists. Once a year a mock search is held. This is an organized tourist attraction, starting in Phoenix and ending in the Superstitions. It is so popular with tourists that reservations have to be made well in advance. The tour, trek, search, picnic —call it what you will—is held every February. Winter visitors to Arizona may ride to the Superstitions in comfort, hike up and down the canyons, scratch their hands and their clothes on cactus, drink cold beer, eat a "cowboy" dinner from a simulated "chuck wagon," and sit around a campfire and have community singing at night. Considering the negative results of the serious searching expeditions during the past sixty years, this tourist attraction is probably as good a way as any to seek the Lost Dutchman, by far the most comfortable, and produces results as effective as any other approach.

Of all the gold mines in the Gila basin none is more famous than the Vulture and the Lost Dutchman. All of the mines have not had such dramatic histories, but all of them come in for their share from litigation to murder. Gold, apparently, is something that unbalances men. And after all is said and done, the stories are not so much a matter of whether men found gold or not, as they are an indication of what the insatiable desire for wealth can do to men.

PART 5

The Critics Are Heard From

1870 to . . .

21

"SHOOT ANYBODY WHO WEARS A HAT"

IN 1702 in his bitter and ironic pamphlet, *The Shortest Way with Dissenters,* Daniel Defoe wrote: "It is cruelty to kill a snake or a toad in cold blood, but the poison of their nature makes it a charity to our neighbors to destroy those creatures, not for any personal injury received, but for prevention; not for the evil they have done, but the evil they may do."

In 1835 another Englishman, whose name was James Johnson, acted upon this principle on the upper Gila River. It is doubtful if Mr. Johnson had read Mr. Defoe (or if Mr. Johnson had ever read a book in his life), but Mr. Johnson was one of the "interlopers," or mountainmen, who invaded the Mexican-owned Gila Valley and defied Mexico to do anything about it. The Mexican power of law enforcement, both legal and military, being utterly pusillanimous, the mountainmen did just as they jolly well pleased until their trails crossed those of another race of men as hardy as themselves. And this race recognized not Spain, Mexico, or anybody else, for they were the Apache Indians. In short, the mountainmen and the Apache Indians soon came to grips, and James Johnson's way of handling the problem was one with Daniel Defoe's essay.

Somewhere along the upper Gila in what is now the state of

New Mexico, probably adjacent to what is now the small settlement of Cliff in Grant County, an area that looks today exactly as
it did in 1835 and is seldom visited by tourists, James Johnson and
a number of other trappers decided to treat the Apache problem
as Defoe recommended the treatment of dissenters—namely, extinction. Johnson let it be known among the Apaches that he was
their friend. There was no reason for them to be enemies. And to
prove it he was giving a big party, free to all Apaches who cared
to come. There would be gifts of flour, saddles, blankets, and
whisky.

Now, the Apaches had never made contact with Americans
(or Englishmen) until 1824 when James Ohio Pattie and his
fellow trappers had entered their country. They were distrustful,
but the gifts were great bait, and about thirty or thirty-five showed
up for James Johnson's party. Among them was one of their chiefs
whose name in Spanish was Juan José.

The results became a part of the Apaches' unwritten history.
The race has never forgotten or forgiven it.

Opposite the gifts for his guests—the food and blankets and
saddles and whisky—carefully concealed by flour sacks and brush,
Johnson had a howitzer loaded with bullets, slugs, nails, pieces of
broken chains, and other metal, all a kind of shrapnel of 1835.
When most of the Indians were examining the gifts, Johnson
touched off the howitzer. About twenty Apaches died, some of
them women and children. The others were badly wounded.
Chief Juan José, who had not been in the line of fire, was shot by
one of Johnson's henchmen. The bullet was not fatal, and Juan
José retaliated at once by attacking the henchman, a man named
Charles Gleason, whose name should go down with that of Johnson in the history of American infamy. With his people dead and
dying before him, Juan José, although wounded, fought with fury
and would soon have knifed Gleason from ear to ear had not

James Johnson shot the Apache chief through the back. Of the thirty-five Apaches present, more than twenty were killed in a matter of seconds, the wounded were shot or had their skulls crushed with axes by the mountainmen, and a scattering of three or four got away.

That was the end of Johnson's famous Apache party, and he vouchsafed that it would teach the dirty redskins a lesson. After that they'd know enough to leave the white men alone. The shortest way with dissenters . . .

Now, the Apache had been no paragon of virtue from his earliest days in the Southwest, long before the coming of the Spaniards. It is impossible to whitewash his record. It is both bold and bad. But never before had he been challenged with a villainy and perfidy equal to if not worse than his own. Apache outrages had been perpetrated on red men and white long before Johnson's Apache party. Johnson, unfortunately, was ignorant of Apache psychology. The reaction was not what he expected.

Quickly the news spread among the tribe. About a week later Apache scouts located fifteen trappers farther down the Gila. A band of warriors attacked these men, who knew nothing of Johnson's treachery, and murdered every one of them. As for individual white men, if a group of Apaches came upon some lone trapper they would hack him into four pieces and impale each quarter on a stake. Then they would dance about these remains and shoot arrows into the flesh. With grim humor they would usually leave the victim's hat on his head.

Chief Mangas Coloradas (Red Sleeves) was the nominal leader of the Apache nation at this time. He had been inclined to be friendly toward the white men. Being a leader of vision and ability he had first reasoned that it might be beneficial to the Indians to become friends of the white men, rather than enemies for no reason beyond the fact that white men were passing through

Apache lands. When he heard the story of Johnson's Apache party, however, he began to reason differently. Just whom to kill next was the only Apache problem from then on. It finally came down to a matter of headgear. The aboriginal Apache never wore a hat. All Americans and Mexicans did. Therefore, the policy of Mangas Coloradas and his people became simple. "Shoot anybody who wears a hat," for he would be certain to be an enemy. And of course the Apache never attacked openly. He never gave his victim a chance. Sudden death stalked the Gila watershed. The few men and women who were spared were taken captive only to be slowly tortured to death. And some of the Apache ingenuity in sadism need not be dwelt upon in print. Perhaps the case of Olive Oatman, as related in a previous chapter, is the only instance of an Apache captive surviving and eventually returning to the white world.

James Johnson, when confronted by white criticism for his brutal and stupid deed, explained that the Mexican government, unable to discipline the Apaches, had placed a bounty upon them of so much per scalp. He defended his treachery by explaining that his Apache coup was held in Mexican territory (true enough in 1835) and that he had a right to take advantage of the Mexican government's offer of $100 for the scalp of an Apache warrior, $50 for the scalp of an Apache squaw, and $25 for that of a child. Johnson and his men estimated that their Apache party yielded over $2,000 in scalps. But they were never able to collect from the Mexican government in Sonora, and eventually Johnson moved on to California, where, it is said, he finally died in poverty. The Apaches never got their hands on him, more's the pity, for they killed hundreds of white men and women in his stead.

Violence was followed by violence, and the more white people the Apaches killed simply dedicated more white people to the killing of Apaches. It was a situation of no quarter given. It actually was a race war.

Raphael Pumpelly, a famous pioneer and mineralogist, and later a professor at Harvard University, wrote in his book, *Across America and Asia,* published in New York in 1870:

> One cannot but look upon the history of our intercourse with the original owners of our country as a sad commentary on the Protestant civilization of the past two centuries. . . . The examples of duplicity set by the early religious colonists of New England has been followed by an ever-growing disregard for the rights of the Indian . . . If it is said that the Indians are treacherous and cruel, scalping and torturing their prisoners, it may be answered that there is no treachery and no cruelty left unemployed by the whites. Poisoning with strychnine, the wilful dissemination of smallpox, and the possession of bridles braided from the hair of scalped victims and decorated with teeth knocked from the jaws of living women—these are heroic facts among many of our frontiersmen.

So, as always, there are two sides to every story and there is no such thing as all bad Indians and all good white men. For more than half a century following Johnson's infamous Apache party all hell broke loose up and down the Gila and along its tributaries. To the white man the only good Indian was a dead Indian and to the Apache it was a case of shoot anybody who wears a hat.

This state of affairs continued from 1835 to 1856, when the United States took formal military possession of the Gadsden Purchase and established such garrisons as Fort Buchanan in 1856 (first called Fort Crittendon) and Fort Grant in 1859, at two strategic points in the Gila basin.

Military posts were no deterrent to the Apaches, however,

who crept up to the edge of such camps and stole supplies, horses, and mules with a dexterity that baffled many a guard and exasperated many a commanding officer.

The military was supposed to protect the settlers from Apache depredations, and it did offer a little security but not enough. The soldiers couldn't be everywhere in that vast area at once, but the Apaches could. Moreover, they outnumbered the army more than a hundred to one, and they played a game of hide-and-seek all over the Gila watershed. The Gila was an Apache river and they knew it thoroughly, and every mountain, canyon, and desert of the entire watershed as well. The soldiers were strangers and the Apaches ran circles around them. About all the two garrisons could really guarantee as protection was the security of the posts themselves.

Then, with the outbreak of the Civil War, Washington recalled all federal troops from Arizona in 1861, and the Apaches ruled the Gila country uncontested. Only Tucson and Tubac survived as towns because of their safety in numbers. Individual ranchers, miners, or prospectors were either killed or forced to give up and get out of the Gila basin. That is, all but one. As always, there is the standout, and Arizona had her example. Try as they would, there was one white man—one lone rancher—whom the Apaches simply couldn't lick. His name was Pete Kitchen, and in his heart and soul were the indomitable courage and persistency of the white race. If the Apaches would shoot anybody who wears a hat, Pete Kitchen's motto was "Shoot anybody who don't."

Pete was born in Covington, Kentucky, in 1822 and arrived in Arizona in 1854. He settled on Potrero Creek, which flows into the Gila's tributary, the Santa Cruz, about six miles north of the present-day border city of Nogales. His old adobe ranch house (what remains of it) may still be seen on a hill just off U.S. Highway 89. Pete laid claim by homestead to about a

1,000-acre ranch of rich bottom land where he raised cabbages, corn, potatoes, fruits, melons, and his pride and joy—pigs. His stock was famous, and stores in Tucson, fifty-eight miles to the north, used to advertise "Pete Kitchen's Hams." His bacon was equally famous from Silver City in New Mexico, near the upper Gila, to Yuma at the river's mouth.

In a sense, Pete Kitchen represents Arizona's transition from lawless frontier to civilization. He has even been called "Arizona's Daniel Boone," but this analogy does not hold, for Pete was not an explorer. He was first and last a settler, and once he settled no power in the white man's or the red man's heaven or hell could move him. This the Apaches found out. One learned it the hard way by poking his head up over a boulder more than six hundred yards from the ranch house. Pete put a bullet through his brain. It was his longest shot on record and he was justly proud of it.

By 1862 the Kitchen ranch was the only place of security between Tucson and the Mexican town of Magdalena in Sonora. The ranch house became a veritable fortress. On a hill, commanding a view in all directions, it was extremely difficult for an enemy to approach, and Pete had a sixth sense about Apaches.

To work his ranch Pete employed a number of peaceful Opata Indians, some Mexicans, and one or two Americans. He married a Mexican girl named Doña Rosa and apparently the marriage was a happy one.

The Apaches decided to obliterate this one last surviving rancher. That would make their victory total. They made raid after raid, by day and by night, and every time they were driven off with great losses. They killed his stock, they ruined his crops, they murdered his foreman, they cut the throat of his stepson, they tried to set fire to the house; and once they made an all-out effort —three attacks within twelve hours. But Pete Kitchen and his ranch personnel fought back. It became necessary to establish a graveyard on his property to dispose of the bodies. "Let 'em come," said Pete grimly to his loyal band. "Just shoot any son of a bitch that *don't* wear a hat."

And that one remaining spark of white civilization was not to be put out. At length the Apaches recognized Pete Kitchen as an enemy worthy of their steel. They gave him up. At times Apache raiding parties, heading toward Mexico or back toward Tubac and Tucson, would pass within half a mile of Pete's house. But they went right on by. They had had enough of this terrible white man. After 1867 they ignored him.

But Pete did not take this victory with unguarded ecstasy. He knew Apaches. Perhaps they were waiting for him to get just the least bit careless. Well, the red devils would have a long wait.

John G. Bourke, who wrote *On the Border with Crook*— General George Crook, whose exploits will be discussed later—offered a vivid description of the Kitchen ranch as he saw it in 1870:

Approaching Pete Kitchen's ranch, one finds himself in a fertile valley, with a small hillock near one extremity. Upon the summit of this has been built the house from which no effort of the Apaches has ever succeeded in driving our friend. There is a sentinel posted on the roof, there is another out in the "cienega" with the stock, and the men ploughing in the bottom are obliged to carry rifles, cocked and loaded, swung to the plough handle. Every man and boy is armed with one or two revolvers on hip. There are revolvers and rifles and shotguns along the walls and in every corner. Everything speaks of a land of warfare and bloodshed. The title of "Dark and Bloody Ground" never fairly belonged to Kentucky. Kentucky never was anything except a Sunday-school convention in comparison with Arizona, every mile of whose surface could tell its tale of horror were the stones and gravel, the sagebrush and mescal, the mesquite and the yucca, only endowed with speech for one brief hour.

Within the hospitable walls of the Kitchen home the traveller was made to feel perfectly at ease. If food were not already on the fire, some of the women set about the preparation of the savory and spicy stews for which the Mexicans are deservedly famous, and others kneaded the dough and patted into shape the paper-like tortillas with which to eat the juicy frijoles or dip up the tempting chile colorado. There were women carding, spinning, sewing—doing the thousand and one duties of domestic life in a great ranch, which had its own blacksmith, saddler, and wagonmaker, and all other officials needed to keep the machinery running smoothly.

Between Pete Kitchen and the Apaches a ceaseless war was waged, and with the advantages not all on the side of Kitchen. His employees were killed and wounded, his stock driven away, his pigs filled with arrows, making the suffering quadrupeds look like perambulating pin-cushions—everything that could be thought of to drive him away; but there he stayed, unconquered and unconquerable.

Pete Kitchen was not a large man. He was five feet ten, spare and lithe, quick on his feet and a crack shot, with blue-gray eyes and a soft well-modulated speech. He had many friends and was generous and even magnanimous. He almost always wore a broad-brimmed sombrero-type hat. He loved children, and he often carried ranch-made candy in his pockets to give to the boys and girls when he made trips to Tucson. He was especially fond of a little girl named Atanacia Santa Cruz (later Mrs. Sam Hughes and mentioned in a previous chapter) and once he brought a little piglet from his ranch to be her pet.

On the other hand, he was a vindictive enemy whose courage was inestimable. Once some Mexicans stole several of his favorite horses. Furious at this insult and theft, he followed their trail in hot pursuit into Sonora. When at last he overtook them, two of the Mexicans fled. Pete captured the third one and retrieved his stolen horses. He tied the Mexican hand and foot and bound him to the saddle. Then he started for home with his prisoner. Exhausted from twenty hours on horseback, Pete (as he often told it) decided to take a nap. He partially released the bonds of his mounted prisoner, placed the horse under the limb of a tree, and put a hangman's noose around the neck of the Mexican, which in turn he fastened to the limb of the tree. Then he took "forty winks."

At this point in his story he would roar with laughter and slap his thigh and say, "You know, while I was asleep that damned horse walked off and left that fellow hanging there!" More laughter. "No use cutting down a dead man, so I rode on home."

Apaches or no Apaches, Pete Kitchen's ranch produce, together with his hams, bacon, and lard, was earning him about ten thousand dollars a year. With the coming of the Southern Pacific Railroad to Tucson in 1880, he found severe competition. But why worry? If the Apaches hadn't been able to stop him, certainly a railroad could hardly be classified as an enemy. He had a small fortune, so he sold his ranch and moved to Tucson. He spent his later years in gambling and drinking, both of which had always been pleasant pursuits to him, although he had seldom had time to enjoy them before. While he lost most of his fortune he was happy all the rest of his life, and died in Tucson on August 5, 1895.

Pete Kitchen represented that spark of survival inherent in the white frontiersman which cannot be extinguished. He beat the Apaches at their own game on their own ground and the Apaches knew it.

But he never quite got over his life of constant qui vive,

and once, in Tucson, rounding a corner he bumped into a friend, reached for his gun, and almost shot the surprised man.

"Why, Pete—would you kill me?" asked his friend.

"Well, God damn it," said Pete quietly, "why the hell don't you wear a hat?"

22

AN APACHE IS AN APACHE

Down near the southeastern corner of Arizona, very close to the border of the state of New Mexico, on U.S. Highway 80, sometimes called "the Broadway of America," stands the Geronimo monument. This bronze tablet commemorates the surrender of the last leader of the Apaches to the victorious United States Army on September 5, 1886, in nearby Skeleton Canyon. That the dreaded Apaches had at long last capitulated forever seemed worthy of monumental commemoration for posterity. And on this metal marker a portion of the lettering states: "Near here Geronimo surrendered, thus ending Indian wars in America forever." At least that is what the monument advises the passing tourist.

The nearest town of any size is Douglas, Arizona, about forty miles to the southwest on the Mexican border. And forty-four years later, in 1930, an Associated Press dispatch dated Douglas, Arizona, November 30, stated:

AMERICANS AND MEXICANS HUNT APACHE BAND

Douglas, Ariz. Nov 30 (AP) Volunteers from many parts of Mexico and the United States have offered their services to a punitive expedition which has for its object the extermination of a band of Apache braves and their women. The depredations in Mexico and United States border towns by these marauders have long been a thorn in the sides of both governments.

About 600 have volunteered. They will be led in the latter part of March by Colonel Hermenegildo Carillo of the Mexican federal army and Leslie Gatliff, chief of Douglas police, into the mountains 168 miles from here where the Indians have gone into winter encampment.

The band has been hunted for several years. In 1928 they ambushed the wife of Francisco Fimbres, killed her, mutilated the body, and kidnapped her eight year old son . . .

And this news release of 1930 continues with the old familiar details, making the information on the Geronimo monument of 1886 a bit silly.

An Apache never quits fighting if he can help it; for countless generations the race's chief business and occupation has been fighting. They fought Indian neighbors before the white man came; they fought the Spaniards and the Mexicans and the Americans. In World War II the Apache boys who bothered to pay any attention to their draft boards found themselves in uniforms and they stoically, if not cheerfully, fought the Japanese in the South Pacific. If and when the future brings a war between capitalism and communism—the United States versus the U.S.S.R.—for the ultimate survival of only one of these systems, undoubtedly there will be some Apache boys stalking Russians.

No group of aborigines apart from the Sioux ever gave the

government more trouble, and for persistency in clinging to his inherent racial character the Apache has far outlasted his plains cousins. The Sioux had some great leaders, particularly manifest in Sitting Bull, Crazy Horse, and Black Elk, and history has come around to acknowledging their abilities. But little kudos is given the Apache leaders with the possible exception of one of their great men—Cochise.

There is an answer to the Apache problem, and it is the only answer to any racial minority within the United States—assimilation. But Apaches don't assimilate easily, and thereby hangs the tale of almost a hundred years of their racial warfare with Americans.

Before bringing the story up to date, it is necessary to cut back to June of 1871 (and even a decade before that), when Washington finally sent a man capable of tackling the job of what to do about the Apaches. He was General George Crook, U.S. Army. He didn't settle it, but he did wonders.

Even before Crook there was an American who knew, perhaps instinctively, how to get along with Apaches. He was not Pete Kitchen, whose policy was to meet the Apaches head on and fight it out until the better man won. Pete was a bulldog; the Apache a wolf. Their contest ended with their leaving each other alone. In truth, the bulldog won the decision.

But there was another man in the Gila country who was confronted with Apache outrages and he handled the problem from an approach that would have been beyond the ken of Pete Kitchen. His name was Thomas J. Jeffords and he came from New York State. Tom Jeffords was a big man, over six feet tall, and had red hair and a long red beard. His first job in Arizona was that of stagecoach driver. Several times his coach was attacked by Apaches and he was wounded by arrows. He carried the scars of these wounds to his grave. Later Jeffords became superintendent of mails between Fort Bowie and Tucson. Fort Bowie, established in 1862 at the east end of Apache Pass, was almost a hundred miles east of Tucson. The pass was one of the most dangerous places on the wagon road across southern Arizona from east to west. It is a rocky defile that winds between desert hills, affording a view to the east over the broad San Simon Valley (San Simon Creek being a Gila tributary) and a view to the west across the long desert plain that led the immigrant wagons and stagecoaches to the San Pedro River, where the town of Benson stands today. With the pass affording a fine command of any approaching wagons or cavalry or infantry for miles in either direction, the Apaches made good use of it for ambuscade. To put a stop to this, the government set up Fort Bowie, although its strategic effect was not felt until after the Civil War.

Jeffords's drivers were paid $125 a month, but he seldom had to pay them. For few drivers lasted out a month without falling victim to the Apaches. Jeffords stated that over a period of sixteen months fourteen of his men were killed.

Cochise was the war chief of the Apaches, having assumed or inherited this office from the long line of leaders who had counted such strong men as Juan José (killed by Johnson's act of treachery in 1835) and Mangas Coloradas (Red Sleeves) who had been lied to, double-crossed, and horsewhipped by white men until his life was dedicated to their extinction. Mangas Coloradas was tricked into surrendering to the army for "peace talks." Stories vary as to what took place, but all agree that Mangas Coloradas was "shot while trying to escape." Only a few of the stories record that the soldiers decided to give him a taste of Apache medicine before killing him. They tortured him with red-hot bayonets and when he refused to scream they shot him. The war leadership of the Apache people then passed to a man hitherto unknown to the white men—Cochise.

Cochise, a Chiricahua Apache, was a man of stature both physically and mentally. Jeffords described him as "a man of great natural ability, a splendid specimen of physical manhood, standing about six feet two, with the eye of an eagle."

It should be made clear that no one chief ruled all of the Apache nation. Each division of the race—the Chiricahuas, the White Mountain, the Mescalero, the Warm Springs—had its nominal leader. An agreement made with Victorio of the Warm Springs branch would have no validity with Geronimo, who some say was a White Mountain Apache (although he was born in Mexico) but who later led the Chiricahuas. It was all very confusing to the officers from West Point to whom an Apache was simply an Apache.

At any rate, Jeffords was irked beyond control at the constant murder of his drivers by Cochise's warriors. He knew approximately where Cochise was encamped. With a courage born of the ridiculous, not only courting but even begging for death, Tom Jeffords rode alone straight into the war chief's stronghold, which, at that time, happened to be in the Graham Mountains just south of the Gila River not far from the present town of Safford. This foolhardy move on the part of a lone white man so surprised the Apache scouts that they let him come on instead of winging an arrow through him from ambush.

In the heart of the encampment, Jeffords dismounted and stated that he had come for a talk with Cochise; and to prove his peaceful intentions he handed his rifle and his six-shooter to a squaw and unstrapped his cartridge belt and tossed it to a nearby brave.

Cochise stared at this tall red-bearded white man who was apparently at ease, and who stood shoulder to shoulder with the chief himself. Jeffords, at that time, was about thirty-eight years old; Cochise was approximately sixty-two.

"I have come to see you," stated Jeffords, "as a friend."

Cochise motioned toward his wickiup. The two men walked over to it and sat down. Following the best Indian decorum, Jeffords sat for a long while without uttering a word. At last he spoke.

"I have heard you are an honest man," said Jeffords in his best Apache.

"I am," said Cochise in English.

"I speak only for myself," declared Jeffords. "I want peace with you. I do not want your men to kill my men."

Jeffords went on to explain that his men were not enemies of the Apaches, were only performing their jobs, and that they had as much right to make a living in the white man's way as Cochise's men had a right to live in the Apache way. He wanted Cochise's word that there would be no more murdering of his drivers.

This honest, daring, and forthright white man won Cochise's immediate respect. He granted the stranger's request. The word would go out. Thenceforth the mail carriers between Tucson and Fort Bowie were not to be attacked. And they never were again.

As Jeffords told it:

"He respected me and I respected him. He was a man who scorned a liar and was always truthful in all things. His religion was truth and loyalty. My name with Cochise was Chickasaw, or Brother. He said to me once, 'Chickasaw, a man should never lie.' I replied, 'No, he should not, but a great many do.' He said, 'That is true, but they need not do it; if a man asks us a question we do not wish to answer, we could simply say, I don't want to talk about that.'"

Jeffords spent two days in camp with Cochise, and these two men, worlds apart in every way, became friends simply because deep in the heart of each was something that each recognized—integrity. They met numerous times after that. So close were they that eventually they became "blood brothers." This mystic Apache rite is indicative of the highest possible regard of male for male. It is performed with the greatest of pomp and circumstance and solemnity, and consists of the union—transfusion —of a small portion of each man's blood and the mutual drinking of it. In the philosophy of the Apache people no higher regard can be expressed.

Cochise's agreement with Jeffords had no effect whatever on the over-all Apache policy to exterminate white men. Murder and rapine continued as before, but Jeffords's drivers were never again molested. That two leaders could meet, reach common understanding, and become friends shed a ray of hope for the future. But as usual, lesser men blundered, and the conditions between red and white became worse than ever.

The blunder was the outrageous Fort Grant massacre of April 30, 1871. There is little point in dwelling on the unpleasant details, which are no credit to the white race. It is sufficient to say that a group of Americans, about forty strong, organized by W. H. Oury and one Mexican, Jesus M. Elias, indignant over Apache raids on San Xavier del Bac and the murder of white men within the very sight of Tucson, led a surprise attack at dawn on a group of Apaches at Fort Grant. These Indians were innocent of participation in the latest outrages and were presumably friendly and willing to take up residence on a reservation. The government had just begun to activate its "peace policy" and for once some progress seemed possible. Believing that they were secure in the army camp the Apaches were unprepared for attack. The American force from Tucson slaughtered 128 of these first peaceful Indians in a matter of minutes. Many were women and children. About thirty Indian babies were spared and taken back to Tucson. And of course this news reached

Cochise as fast as the scouts could report it. And again all hell broke loose throughout the Gila country.

This deplorable state of affairs had no effect whatever on the relationship between Cochise and Tom Jeffords. Some of Jeffords's blood now ran in Cochise's veins, and some of Cochise's ran in Jeffords'. Blood brothers never betrayed each other. They remained friends until death parted them.

Cochise, while all Apache with an indomitable fighting heart, was not all extravert. Terrible as were some of his deeds, such as having white prisoners dragged to death behind galloping horses and staking down naked Mexicans over ant hills to be eaten alive, there was another facet to his character. Along with the fact that he was proud, cruel, vindictive, and passionate, he was also something of a mystic. He liked to reflect on the meaning of life and the probability of life after death. He discussed these eternal riddles of mankind with Jeffords. On the other hand, it was said that he enjoyed getting drunk now and then, and would occasionally and mercilessly beat his wives.

On June 7, 1874, Jeffords and Cochise met for the last time. Cochise was very ill. Jeffords had brought him medicine, but he soon realized that the war chief's hours were numbered. He decided to ride at once from Cochise's stronghold, high up in the Dragoon Mountains, to Fort Bowie in Apache Pass, and if necessary, force the army surgeon at the point of a gun to ride back with him in a desperate effort to save his blood brother's life. Frank C. Lockwood, in his *Pioneer Days in Arizona,* has described this scene to perfection:

As Jeffords was about to depart Cochise asked:
"Do you think you will see me alive again?"
"No, I do not think I will," Jeffords replied.
Said Cochise, "I think I will die about ten o'clock tomorrow morning. Do you think we will see each other again?"

Jeffords was taken aback at this, but said, "I do not know. What do you think about it?"

The Cochise replied: "I do not know; it is not clear to my mind; but I think we will, somewhere up there."

Then they parted for the last time pondering the great question that has immemorially perplexed pagan, saint, philosopher, and savage.

Cochise died at ten o'clock the next day as he had said. As the end drew on, he requested his braves to carry him up on the west slope of the Stronghold so that he might see the sun rise over the eastern ridges once more. He was buried somewhere out on the mesa near the entrance to the Stronghold. No one knows just where his grave is. The Indians rode their horses over the burial place, trampling the ground all about so that it would be impossible to identify the spot. Jeffords knew where he was laid, but he held the secret as a sacred trust and never divulged it during the forty years that he survived Cochise.

Today a mountain peak and an Arizona county bear the great chief's name. The white race has given him an inevitable salute.

Cochise's first son, Taza, became the next leader of the Chiricahua Apaches. Little has history heard of him. In all likelihood he was a peaceful man. He did not last long as chief; the Chiricahuas demanded a fighting leader and they got him in Cochise's second son, Natchez. To annihilate the white race was his creed, and while he lacked his father's exceptional abilities, he left the mark of terror throughout the Gila watershed.

In June of 1871 the man who was to do more than anyone else to help resolve the Apache problem had arrived in Arizona. He was General George Crook, sometimes called "the terrible and the just." He was born in Dayton, Ohio, on September 23, 1829, and was forty-two years old when he arrived unostentatiously in the battle-scarred area designated by Washington as the

Department of Arizona. Crook was a superior soldier but never looked it. He had little use for dress uniforms, and although holding the rank of major general, he liked to wear a white duck shirt, corduroy trousers, and a canvas helmet. He preferred a mule to a horse, and called his mount Apache. He was neither a smoker nor a drinker and did not use profanity—traits that made him unique in the Gila Valley.

General Crook was assigned to Arizona while on duty in Oregon. He entered the Gila Valley from California via Yuma and Tucson. Between Tucson and Fort Bowie he never saw a single Indian, and he had been in Arizona for several weeks before he so much as looked upon an Apache. But this was merely the lull before the storm.

George Crook was slightly over six feet tall, had light-brown hair, blue eyes, and was spare and sinewy. Seriousness and determination of purpose were an inheritance from his Scotch ancestry. His speech was quick and to the point. There were no wasted words. He had a sense of humor but it was not on the surface of his character, and he especially loathed a pun. When a job was done he was modest about taking credit. He was more interested in the next job.

Once in command in Arizona, Crook was dissatisfied with the looseness of the Indian policy. It was too feckless to suit him. The Apaches were pressing the war, and the soldiers were on the defensive. He planned to reverse this. Rather than wait for the next Apache attack, Crook decided to take the offensive. But he did not make this move without careful planning, and proper training of his troops. Instead of wasting away the hours and days in the monotony of garrison life, Crook instigated long and hard forced marches. He reasoned that the soldiers could never conquer the terrain, much less conquer the Apaches, by remaining within Fort Bowie or Fort Grant and playing poker. Moreover, he himself wanted to know the topography of the Gila watershed. The only way to learn it was to see it.

He wasn't spoiling for a fight, but an army was supposed to be an army. It had to become as tough as the Apaches. By mid-summer of 1871 Crook was scouting all of the Gila country with five companies of cavalry, and a retinue of scouts and supplies. His approach was always peaceful; first justice, and then, if necessary, the sword. He made overtures to the White Mountain Apaches of the Tonto region of central Arizona. At a conference with such White Mountain leaders as Miguel and Alchisay, Crook outlined a plan for peace. He explained that the white man was in the Gila country to stay and the Apache had equal rights with him. If the Apaches would plant crops and raise cattle and horses, there would be enough for all. The past must be forgotten. There would always be good white men and bad white men, good Indians and bad Indians, but it was the duty of the good to convert and educate the bad. If that couldn't be done, the next and sure medicine for the bad was this—the rifle. Good Indians must help bad Indians; bad white men must be punished by good white men. Could they understand that? They could? Good. The next thing was to pledge their sacred honor to make this plan work. The White Mountain Apaches were impressed. Without firing a shot—or stubbing his toe—George Crook had cleared the first hurdle on the long road toward peace.

And then, incredible and as exasperating it may be, all of Crook's careful preliminary work was upset by Washington. Even while he was using persuasion backed by obvious force, Crook learned that President Grant, justly incensed over the intolerable Fort Grant massacre on the part of white men, had sent two representatives of a "peace commission" to Arizona. They were a civilian, Vincent Colyer, and a military man, General O. O. Howard. Crook was to bide his time, and then, if force were needed, he was to attack the Apaches. Crook, with marked patience, courteously stood by and waited to see what Colyer and Howard could accomplish—if anything.

Colyer, a stranger to the Gila country, arrived with a belief the Apaches were the victims of white oppression. He remained for a few months, selected a few sites for temporary reservations, met a number of Apaches but none of the key men of the tribe, declared that all Indians would be friendly if they were fed, sent a report back to Washington that the situation was well under control and that there would be no future trouble, and went on to California.

General Howard approached Tom Jeffords and asked him to take him to see the aged Cochise. Jeffords led the general to the old war chief, who had only two years to live. Cochise trusted his blood brother or he never would have deigned to see Howard. He assured Howard that he wanted peace as much as did the white men—a double-entendre, for Cochise firmly believed the white men wanted to kill all Apaches. But they managed to reach a verbal understanding, and Howard came away believing that he had won a pledge of peace from Cochise. And this news went back to Washington.

Howard also selected the site for the San Carlos Indian Reservation on the Gila River, and another location in the Chiricahua Mountains, where Cochise and his people were to reside. It all looked splendid—in reports to Washington.

But it was far too superficial. The feeling between red and white was too deep and bitter to be rectified by a few words. And the Peace Commission did not meet such young and important Apache warriors as Natchez, Juh, and Chatto, of the Chiricahuas, or Victorio, Loco, and Nana, of the Warm Springs— all destined to be leaders in the near future. And Geronimo was as yet unknown.

The unhappy result was that Crook's efforts marked time, and he lost face with the Apaches; and white men continued to shoot Apaches on sight and Apaches continued to ambush white men. Within a year of Colyer's efforts, unconvinced and renegade Apaches made almost sixty separate attacks and killed more than a hundred citizens. Washington asked Crook why this should be. Couldn't he control these people after all that Colyer and Howard had done? Reluctantly Crook took up the sword.

To describe his campaign battle for battle belongs to a military history of Arizona. It is sufficient to say that this was a methodical closing-in and mopping-up operation in which any Indians who would surrender and come over to Crook's side were spared, fed, and the best of them enlisted as scouts—while all others who refused his amnesty were to be exterminated. This was a policy the Apaches could easily comprehend. At first the vast majority defied Crook.

Crook divided his command into five separate units, each unit acting independently of the others and each unit assigned to a specific area. Women and children were to be spared whenever possible, and prisoners were to be well treated. The Apaches were to be pursued relentlessly and never given an opportunity to stay in one place and get set for a counterattack. They had to be kept constantly off balance, sorely pressed for supplies, and often faced with starvation.

Meanwhile, the great Cochise had died; Taza, his first son, had little taste for war; and Apache leadership passed to the younger men such as Victorio and Loco, of the Warm Springs, and Natchez and Juh, of the Chiricahuas.

The army slowly closed in on these units, and by spring of 1875 many of the Apaches, either willingly or grudgingly, surrendered to Crook, whom they called the "Gray Fox," and took up life on the San Carlos Reservation, a vast mountainous area between the Gila on the south and the Black River and the White River on the north.

Then, with this policy of the sword a success, and more and more Apaches assenting to Crook's terms of peace, and with victory almost within sight, Washington suddenly transferred Crook to Nebraska and the Department of the Platte to fight the Sioux!

Apaches had learned to trust the Gray Fox, for he always kept his word. If he promised forgiveness and food, they could depend upon it; if he promised death, they could depend upon it. But now the Gray Fox was gone. What is worse, the new government policy made it necessary for all avowed peace-loving Apaches to live on the San Carlos Reservation. White Mountain Apaches preferred their own White River country high up in the mountains north of the Gila. The Chiricahua Apaches preferred their own mountain and desert terrain of southeastern Arizona. The Warm Springs band wanted to live in the Mogollon Mountains and roam all over southwestern New Mexico.

For a while a tenuous peace was held together by the good work of John P. Clum, who was Indian agent at San Carlos from 1874 to 1877. He organized a system of Indian police made up of the most trustworthy of the surrendered Apaches, and used them to help keep the recalcitrants in order. His work was a labor of love, and its constructive policy was never understood in Washington. Disgusted, Clum resigned in 1877. Meanwhile the "Indian Ring," made up of politicians who let contracts to feed the surrendered Apaches, was making a good thing for itself out of a combination of easy opportunity and public ignorance of what was going on. A beef weighing 500 pounds, for example, would be bought by the government to provide meat for Uncle Sam's now peaceful wards. But insiders in the Indian Ring would tinker with the scales and charge the government for

1,500 pounds of beef. The government paid for 1,500 pounds; the Apaches received 500 pounds; and the money for the non-existent 1,000 pounds went into white men's pockets. Graft, greed, and corruption ran rampant, and meanwhile several thousand Apaches were forced to live on the San Carlos Reservation, where they did not wish to be. To put them all on one reservation was validated on the basis of economy. It would have been just about as sensible for the federal government, after the Civil War, to try to make all Southerners move to the state of Arkansas and stay there.

Trouble came quickly.

Some leaders and a medicine man of the White Mountain Apaches rebelled. The Indian Bureau ordered the medicine man arrested. During the fracas, he was shot. That was enough for the White Mountain Apaches. They left the reservation and went back to their own country. In the melee some were killed, and in turn a number of soldiers of the 6th Cavalry lost their lives. The White Mountain people had gone "on the warpath" and that was the match that started the holocaust all over again. Immediately the discontented Chiricahuas left the reservation. Under Chief Juh, and a new leader unknown so far, named Geronimo, the Chiricahuas murdered the agency chief of police, slit the throat of the subagent, and went home. If the soldiers didn't like it, let them come after them. They would get a warm welcome. Shades of Cochise!

Indignant as were the people of Arizona over years of Apache depredations, they were even more indignant over the stupid and calamitous policy of the Indian Bureau. The Tucson *Star* published in its columns in 1882:

For several years the people of the Territory have been gradually arriving at the conclusion that the management of the Indian reservations in Arizona was a fraud upon the government; that the constantly recurring outbreaks of the Indians and their consequent devastations were due to the criminal neglect or apathy of the Indian agent at San Carlos. . . .

The investigations of the Grand Jury have brought to light a course of procedure at the San Carlos reservation, under the government of Agent Tiffany, which is a disgrace to the civilization of the age and a foul blot upon the national escutcheon. . . . The investigations of the Grand Jury also establish the fact that General Crook has the unbounded confidence of all the Indians.

And so, with the Indian problem as bad, if not worse, than it was when he first arrived in Arizona, Washington recalled General George Crook and handed him the Apache Indians all over again.

From 1882 to 1886 Crook did his best, and most of it had to be done not with justice, but by the sword.

Again, there is no point in recording battle after battle as Crook's superior strength slowly wore the Apaches down. He pursued them through southern Arizona, New Mexico, Sonora, and Chihuahua, and at last the remnant who had not surrendered or had not been killed were a band commanded by Natchez and Geronimo.

In March of 1886 Crook arranged for an armistice. He met Natchez and Geronimo on the Mexican border and offered them peace terms. The terms called for an unconditional surrender and two years in prison outside of Arizona for the leaders. If they wouldn't accept, Crook promised them they would be hunted down to the last living Apache if it took fifty years.

Geronimo finally agreed to give himself up. Several lesser leaders also sent word to Crook that they would surrender if he would guarantee their safety and that of their women and children. This appeared to be the end at last, and Crook sent this news to Washington. But at that very moment a white man named

Tribollet sold Geronimo gallons of whisky. Inflamed by these spirits Geronimo and part of his warriors took to the hills and refused to surrender.

Washington, of course, blamed Crook. Out of patience, exasperated at last, Crook asked to be relieved of his command. He was followed by General Nelson A. Miles. But it was one of Crook's men who finally saw Geronimo and arranged for his ultimate surrender. This man, who has never received the popular acclaim that was his due, was Lieutenant Charles B. Gatewood.

The surrender of the last of the incorrigibles took place in Skeleton Canyon not far from what is now U.S. Highway 80, and that is why the Geronimo monument is located on the highway today.

There is a curious side angle on this surrender, and quite possibly it is true. Ross Calvin, in his book *River of the Sun,* states that later evidence proved that Geronimo was suffering from a severe case of gonorrhea. He therefore surrendered because he knew he had to get to a white doctor. "What the bullets couldn't do, the bugs did."

Those who were designated "good" Apaches were permitted to remain in Arizona and New Mexico. Those who were "bad" were sent to a prison camp in Florida. This was contrary to the government's promises, but who cared?

Geronimo never saw Arizona again after September of 1886. He was first sent to prison at Fort Pickens, near Pensacola, Florida, and later transferred to Fort Sill, Oklahoma. Geronimo had never been a chief by inheritance, but was more or less a usurper of such a position. He lacked the superior character of a man like Cochise; and while his courage and tenacity were unquestionable, he was something of a liar, thief, hypocrite, cheat, roué, and drunkard. And with all these traits, Geronimo was an opportunist. For the remainder of his life after 1886 he was technically a prisoner of war (although Crook had promised him no more than two years of imprisonment, the government acted otherwise), but prisoner or not, he contrived to have a pretty good time. Also his name and personality had caught on with the public. He came to represent the quintessence of Apache-ism, which he was not. Cochise, or Natchez, or the Chiricahua sub-chief Chatto—or the Warm Springs Loco and Nana—all wer better representative Apaches than Geronimo. But it was Geronimo who was exploited as a dreaded ex-war chief while at Fort Sill. This appealed to his vanity (a characteristic not typically Apache) and he was exhibited at the St. Louis World's Fair, and at several other cities, where the public could come and stare with awe and shake his hand. He was even permitted to sell bows and arrows and photographs of himself. And when he grunted and said "Ugh" or "How" the public loved it. He had never said "Ugh" or "How" as an Apache but he quickly learned that such meaningless monosyllables were what the public took for Indian talk and were what the public wanted to hear. A strong strain of Barnum ran in the old reprobate. One of his biggest moments occurred at the inauguration of Theodore Roosevelt. Mounted on a pinto horse, he all but stole the show during the inaugural parade on Pennsylvania Avenue in Washington.

In 1903 Geronimo joined the Dutch Reformed Church, but was soon bored with services. There wasn't enough adulation for himself to please him.

In 1909, with money earned by selling some bows and arrows, he bought whisky, got drunk, fell out of a wagon, and lay in a cold rain all night. A few days later, on February 17, he died in the military hospital at Fort Sill. His name has persisted through history. The Sioux chief, Sitting Bull, and possibly the Sioux warrior, Rain-in-the-Face, are about the only Indian names equally or better known to the public. But the greatest Sioux of them all was Crazy Horse, and the greatest Apache of them all was Cochise.

General George Crook left the Gila country in 1886, his work all but done, and yet he left with a feeling of disappointment. For there were a few renegade Apaches yet to be captured. Possibly Crook was as critical of the white man and his government as he was of the Indians he so relentlessly pursued. He summed up his point of view, attained from years of Indian fighting, as follows:

It should not be expected that an Indian who has lived as a barbarian all his life will become an angel the moment he comes on a reservation and promises to behave himself, or that he has that strict sense of honor that a person should have who has had the advantage of civilization all his life, and the benefit of a moral training and character which has been transmitted to him through a long line of ancestors. It requires constant watching and knowledge of their character to keep them from going wrong. They are children in ignorance, not in innocence. I do not wish to be understood as in the least palliating their crimes, but I wish to say a word to stem the torrent of invective and abuse which has universally been indulged in against the whole Apache race. . . .

I have no knowledge of a case on record where a white man has been convicted and punished for defrauding an Indian. Greed and avarice on the part of the whites—in other words the almighty dollar—is at the bottom of nine-tenths of all our Indian trouble.

George Crook lived only four years after turning over his command in Arizona to General Miles. He died in Chicago on March 21, 1890, at the age of sixty-one. The reaction to this news in the Gila country is somewhat surprising. For eight years Crook had fought the Apaches. During those years many hated him, many tasted defeat or death, and a great number finally came over to his side. At Geronimo's first and spurious surrender there were more Apaches working for Crook than there were Apaches left to fight him. He tried to make all good Indians his scouts, or else induce them to take up farming or cattle raising. According to John G. Bourke, in *On the Border with Crook*, "When the news of Crook's death reached the Apache Reservation, the members of the tribe who had been his scouts during so many years were stupefied: those near Camp Apache sat down in a great circle, let down their hair, bent their heads forward on their bosoms, and wept and wailed like children."

It can safely be said that in the long and bloody history of the Apache and white conflicts, General George Crook was the only white man who ever made the Apaches cry. In spite of all the hell that had gone on, he understood them and the best of them loved him. It is a great pity he couldn't have guided their destiny for another twenty years.

The Apache is not a dying race. There were more than six thousand of them in 1950 living on two huge reservations which are contiguous, the San Carlos and the Fort Apache. Soldiers were stationed at Fort Apache itself as late as 1923. Then there are two other Apache reservations outside the Gila watershed in New Mexico, the Mescalero and the Jicarilla.

And what is the Apache like in 1950?

In many ways an Apache is still an Apache. It will take several more generations to eradicate from the race the fact that less than seventy-five years ago, even fifty years ago (and there were sporadic outbreaks in the 1920's and 1930's), these people were savages. Deep within the reservations the medicine man still functions. Apache youths and maidens still have maturation ceremonies when they reach adolescence. The Devil Dance, the Apache's most famous ceremonial, is still performed; and all through a starlit and firelit night a tom-tom will throb. The Apache language, a form of Athapascan, is still spoken. The wickiup is still used. Papooses are still carried in cradle boards. A horse is often killed to accompany his late master to heaven. Food is still occasionally placed on graves. In the old days a wickiup in which a person died would be burned, and the body along with it. This is no longer a common practice, it is said—but note the qualifying adjective "common." Oldsters will still not eat fish or bear, and to them the owl is always a bird of evil omen. Polygamy is never practiced—what, never?—well, hardly ever. But gambling and drinking, two indulgences beloved by almost every Apache, go on constantly. Both are frowned on by white authorities, especially the drinking. But within the reservations there are tizwin and tulapai parties, and there are always white men who are willing to bootleg whisky for a profit. Fighting, murder, stoicism, force, brutality—all have their incidents from time to time.

In contrast to these indigenous traits, there are a few new ones that stamp the present-day Apache as living in a period of transition.

The men now wear trousers and hats, and the women like gay cotton print dresses. The wickiup has been supplanted in many instances by a house, even though it may be little more than a crude shack. Every Apache brave once owned a horse, and most still do, but some own automobiles. A few of the cars are new and in good running order, and many are jalopies but still manage to run. Virtually every family boasts one sewing machine, and a few families have radios. Woolworth jewelry has replaced native arts and crafts; and basketmaking is slowly disappearing as an occupation for squaws. As one local rancher put it, "the next generation is raising cattle instead of hell." Farming is important, but stock raising is the basis of their economy, such as it is. There is also a tribal herd, apart from privately owned stock, which is made up of a fine grade of Herefords used for breed-

ing purposes. Most men patronize a barbershop once a month or
so, and it is only far back in the reservation that the tourist is
likely to see Apache men with hair falling to their shoulders. A
few have become Christians and are habitual churchgoers (although in the main the race is unimpressed by the white man's
religion) and a few have become drunkards and are habitual jail
residents. Young girls like rouge and lipstick and have even been
seen on the streets of Globe wearing bobby sox.

But to show how the Apache will always have an uphill pull,
the town of Globe adjacent to the San Carlos Reservation is a
good example. Globe began as a silver town, and later, of course,
became famous for copper and the great Old Dominion Mine. But
this rich mining area, between the Apache Mountains to the
northeast and the Pinal Mountains to the south and west, was at
first included within the San Carlos Reservation. As soon as mineral wealth was discovered in 1876, the white race decided that
this area didn't really belong within the reservation at all. No use
letting the Indians have that plum! So a change was made in the
boundary of the reservation and a 12-mile strip, rich in ore
and some pure silver, was declared outside the Indian-owned
land. The more intelligent Apaches questioned this theft. One
said that the term "Indian giver" should be applied to the white
race and not to the red. But there was nobody for the Apaches to
appeal to, so they watched the town of Globe develop, and
watched white men get rich on the silver and copper that, in all
justice, should have been theirs.

But the Indians were allowed to work in the mines for a
pittance, and were exploited in a number of other ways in the
town. For example, one merchant began selling potatoes and
whisky. The Apaches soon became good customers for the whisky.
When warned that it was illegal to sell whisky to Indians, this
resourceful merchant shrewdly sold any Indian a potato for two

dollars, and the purchase included a pint of whisky free. There was nothing to stop him until he ran out of potatoes, and he soon got more of those.

So the present-day Apache can be said to be in a state of transition from the old generic tribal customs to something resembling a low standard of living according to the white man's appraisal. Where the Apache will be in another hundred years is anybody's guess. Assimilation is going on. Younger generations are attending white schools. On the whole they range from fair to very good students, with a few excellent; but this may be due to the fact that those who would be poor never start school in the first place.

Anomalies are found frequently. A medicine man may be the leading participant in a primitive and pagan Devil Dance far back in the mountains and on that same night his granddaughter may be attending the movies in Globe. In fact Ross Santee, who has so ably illustrated this book, wrote in his own *Apache Land:* "A few years back I had gone to San Carlos to see an old Apache friend. Down on the reservation I was informed that he had driven to Phoenix with his family to see *Gone With the Wind,* the round-trip calling for better than two hundred miles."

Another choice item from Mr. Santee's book is this tidbit about an Apache boy, returned from the South Pacific, who decided to go to high school:

One Apache boy, back from the Navy, was asked the meaning of Democracy. He couldn't answer. The instructor suggested: "Of the people, by the people, and for the people." He questioned the Apache boy again the next day. "Of the people, by the people, and for the people," repeated the Apache. "Can you tell us anything more about Democracy?" asked the instructor. "That's all I know," said the Apache. "I just got out of the Navy. I didn't learn anything about Democracy there."

And so the inscrutable, unpredictable Apaches—six thousand strong—continue to live in the Gila watershed. Dreadful as the history of the Apache may be—liar, thief, murderer, torturer, hypocrite—there remains something admirable in the heart of a race that has fought for its identity, for its way of life, for over four hundred years of contact with the white man. And if an Apache is literally all the derogatory nouns listed above, it must be remembered that to an Apache a white man is a liar, thief, murderer, torturer, and hypocrite. And in spite of the white race, in the mid-twentieth century a great deal of the Gila watershed is still Apache country. You may never meet one of his kind, but if you do it will be well to remember that an Apache is always an Apache.

23

WHAT'S THE NAME OF THAT TOWN AGAIN?

THROUGHOUT THE Gila watershed there are some remarkable cities, towns, and hamlets—or "a wide spot in the road," as some of the lesser communities are designated. Nearly all of them came into existence in the nineteenth century, and many of them after 1875. It can certainly be said that there are no two Arizona towns alike. Oil towns in Oklahoma are somewhat of a pattern; farming communities in Iowa all more or less resemble each other. But in Arizona there is a distinction to every community, and it is caused largely by the fact that the entire Gila watershed is a land of sharp contrasts: burning deserts and snow-capped mountains, deep canyons and high peaks; red, yellow, black, and golden earth, radiant sunshine and exhilarating air.

No less distinctive than the towns themselves are their names, which amaze Easterners and recall the wild West of yesterday. Here are a few: Oracle, Paradise, Gunsight, Snowflake, Christmas, Bumble Bee, Garlic (Ajo), Honeymoon, Hot Water (Agua Caliente), Brewery Gulch (Bisbee), Show Low, Gourds (Calabazas), Walnuts (Nogales), Saw Mill, Salome, Rodeo, Jackrabbit, Sombrero Butte, Two Heads (Dos Cabezas), Plenty, Copperosity, Cocklebur, Skull Valley, and of course the perennial favorite—Tombstone.

Some of these towns have "gone ghost," others have disappeared entirely, but the majority are still there. With the slow but sure federal domestication of the wild Apaches, it became safe for settlers to take up residence in lonely parts of the Gila country, and Arizona's communities began to develop between 1875 and 1880. Many of the towns grew up around a mine or a group of mines—Tombstone being a perfect example. Others developed as supply towns for mines in remote areas—Florence and Winkelman, both on the Gila, the latter near the Christmas Mine, although later Christmas became a community and post office in its own right. Some got their start by being in strategic or focal points geographically, such as Yuma and Phoenix. Some began as forts or army posts, such as Prescott near Fort Whipple. Agriculture and stock raising brought many towns into existence, notably Duncan and Safford on the Gila, and Casa Grande (not the Hohokam ruins), Chandler, and Mesa near Phoenix. Railroads or industry, or a combination of the two, developed other communities, such as Flagstaff and Williams (lumber and stock raising), north of the Gila watershed; Silver City (mining) in New Mexico in the Mimbres basin east of the Gila, and Willcox, a shipping point on the railroad near Apache Pass for Fort Grant, the San Carlos Reservation, and the mining town of Globe.

The Apaches had successfully retarded white civilization from the days of Coronado up to the campaign of General George Crook. In 1874 the population of Arizona Territory was less than 11,000 whites. The Indian population, counting all tribes —Apaches, Navajos, Papagos, Pimas, Maricopas, Yumas, Cocopahs, Hopis, Mojaves, Opatas (laborers from Mexico), Paiutes, Walapais, Havasupais, and a few lesser groups—is inestimable with any degree of accuracy, but possibly 40,000 would be a reasonable guess for 1874. Instead of dying out (the popular fallacy), Indian population is increasing. In 1950 the number of Indians living in Arizona was approximately and conservatively 70,000.

By 1880 Arizona Territory had increased its white population to 40,000 from the 11,000 of only six years before. And the main reason for this was the gradual disappearance of the Apache menace. By 1950 the white population had reached 600,000. Thus the state's population in its entirety is less than that of the city of Pittsburgh. There is still plenty of room in the West.

It would be impracticable to tell the story of every town in the Gila basin. And quite a bit of information about Tucson and Tubac has already filtered through previous chapters. But a few of the more important communities have colorful histories and are well worth a closer scrutiny. To begin at one end of the Gila River and work upstream, Yuma at the river's mouth makes a logical starting point.

Beginning as Arizona City in 1854, merely Charles D. Poston's jest and device for free ferry passage, Yuma, with a population of about five thousand in 1950 is nearing its first centennial. It is a pleasant, quiet, hot, sultry town to the transient visitor, and in spite of its salubrious climate it does not convert many of its passing parade into permanent residents. Nevertheless, there are worse places in the world in which to live than Yuma, Arizona. If it is sunshine you want, Yuma has it. The fact that the sun always shines 365 days in a year, and 366 in leap year, has been a municipal boast for half a century or more. One hotel proprietor long advertised "free meals and lodging any day the sun doesn't shine." This story has had many tellings, but it is generally agreed that only once in half a century was there no sunshine in Yuma, and on that day the hotel owner made good his promise. But the lucky public had to wait all day in order to collect because one ray of sunshine just at sunset would have exempted the obligation. So each claimant received but one meal —supper. And with the following dawn came the dependable sun. This was somewhere back in the 1890's and the sun has shone every day since.

In fact, Yuma's sun has been mentioned in print many times. J. Ross Browne, in *Adventures in the Apache Country,* wrote in 1864:

The climate in winter is finer than that of Italy. It would scarcely be possible to suggest an improvement. I never experienced such exquisite Christmas weather as we enjoyed during our so-journ. Perhaps fastidious people might object to the temperature in the summer, when the rays of sun attain their maximum force, and the hot winds sweep in from the desert. It is said that a wicked soldier died here, and was consigned to the fiery regions below for his manifold sins; but unable to stand the rigors of the climate, sent back for his blankets. I even heard the complaint made that the thermometer failed to show the true heat because the mercury dried up. Every thing dries; wagons dry; men dry; chickens dry; there is no juice left in any thing, living or dead, by the close of summer. Officers and soldiers are said to walk about creaking; mules, it is said, can only bray at midnight; and I have heard it hinted that the carcasses of cattle rattle inside their hides, and that snakes find a difficulty in bending their bodies, and horned frogs

die of apoplexy. Chickens hatched at this season, as old Fort
Yumers say, come out of the shell ready cooked; bacon is eaten
with a spoon. . . . The Indians sit in the river with fresh mud on
their heads, and by dint of constant dipping and sprinkling manage to keep from roasting, though they usually come out parboiled.

This extravaganza was substantiated in 1870 by Stephen
Powers, who walked from Raleigh, North Carolina, to California's
Golden Gate over the southern route. Mr. Powers wrote a book
called *Afoot and Alone, a Walk From Sea to Sea*, which was
published in 1872.

In it, in a chapter called "Home of the Heat," he stated:

What kind of a town Arizona City [later Yuma by official
proclamation] may be, is known to the gods. I only remember a
batch of mud-houses, among which were moving about some
ghostly umbrellas, with a faint suspicion of whey beneath
them. . . . Keeping cool is one of the principal concerns of life
at Fort Yuma. The Yumas have a method of doing so peculiar to
themselves. They fill their long black hair with mud, which
crushes the inhabitants thereof as effectually as Mount Aetna does
the wicked Enceladus. Then they take a log into the river, and
float tranquilly down with the current, with nothing but a shining
orb of mud visible above the waters. Doubtless the Yuma Indian
could conceive of no more ecstatic experience, than one wherein
he might float down unwearied through long summer days, lapped
in the soft, warm waves of the River of Paradise.

Five years later Yuma broke into print in book form again.
This time the author was not at all atrabilious, but was observant,
factual, and a little dull. He was Hiram C. Hodge, and his
book, *Arizona As It Is*, was published in 1877. But one paragraph
from Mr. Hodge's book will serve to show the progress in Yuma
from Poston's jest and Jaeger's purchase in 1854, which created

the town, up to life in the community twenty-three years later. Hodge wrote:

At Yuma is the Territorial Prison, which is now partly completed, and when fully finished according to the plans and specifications, will be a model of strength, utility, and architectural beauty. Among the other important buildings are the county courthouse, jail, public school-house, Catholic school-house, two hotels, printing-office, and a large number of fine stores and saloons and private dwellings. The "Sentinel" is a wide awake newspaper, is well established at Yuma, and thoroughly devoted to the interests of the county and territory. It is now under the management of George E. Tyng, Esq. . . . The Southern Pacific Railroad of California will, it is expected, be finished in a few months to Yuma, when the town will receive a new and fresh impetus.

The Southern Pacific, pushing eastward from Los Angeles, was completed within a year of Mr. Hodge's estimate. That it did change the town a bit and was of wondrous interest to the populace was soon recorded in another book by a man whose soul loved brevity and who wrote under the name of E. Conklin. His book, *Picturesque Arizona,* appeared in 1878, and of Yuma he said:

Distance often gives erroneous interpretation, as well as enchantment. We think this is somewhat the case with Yuma. It is not an Indian village; though an Indian village exists contiguous to it, and a full representation of the old Yuma tribes constitute an equal half of its daily population. Blanketed and half-nude Indians associate as intimately with the whites (what few there are here) as do the Mexicans themselves.

The town itself, is strictly of Mexican origin, and savors of all the looseness and primitiveness characteristic of the smaller, out-of-the-way towns in the Republic of Mexico. . . . One sees a mass of one story buildings, built of adobe, and roofed with

mud. . . . Some are whitewashed and present a cleanly appearance; while others are the embodiment of the filth of the greaser.
One or two genuine Spanish houses built in the quadrangular
form with the garden plot in the center, and two stories high with
a veranda, where flower-stands bedecked with flowers, cheer
this otherwise barren place. The town now numbers about two
thousand persons of all classes, including Indians.

The hour of eight, every morning now, when the train comes
in, is an interesting one in Yuma. There is then congregated, with
eager eyes, Indians, Chinese, Americans; Jew, Gentile, and Pagan.
In fact, most every nation and condition of men on the earth, one
might be inclined to say, is represented.

At night, the Indian huts and camp fires may be seen glim-
mering around the city. As one approaches these and sees, crouched
together, a handful of half-clothed, beggarly Indians, a feeling of
sadness steals over him. They will sit with stoic stillness and stare
at you with an awe-stricken expression as if they knew that their
hour for final extermination was at hand.

And so Yuma, Arizona's second city by the 1870's, impressed, or failed to impress, its visitors. Only Tucson was
larger, as Tubac, by this time, was fast becoming a ghost town
due to the curtailment of mining activity in its immediate
vicinity.

Yuma's next peripatetic author was William Henry Bishop,
who had published in 1883 a book called *Old Mexico and Her
Lost Provinces.* Since his reaction gives one or two varied facets of
life in Yuma, here is an excerpt from Mr. Bishop's book:

The heat in Yuma is proverbial. The thermometer ranges
up to 127° in the shade. There is an old story of a soldier who
went to the place which Bob Ingersoll says does not exist, and,
finding it chilly there by comparison, sent back after his blankets.

Great heat, nevertheless, is not equally formidable everywhere.
It is well attested that there is no sunstroke here, and no such suf-

fering as from a much lower temperature in moister climates. Distinct sanitary properties are even claimed for this well-baked air. So near the sea-level, it is said to be less rarefied, and to comprise, therefore, a greater quantity of oxygen to a given bulk, than that of mountain districts, which, in purity and dryness, it resembles. It is thought to be beneficial in lung troubles. Yuma, among its arid sand-hills, has aspirations to be a sanitarium.

The town is a collection of inferior adobe houses, a few of the very best being altered from the natural mud-color by a coating of whitewash. . . . The houses consist of a framework of cottonwood or ocotillo wattles, plastered with mud inside and out, making a wall two or three inches thick. The roof is thatched and the floor is bare ground. Around them are generally high palisades of ocotillo sticks, and corrals of the same adjoining.

The waiters in a Yuma hotel are of a highly miscellaneous character. You are served, in the same dining-room, by Mexicans, Chinamen, Irish, Americans, and a tame Apache Indian. One and all had a certain astounded air, ending in something like confirmed depression, on finding that we were to remain, and would dine at our leisure, and did not wish to have the dishes shot at us as if out of a catapult, after the practice of the ordinary traveller pausing here his allotted half hour. One does not expect too much of his waiter in Arizona, however. There are reported instances in which he makes you eat your steak with his hand on his pistol-pocket, and the threat of wearing it out on you if you object.

It may be noted that only one of the passing authors quoted above mentioned something that became Yuma's pride and joy, the Territorial Prison. This institution "opened for business" in 1876 with seven prisoners. But "business" was good, and at one time the penitentiary held nearly four hundred convicts. The buildings stood (and most of them still stand) on a bluff overlooking the confluence of the Gila with the Colorado.

In the bright sunshine it is hard to catch the grim and

gloomy spirit that once must have pervaded the place. There was a row of dungeon cells cut into the rocky hillside. Rings on the floor indicate where men were chained. Also there were special cells for incorrigibles. A guard tower and a Gatling gun discouraged escapees, and it is said that the Yuma Indians were offered $50 for every escaped convict they could capture and return alive. Not only was escape a great risk for this reason, but miles of desert faced every seeker of liberty, and the wretch had no supplies of food or water. Nevertheless, so great is the desire for freedom that some prisoners did manage to escape. Far more have left their bones in the dreary little prison cemetery near the riverbank.

In 1909 the Territorial Prison was removed from Yuma to Florence. The buildings gradually became ruins, and as they crumbled with the years the site became a place for occasional picnickers, and later a haven for tramps. A hobo town was a public nuisance and the city made an effort to rid itself of this element. In recent years the old prison has been restored and now serves as a local museum.

At least one female was incarcerated at Yuma's penitentiary. She was Pearl Hart, about eighteen years old, known as the "girl bandit."

Pearl and her lover were reported to have robbed a train in 1899. This would seem a difficult feat for one holdup man and a girl. But there was no doubt about other crimes the pair committed, from robbery to murder. Their victims were always lone travelers far out in the desert country. The local newspaper stated on October 23, 1899: "Pearl Hart, the alleged train robber, is still enjoying her freedom and it begins to look as if she were safe from capture. It is thought that she may be hiding in this city, but it is more probable that she is in Mexico."

A few days later Miss Hart was caught, along with her

lover, by a local posse, and summarily deposited in jail. Later the newspaper reported: "The life and experiences of Pearl Hart, the female bandit who broke into print about four months ago will appear in one of the monthly magazines. She is still in the local jail, smoking Perfectos and wearing the jeans."

Pearl got five years in the Territorial Prison and her partner-lover got thirty. While languishing in a cell for incorrigibles she wrote a poem. This bit of doggerel may be seen in the prison-turned-museum today. After serving her sentence Pearl was released and disappeared. Since she would be about sixty-eight years old at the present writing she may conceivably be still living somewhere in the Gila Valley.

But the aura—or stigma—of Yuma's prison still haunts the little city. Even some of the street names are indicative. There are Maiden Lane, Lovers Lane, Prison Lane, and Penitentiary Avenue —a progressive sequence worthy of a second thought. And the 1950 Yuma High School football team, instead of having such a commonplace totem as panthers or lions or wildcats, is known as the Criminals.

One of the interesting features about Yuma has been the long battle between men and the two rivers—the Gila and the Colorado—to make use of water for desert reclamation. This project began in 1902. In 1906 the Gila went on a rampage and all but flooded Yuma into oblivion. With the Colorado already high, the Gila roared over its banks and through the town and made an island out of the prison high up on the bluff, with the Colorado on one side of it and the Gila on the other, with Yuma itself under water. Godfrey Sykes, in his book *A Westerly Trend* describes a Yuma but rarely seen:

Yuma had just been through the throes of a major catastrophe . . . the place was almost unrecognizable. The main, and only, street was a muddy gully, adobe and willow-pole houses, stores and saloons were mostly heaps of ruin, and the inhabitants were either grubbing about in the piles of debris in search of treasured belongings, or sitting perched upon the higher heaps, considering matters.

The cause of the disaster was the Gila River, which had suddenly and almost without warning risen to an unprecedented height and practically washed the business section of the town away. Structures of the types of which pre-diluvian Yuma consisted, readily dissolve under such circumstances, and the heavy heat-resisting earth roofs which were almost universal had merely added to the volume of the mud heaps.

This was the famous flood of 1906, which caused the combined waters of the Gila and the Colorado to overflow farther downstream and spill into Mexico and California until the Imperial Valley suffered as did Yuma and the runaway rivers created what is today California's Salton Sea.

It is difficult to visualize such a Gila today. For almost five years not a drop of water has come down the dry sandy river bed. This is due not only to a series of dry years but also to the fact that the Coolidge Dam and the Roosevelt Dam check the flow of the Gila and the Salt, respectively. There is plenty of water, roaring and surging through its colubrine canyons in the upper Gila, but this fluid, so precious to Arizona's economy, is impounded and used for power and irrigation. Yet if a new bridge should be constructed anywhere across the lower Gila between Florence and Yuma, it would have to have a span of at least a quarter of a mile for security. For the whims of the Gila are utterly unpredictable, and man can never be too trusting. As one citizen put it: "When she rolls, she *rolls;* and it's a good time to be somewhere else."

The Yuma Project of the Bureau of Reclamation comprises

65,000 acres of desert land that have now been made available for planting. Auxiliary projects have increased this area of potential fertility. Colorado River water flows through the Gila Gravity Main Canal, is further boosted by a pumping plant, and makes the rich desert soil blossom like the rose. Farther up the Gila, above the town of Roll, is the Wellton-Mohawk Division, continuing along the river for some forty miles, and containing about 75,000 irrigable acres. This project is in the development stage and it will be a number of years before this section of the Gila Valley will be burgeoning. But the day will come.

Considering that everything around Yuma for many a mile—even hundreds—had long been considered worthless desert, it is somewhat surprising to learn that this area now produces alfalfa, flax, barley, wheat, maize, grass seed, lettuce, carrots, cantaloupes, watermelons, honeydew melons, grapefruit, oranges, lemons, limes, pecans, and dates.

With all this emphasis toward agriculture, there is one other business that Yuma excels in, and that is the marriage business. California's "no gin marriage" law makes it necessary for couples to wait three days after registering for marriage. This is not the case in Arizona. Therefore, impatient couples come from California by train, plane, or automobile, and can be married in a matter of minutes.

As you drive east across California's Colorado Desert on U.S. Highway 80, and are nearing the town of Winterhaven, which is just across the Colorado River from Yuma, a large billboard greets you with "In Yuma—Marriage Information." Now, these are admittedly days of rather general and popular sex education, and commendably so. But still, it is a rather astounding sign. But you soon learn that it signifies only the technicalities of Arizona's laws about getting married and nothing further.

Because of the influx of couples, Yuma has a number of "wedding chapels." Most of them are painted white, and have trellises with flowers, or perhaps painted flowers on a white stucco building. There is 24-hour service. Signs such as "Weddings— any time, day or night. Ring bell" are not uncommon. And one "chapel" advertises "Get Married Here! Choose Minister or Justice of Peace. No Delay."

Well, business is business, and modern Yuma has as much right to make a living as any other community. After all, these are visitors from California that the town is striving to assist and please. And it is probably totally without premeditation on the part of either property owner that not only close-by one of the "wedding chapels" but actually next door to it is a motel advertising in neon lights "Best Beds In Town."

So that is Yuma in 1950, ninety-six years after Charles Poston bluffed L. J. F. Jaeger into providing a free ferry ride, and unbeknown to himself was thereby the founder of the town. The community in 1950 would be a surprising sight to Hernando de Alarcon and Melchior Diaz, both of whom trod its ground in 1540 —four hundred and ten years ago—long before there was a white man from Maine to Florida.

For all of its geographical importance, Yuma was never seriously considered as a city to be the capital of the territory. Possibly this was due to the fact that the town is at one extreme end of the area, and a more central site was desired.

The first capital was a provisional government established at Fort Whipple in 1863, with John N. Goodwin as governor, but was soon moved to a location eighteen miles south. Here a governor's mansion (made of logs) was erected and the town of Prescott grew up around it. Prescott can be said to be Arizona's first capital. The town was named in honor of the historian,

William Hickling Prescott, who died in 1859. Tucson, of course, would have been the logical site, but Tucson was being punished for being pro-Confederate, and feelings were running high in 1863.

Tucson received the capital honor in 1867 and held it for ten years. Then the capital was relocated at Prescott, and in 1889 Phoenix became the final choice. There was a movement at one time to call Prescott Gimletville, but happily it is still Prescott. In its infancy the town had only a few hundred citizens made up of cowboys and miners and a few shopkeepers. As soon as the Apache Indians comprehended its gubernatorial importance to the white men, they promptly attacked and all but destroyed it. But the town survived arrows and bullets and arson, and grew slowly. By 1870 it had ten saloons and twice as many gambling halls and one "eating house." This establishment was run by a woman who was always known as "Virgin Mary." When newcomers scoffed at the name, or even took umbrage at its use, older residents assured the critics that the name was perfectly reasonable.

"We know her last name is Mary," they explained. "Any female's got a right to select any first name she likes. This here's the West. There's only one other female in town, and her first name's not Virgin." And that usually ended the discussion. And it was best to be friendly with Virgin Mary, for she ran the only dependable place to eat in Prescott. "Meals $25 in gold per week payable in advance" said the notice outside her log cabin on Goose Flat. Her menu was simple. It habitually read:

BREAKFAST
Fried venison and chili
bread
coffee
milk (goat)

DINNER

Roast venison and chili
bread
coffee
milk (goat)

SUPPER

Chili
(got any complaints?)

If Virgin Mary were still running her restaurant in Prescott she would have some sharp competition. In 1950 this mile-high city in the pine belt has a population exceeding six thousand, and its excellent summer climate is attractive to tourists. And it has been the home of some contrasting personalities: the late Fiorello LaGuardia, former mayor of New York; Bucky O'Neill, the organizer of the famous Rough Riders of the Spanish-American War; Earl Sande, the nationally famous jockey; Ottmar Mergenthaler, inventor of the Mergenthaler linotype; U.S. Senator Henry F. Ashurst; and the now-forgotten Virgin Mary, who died in 1888 at Lynx Creek and whose remains lie in an unmarked grave. Incidentally, Pauline Weaver, who has been mentioned a number of times in previous chapters, also is buried in Prescott.

Today the city of Phoenix has superseded the former capitals, and with a population of 75,000 or more, is the largest city in the Gila basin. It is a clean, attractive, pleasant city, hot in summer but ideal in winter, situated on the Salt River not far from its junction with the Gila.

No native of Phoenix is ever called a "hayseed" although he might well be since the town began as a hay camp in 1864. The owner was John Y. T. Smith, who supplied hay for the animals, and a little provender for the soldiers, at Fort McDowell, an army post thirty miles to the northeast on the Verde River. Another pioneer was Jack Swilling, who established a flour mill on the Salt River and made use of the ancient Hohokam canals (still serviceable with a little repair work) to bring water to nearby ranches.

On October 20, 1870, a mass meeting of residents of the Salt River Valley was held for the purpose of appointing a committee to select a townsite. John Moore, Martin P. Griffin, and Darrell Duppa formed the committee and selected the location that is now Phoenix. Of the three civic-minded committeemen, Duppa was by far the most colorful. He was an Englishman; and an adventurer, a charlatan, a spurious "lord," a scholar, a linguist, an opportunist, and a dipsomaniac. Jack Swilling wanted to call the new town Stonewall because he was an admirer of Thomas ("Stonewall") Jackson. John Moore and Martin P. Griffin wanted to call the place Salina because the Salt River was first named by the Spaniards and was Rio Salina. While these suggestions in nomenclature were being debated, "Lord" Duppa had a few drinks and then waxed eloquent. He made a great speech to the awed mass meeting in which he used Latin and Greek and pointed out the evidence in the old canals and mounds of the pre-Columbian Hohokam civilization.

"A great race once dwelt here," he stated with solemnity. "And another great race will dwell here in the future. I prophesy that a new city will spring Phoenix-like from the ruins and ashes of the old. I prophesy that . . ." and then he slipped off the rostrum. But his words were enough; the town was called Phoenix. The story goes that it was discovered later that the brand of whisky that Lord Duppa had been drinking was also called Phoenix, thereby lending not a little of the power of suggestion to his inspiration. But this elaboration of the city's founding has no authentication whatever.

The first building, constructed in 1870, was Hancock's store. Since buildings were at a premium, this store served not only as a market place, but also as courthouse, saloon, judge's chambers, school, and public abattoir, and often provided all these services simultaneously.

The next building was Mike's Brewery. And from then on Phoenix enjoyed a building boom. The Prescott *Miner* for December 7, 1870, carried an advertisement which read:

Great Sale of Lots
at
Phoenix, Arizona
On December 23 and 24.

A Prescott citizen, Judge Berry, bought the first lot in this great sale for $104. It was located (this is by hearsay) at what is now the intersection of Washington Street and Central Avenue in the heart of present-day downtown Phoenix. And in 1950 $104 wouldn't buy one front foot of the same lot. Yet there were many who believed the judge was badly taken in at that 1870 sale. Most residents thought that anything over $25 for a city lot, where there was no city, was outrageous. And many of these residents lived long enough to regret their shortsightedness.

The best way to see modern Phoenix, of course, is to drive all over it. But for a quick view which will afford a topographical understanding of the entire city and its setting, the Salt River Valley, the Gila River, the Estrella Mountains, the famous Camel Back Mountain, and numerous other local landmarks—go up to the fifteenth floor of the Westward Ho Hotel, and before you, in all four directions, lies the heart of Arizona.

A town that is often forgotten by history is Calabazas. The name means "gourds" or "squash" or even "pumpkins" and the town is sometimes remembered as Arizona's Pumpkin Center, which it definitely was not. It epitomized the publicly accepted notion of what a raw western town should be—fighting, shoot· ing, gambling, drinking, whoring—but it had something more than that. Today it is a ghost town (it died in 1870) and its remains may be seen by turning left off the Tucson-Nogales road about fifty-six miles south of Tucson. The story of Calabazas (sometimes spelled Calabases) was told in book form by James Cabell Brown in 1892, a volume which the author subtitled "Amusing Recollections of an Arizona City" under the main title *Calabazas*. The one thing "more" that the town had beyond the usual raucous characteristics of a frontier community was a gen- tlemen's athletic club, and the gentlemen of the town came to re- gret it. And thereby hangs a tale.

Into Calabazas came a Mr. Murphy who was an itinerant bar- ber. The town needed a barber, so Murphy opened a shop in a tent. His love, however, was not tonsorial art, but athletics. He would entertain the entire male population of the town with his stories of pugilism and wrestling and racing. Murphy himself was a sprinter.

And into Calabazas came a young man named O'Connor. He seemed to have no especial trade. In fact he came to Calabazas to look for work of any kind. But he was interested in athletics too, and occasionally he would engage in a footrace with Murphy. Murphy always won easily, but the young man kept trying, just for the sport of it. Then Murphy had the idea of forming an athletic club for all able-bodied males. The Calabazas Club was born—for gentlemen only. There were no dues; this was not a money-making scheme.

About this time into town came a Mr. Riley. He had a wagon and what he called a worn-out crow-bait horse. So Riley went into the express and hauling business. But he, too, was sports minded, and he quickly became one of the most ardent and, when drunk, which was often, one of the most vociferous of club members. Mr. Riley, it turned out, loved to wager.

But Riley had no love for Murphy. He would often make vilifying and scathing remarks about Murphy, and all too often within Murphy's hearing. Things like this, of course, can happen in any club. But unquestionably a crisis was approaching.

At last, very drunk, Riley scoffed at Murphy's abilities as a sprinter; and further declared that young O'Connor could beat him in a 100-yard dash if O'Connor would merely put in a week of good training. Murphy challenged the statement and offered to bet $100 on himself. Riley wanted to make it $200. Murphy accepted. Everybody felt sorry for Riley, but a fool and his money . . .

The great event was scheduled for the next Sunday. And Riley, nothing if not a sport when in his cups, suggested a horse race as well. He would put up his poor tired old bay horse against any animal of equine ancestry in Arizona, and he would bet $100 that his nag would win. Moreover, he would ride his nag himself.

A Calabazas Club member named Curly Pete had a handsome little filly that was all legs and could race like the wind. He offered to enter his filly against Riley's sorry-looking bay. He hated to accept the bet of $100, even money, but Riley insisted.

All Calabazas turned out at the track on the following Sunday. Even the lone preacher said, "No services today—too much competition. See God at the races." And he put $100 on Curly Pete's filly, which Riley covered at once. The preacher made haste to explain that if he should win, the money would, of course, go to the purchase of hymnbooks for the church.

The first event was the foot race between Murphy and O'Connor. No money had been bet on it except by Riley. Nobody in Calabazas had any confidence in the amateur O'Connor, even if he had trained arduously for a week. The $200 between Murphy and Riley were all that were at stake. But the girls from the red-light district—"hurdy-girls" was the local name—all favored the younger and more attractive O'Connor. But even they were afraid to bet on him.

Riley was drunk before the first event, and was only prevented from drinking more by being reminded that he was to be the jockey for his bay against Curly Pete's filly in the next event.

"I can ride my own horse, drunk or sober—and that goes for the horse too," boasted Riley. And again most citizens of Calabazas felt sorry for him.

A 100-yard cinder track had been laid out by club members. There was an official starter and an official judge. But it turned out that the judge wasn't necessary. In the first event Murphy outsprinted young O'Connor and won by ten yards. Everybody agreed that the outcome was exactly what had been expected. Riley, always a sportsman, paid Murphy $200. The loss seemed to sober him considerably. "I got to win this next one," he muttered.

The horse race was one-quarter of a mile. And while the track, laboriously cleared by club members, wasn't too good, it was at least a straightaway, and certainly could be considered "fast," since not a drop of rain had fallen upon it.

Again there was an official starter, and again all of Calabazas gathered near the finish line. And again all of Calabazas said I told you so. For Curly Pete on his filly came racing down the quarter-mile stretch in fine form, and far behind him came Riley on his clumsy bay, in imminent danger of falling off at any moment.

Curly Pete declined to accept the bet but Riley insisted. The preacher, in contrast, had no compunction about receiving his winnings. After all, they were for God. Riley paid both bets.

It was still early in the day. Everyone had enjoyed these two events, and everyone wished there were more. That gave Riley a great idea. After all is said and done, a sportsman is a sportsman, and he doesn't do things by halves.

"Let's do it all over again!" was Riley's roaring challenge. "I'll double every bet I made and I've got my life's savings right here around my waist—" he patted a money belt—"and I'll bet any man or group of men here a thousand dollars that O'Connor beats that rat Murphy, and another thousand dollars that my bay will nose out that filly. Any takers?"

Everybody laughed, and some, who had partaken of plenty of whisky as had Riley, said, "Why not?"

So the whole sporting event was repeated, much to the delight of the populace. Riley doubled his previous bets except for the one with the local minister. The man of God cautiously made the same bet over again. Riley fussed and fumed and boasted and belched until he annoyed and irritated other club members into betting against him. When it was all tallied up he had $1,400 on O'Connor over Murphy, and $1,600 on his bay over Curly Pete's filly.

Then came the second foot race. It was simply the first race over again, with Murphy apparently leading all the way. But instead of being ten yards behind, O'Connor stayed on his rival's heels to the three-quarter pole. Then Murphy cut loose in a burst of speed and the Murphy bettors roared their approval. But while the crowd watched, O'Connor amazingly stayed right behind him, and then astoundingly put on his own burst of speed and passed the tiring Murphy a few yards from the finish line and won handily.

Murphy was so exhausted that he had to be carried to his tent. But young O'Connor seemed hardly out of breath. The crowd was stunned; and Riley, roaring and drunk, collected his winnings. Even the minister had to pay back his hundred dollars, and the hymnbooks for the church were as mythical as before.

Next came the second horse race. Many, annoyed and frowning over their unexpected losses, approached Riley with more money. And the drunken fool took every bet.

The horse race was no repetition of the former exhibition. Curly Pete's filly broke nicely and enjoyed a half-length lead for a few yards. Then the bay surged ahead and flew down the track leaving the filly far to the rear. And Riley, instead of hanging on for dear life as he had in the first race, rode his bay like a jockey, leaning far forward and almost whispering into his mount's ear. The margin between the two animals was so great that somebody called, "the filly'll be in next Sunday!"

This exhibition of superior horsemanship sobered Riley com-pletely. He collected his bets politely from the speechless and shocked losers, and went at once to Murphy's tent to collect from him.

The great athletic contest was over. Riley had won at least $3,600, if not a little more. Nearly everybody else in Calabazas was broke; and that was certainly true of every member of the Calabazas Club. But there was nothing anybody could do about it. Facts were facts.

Club members gathered in the late afternoon in their favor-ite bar, the Golden Fleece. There were no high spirits. And un-less a man's credit was good he had no way of bolstering his mental spirits with alcoholic spirits. It was a sorry and lugubrious meeting of the only gentlemen's club in Arizona.

And then, slowly but steadily, into every member's mind came the persistent and unpleasant and at length horrible thought that possibly they had all been taken in. All the members of the club were present with the exception of Messrs. Murphy, O'Connor, and Riley. It was unlike Riley not to be on hand and squandering his new wealth. Where were these three?

This question occurred to half a dozen members almost simultaneously. The half dozen voiced their query. All others echoed the question. Where were Murphy, O'Connor, and Riley?

The club marched in a body to Murphy's tent. He wasn't there. They went to O'Connor's shack. He wasn't there. They went to Riley's Express Office. He wasn't there.

And then, without having to put it into words, everybody knew the answer. The Calabazas Club, and all of Calabazas as well, had been taken in.

Some of the more desperate citizens and club members agreed to ride to the border. And sure enough, at the little border station of Nogales ten miles to the south, they learned that three laughing and jovial friends had paused there only to buy some whisky, and then had ridden into Mexico. Their names were Murphy, O'Connor, and Riley.

"Gentlemen," said Curly Pete, "the Calabazas Club is hereby dissolved."

The motion was unanimous.

About a week later a stranger rode into a poverty-stricken Calabazas. He was "totin'" two guns.

"Lookin' for some con men," he advised. "Three crooks."

"Bet one was named Murphy," said one former club member.

"And another named O'Connor," said somebody else.

"Sure as shootin'," said the stranger. "And the third's name is Riley."

"What do you know about 'em?" asked Curly Pete.

"Well, this here is their little game," explained the stranger. "Murphy comes into a town and sets up as a barber. O'Connor comes in lookin' for work. Murphy starts a sportin' club, and beats O'Connor in runnin'. Riley comes in with what he calls an old plug and pretends to be drunk all the time, but Riley is really a teetotaler and the plug is really a race horse. Riley bets the wrong way twice, once on the foot race and once on the horse race, and loses—then they double-cross the town when the real money is down, collect, and fade away. That's their business and they been operatin' from Indiana through Tennessee and Arkansas and Texas—and I've been trailin' 'em all the way."

"Did you lose a lot of money?" asked a former club member.

"Hell, no," said the stranger. "I'm the man who taught 'em the idea, and they never paid me a red cent!"

"Boys," said Curly Pete, "here's one way we can collect."

And to his surprise the stranger was the first and only visitor to Calabazas to be stripped of his clothes, plastered with adobe mud, and ridden out of town on a rail.

Now this entire story may be open to doubt. But James Cabell Brown, once a member of the Calabazas Club, has told it in a matter-of-fact account, although in far less detail than recounted here, and declares it is veracious. Embroidered or not, the yarn belongs to the literature of the Arizona frontier.

Literary merit was not limited to Calabazas. Brewery Gulch had its claim to letters too. Brewery Gulch was probably the first Arizona town to boast of having a public library, but just what percentage of Gulchers patronized it is problematical.

Brewery Gulch is Bisbee today, situated in the Mule Mountains of southeastern Arizona. This unique city, located in a major canyon and a number of side canyons (one of which is still Brewery Gulch), has no level ground. Every foot of the town is either uphill or downhill depending upon which way the pedestrian is going. And the pitch is steep. There are no mail deliveries in spite of the fact that the population is close to ten thousand, simply because no letter carriers can stand the grueling and exhausting ordeal of never walking on the level. You call at the post office for your mail or you don't get it.

Bisbee owes its life to mineralogy. The outstanding mine is the great Copper Queen. But it is no less sensational in its history than another called the Irish Mag which has earned more than $15,000,000. The town was named for Judge De Witt Bisbee, an investor in the Copper Queen, although it might have been called Dunn, since John Dunn first found promising ore in the vicinity in 1877. Brewery Gulch was its first name and it has hung on in spite of the fact that the town has sprawled over the mountains and through other canyons. To visit Bisbee and miss Brewery Gulch and O.K. Street is to miss the heart of the matter.

In 1880 the Phelps Dodge Corporation of New York sent Dr. James Douglas to Arizona to purchase likely copper prospects. Dr. Douglas held two degrees, M.D. and D.D., but he also had a hawk eye for minerals. He purchased a tract near the Copper Queen. In good time, as both units expanded, a merger was arranged. Gradually the Phelps Dodge Corporation took over control of many smaller mining companies until at last Bisbee became virtually a Phelps Dodge town. Today the company controls approximately ten thousand acres of potential mineral wealth. Copper, of course, is king. When the price is up, the town booms; when it falls, the town suffers a depression. Its history is the usual run of shootings, hangings, drinking, gambling, red-light districts, dance halls, holdups, and all the lawlessness germane to what was known as "the wild West." It has a weekly newspaper called the Brewery Gulch *Gazette,* and every issue states proudly on its front page: "The sun shines on Brewery Gulch 330 days in the year, but there is moonshine every day."

The moonshine, or whisky, known locally as "bug juice" in

the old days, provided the inflammatory spirit that gave the town its sensational aspects. And also, although indirectly, the bug juice got the town the honor of having a library.

This asset came about because some of the boys were "bucking the tiger" (betting against the house) in the Bon Ton saloon. The usual drunken argument took place and a Mexican, involved in the dispute, shot a miner named James Kehoe. He only wounded Kehoe, but his second shot killed an innocent bystander and a third shot passed through the wall into the saloon next door and broke the surprised bartender's jaw. The Mexican fled, but was tracked to a shack in the Mexican quarter called Chihuahua Town.

With the dawn the miners exercised their public duty. The Mexican was promptly hanged from a cottonwood tree in the center of town. Then the self-appointed servants of justice went back to the Bon Ton and played a game of twenty-one. The loser had to stand for a round of drinks and, worse, had to cut the swinging corpse down and carry it to the "boneyard." Nobody wanted to do this, and the end result was that another dispute took place over who lost; this resulted in further shooting. Meanwhile the dead Mexican still dangled in the sunshine for all and sundry to see, and to learn the great lesson that crime doesn't pay.

At this time who should pass by but Dr. James Douglas, and with him were two gentlemen from New York who had come out to see their newly acquired property. They were Mr. Phelps and Mr. Dodge. All three were horrified at the sight of the swinging corpse. It made such an impression upon them that they carried the unpleasant vision all the way back to New York. Dr. Douglas suggested that something be done to better such brutal conditions, and he further suggested that if the miners only had some pastime or avocation to interest them in their moments of relaxation they would doubtless develop their better natures. Mr. Phelps and Mr. Dodge agreed. So a new building was erected in Bisbee near the lower end of Brewery Gulch and was endowed as a town library. Here the miners could gather, and sit and read quietly such classics as the works of Homer and Horace, and Tacitus and Thucydides, and Caesar and Cicero, and Seneca and Shakespeare—to say nothing of Chaucer, Spenser, Dante, Milton, and Goethe.

The library is still there.

But the number of miners who have held library cards is unrecorded. To get such information a stranger would do best to inquire at the Bon Ton saloon. But he should be careful not to interrupt a poker or faro or monte or blackjack game, for if he should do so, he might receive more than the mere information that he is seeking.

From Bisbee it is not far to Tombstone. And because of its name, this town has captured and long held a place in the folklore of the American West.

Relations were not always friendly between the two mining towns—Bisbee and copper, Tombstone and silver. In the Tombstone cemetery, known as "Boothill," is the grave of John Heath, and his headmarker states:

Taken from
County Jail &
LYNCHED
By Bisbee Mob
In Tombstone
Feb 22nd 1884

The little graveyard is anything but lugubrious and ghoulish in the bright Arizona sunlight, but behind it lies violence. In fact, only those who died violent deaths, such as John Heath, seem to have been remembered for posterity.

Tombstone likes to call itself "The town too tough to die." Its story has been told so many times in print that it is probably the best known bad town in the West.

Ed Schieffelin, a prospector, was warned to avoid the area because of the Apache Indians. "You'll never find anything over there but your tombstone," he was advised. Schieffelin found pure silver and plenty of it in 1877. With his brother, Al Schieffelin, and a mining promoter named Dick Gird, he located what Al called the Lucky Cuss Mine in honor of Ed. Later they struck other rich veins, and the results were three more mines—the Contention, the Tough Nut, and the Good Enough. When they eventually sold their interests in these properties they were the richer by about $800,000. A tent and shack town sprang up almost overnight at these mines.

"What's the name of this place?" asked a new arrival.

"This is my tombstone," declared Schieffelin. "They told me that's all I'd find."

So Tombstone the town was called.

John P. Clum, who did such good work with the Apache Indians during the interlude that General George Crook spent in Nebraska, became the editor of Tombstone's first newspaper, and fittingly called it the *Epitaph*. The paper has never ceased publication since its first issue came off the press in May of 1880. At the age of seventy, there are indications that the *Epitaph* will go on as long as men live in Tombstone.

From a tent and shack town Tombstone grew rapidly. What had been cactus-studded desert hills overlooking the San Pedro Valley and the Dragoon Mountains became a town of 15,000 people in a few years. Seventy-odd years later there are many buildings still standing that were constructed between 1877 and 1882. Today the visitor may see the famous old Crystal Palace Bar, opened in 1880 and still serving "all brands of choice liq-

uors"; or the Can-Can restaurant, the Oriental saloon, and the
Bird Cage Theatre. The Can-Can was run by a Chinese named
Ah Lum, and if there was a delicacy in the West Ah Lum had
it. The slogan was the "finest restaurant between New Orleans
and San Francisco." The Oriental saloon was the rival of the
Crystal Palace and had its share of events, from horseplay to
gunplay.

The Bird Cage Theatre is now a museum. It was a play-
house at times, but more often a variety house, and for three
years it never closed, day or night. This may seem an extreme
statement, but it is qualified by the fact that the theater was also
a saloon. If the actors were exhausted, the bar was always open
to cater to a waiting audience. The name Bird Cage was given to
the theater because the four boxes, upper and lower and two on
each side, were similarly shaped and resembled cages. One miner
was so theater minded and entertainment hungry that he rented
a box for two years at $25 a night and always had it available
for the use of his girl friends from the red-light district if he
happened to be out of town. The queen of the red-light district
was Dutch Annie, and she became a socialite of Tombstone by
having a box at the theater. Other red-light belles were Rowdy
Kate, Blonde Mary, Crazy Horse Lil, and Gold Dollar Gertie.
They, too, were frequent patrons of the Bird Cage. The owner
and manager of the theater was Joe Bignon, and his variety bills
offered everything from burlesque queens in tights to Shakespeare's As You Like It. One of the burlesque girls was Joe's wife,
Big Minnie. She was six feet tall, weighed two hundred and thirty
pounds, and always wore tights on stage and off. Also she served
capably as a "bouncer" if any members of the audience should
prove objectionable and annoying to others. Visiting stars of the
day were Eddie Foy and Lotta Crabtree, and in lieu of "road"
talent, entertainment created from local "artists" was often pro-

duced. One cowboy used to sit in an upper box, relax, and put his feet over the rail. This went on from performance to performance, and so irked a miner in the audience that right in the middle of an aria by a pretty soubrette he drew his gun and shot the heel off the cowboy's boot. After that the chap kept his feet on the floor, where they belonged. Decorum was the order of things within the Bird Cage.

Somebody once counted the saloons between Tough Nut Street and Trigger Alley, and was surprised to find that every building was a saloon with the exception of the Can-Can restaurant, which, of course, served liquor. If you could have strolled along that block in Tombstone in 1882 you would have passed, upon leaving Tough Nut Street, the Sunshine Bar, the Eagle, the Can-Can, Brown's Saloon, Riley's Saloon, Kelly's Wine House, the Grotto, the Friendly Miner, the Fashion Saloon, the Tivoli, the Alhambra, Casey's Place, the City of Paris, and the Silver King. That would bring you to the Bird Cage Theatre, where, if the show wasn't on, you could go into the bar!

When the silver veins were worked out and water filled the lower levels of the mines, Tombstone was almost deserted. The town, on U.S. Highway 80, managed to survive, but the financial crash of 1929 and the subsequent depression years all but killed the community. It never became a ghost town, but the population dropped to a precarious 700 in 1940 as compared with 15,000 in 1882.

In recent years Tombstone has had a renascence, and not of the mining industry, but of the health business. The climate is excellent. The elevation is approximately 4,500 feet. The air in this pure high desert atmosphere is a boon and a blessing for the city dweller to breathe deeply into his lungs. In Tombstone there is no pollution from smoke, burnt gasoline fumes, and smog. The summers are warm and pleasant and the winters are cool but al-

ways brilliant with sunshine. Modern Tombstoners, quite naturally, claim that the climate will cure anything; but specifically it
has been proved an aid to pulmonary troubles and sufferers from
rheumatic fever, lumbago, and arthritis. "You will delay your
tombstone if you come to Tombstone" has been suggested for the
masthead of the *Epitaph* to replace "The town too tough to
die." Also windshield stickers, designed in the shape of Ed
Schieffelin's monument, are provided for any passing motorist who
will take them. And they state a combination of values: "Excellent water from mountain springs, sun's infrared rays stronger
here than any place in U.S.A.; and historical points of interest."
Or if you come to the town and don't like it after all, the
Chamber of Commerce will suggest that you "Boost for the town
you're living in—or live in the town you're boosting for." The
new health boom has brought Tombstone's population back to
about twenty-five hundred and it is still growing. It can be
safely said in 1950 that Tombstone will never die, not because of
its childhood pranks, when it was "too tough," but because of its
middle age, when it is "too healthy".

Nevertheless, what Tombstone has to sell in the way of
glamour all stems from its storied past. In 1950 the town staged
a "Helldorado"—a combination of fair, pageant, and circus dedicated to the recapturing of the spirit of its old days when it was
a "he-heller." Even certain outstanding fights and murders were
re-enacted in a mock performance. But this civic narcissism back-
fired a bit. The old wild oats could not be sown again. Instead,
the Helldorado turned out to be a pleasant sunny weekend party
with games and street races, children everywhere, a balloon man, a
merry-go-round, popcorn venders, and ice-cream salesmen. There
were two-legged races and potato races. In place of drunken cowboys and boisterous miners, a few kiddies got tummyaches from
too much candy, and soft drinks outsold hard liquor. The

murder and mayhem of 1880 had evolved into something akin to a Sunday-school picnic.

But Tombstone will always look back at its youth with a wistful sigh. Old residents are bound to show visitors the O.K. Corral, scene of the famous Earp-Clanton street fight in 1881— a fight which lasted only thirty seconds, but which left three men dead and two wounded, and an argument which to this day has never been settled. Some historians assert that Wyatt Earp, a peace officer, was in the right and that the Clanton faction was a group of drunken killers. Others believe that Earp, his brothers, and the belligerent Doc Holliday were in cahoots with bandits, and victimized the Clantons to vindicate themselves.

The most succinct account of this famous fight is told by a bartender in the Crystal Palace saloon. He has recounted it to visitors so many times that he is sick and tired of it, and he has reduced it to its least common denominator. Perhaps his version is a perfect summing up of most of Arizona's frontier history. His narrative states:

"It all begun over liquor. First came the argument, then the shootin', then the buryin'. What'll you have to drink?"

24

IT'S POISON!

I F YOU touch it, it stings you; if you pet it, it bites you; and if you eat it, it kills you" is the way a pioneer summed up the indigenous flora and fauna of the Gila Valley.

While this is a bit extreme, the Gila country from the age of dinosauria has afforded a home for some odd, bizarre, and often shunned creatures and unwelcome vegetation. The first chapter of this book began at a point in time about 200,000,000 years ago. Life has persisted in the Gila area ever since; and it existed, of course, even long before that fulcrum date of 200,000,000 years ago, or premammalia.

While this tremendous subject of natural history can barely be touched upon in one chapter from 200,000,000 B.C. to A.D. 1950, the chain of life during that great span of time was never broken in what is today the Gila watershed. In order to make a quick survey of this subject and to emphasize the contemporary flora and fauna of the area, there will be no people in this chapter. Therefore, there will be no theft, bribe, arson, graft, rape, torture, mayhem, mutilation, kidnaping, betrayal, double-crossing, duplicity, and murder—all indicative of the cruelties of man toward man that infest history. For information about human behavior in the Gila Valley, this chapter may effectually be skipped.

Nature, however, is no sentimentalist either. Animals have preyed upon animals from the flesh-eating allosaurus to the coyote and the rattlesnake, all of which makes it impossible to be squeamish. When the great age of dinosaurs came to an end at approximately the culmination of the Mesozoic era, plants, flowers, and fruits continued to evolve. And the inheritors of the earth were no longer saurians, but mammals.

Vertebrate paleontologist, Dr. George G. Simpson has written:

The most dramatic and in many respects the most puzzling event in the history of life on the earth . . . is the change from the Mesozoic, Age of Reptiles, to the Tertiary, Age of Mammals. It is as if the curtain were rung down suddenly on a stage where all the leading roles were taken by reptiles, especially dinosaurs, in great numbers and bewildering variety, and rose again immediately to reveal the same setting but an entirely new cast in which the dinosaurs do not appear at all, other reptiles are mere supernumeraries, and the leading parts are all played by mammals of sorts barely hinted at in the preceding acts.

This abrupt change in evolution's great pageant of production is manifest in Arizona. In the Gila watershed throughout the entire Pleistocene period—from 1,000,000 to 25,000 years ago —an astounding number of animals roamed the hills and valleys. The skeletal remains of mastodon, mammoth, eohippus (small horse), peccaries (wild pigs), deer, and camels have been identified. And it is most likely, although so far unauthenticated, that the Gila country supported carnivores of species including wolves, bears, foxes, badgers, skunks, weasels, pumas, lynxes, raccoons, and otters as long as a million years ago. All of those animals are present today. Some, such as the timber wolf and the grizzly bear, are all but extinct.

But it would be a reasonably safe statement to make that the flora and the fauna of the Gila watershed from the ice caves of the Mogollon Mountains at 10,000 feet above sea level to Yuma at virtually sea level, looked 25,000 years ago very much as they do today. There has been too slight an evolutionary change in the vegetable and animal life of the region over that short space of time, geologically speaking, to make any appreciable difference.

The flora of the Gila can be classified into three divisions: desert plains, grasslands, and mountain country. A more specific division would be the "life zone" system as set up by Dr. C. Hart Merriam of the United States Biological Survey. This system takes into account the determining factor of altitude in relation to life, both plant and animal. Thus flora and fauna show a relationship between latitude as measured in miles on the flat surface and altitude as measured in feet. A latitudinal division offering a definite type of life was considered by Dr. Merriam as a life zone, and for every latitudinal division there was a corresponding altitudinal division. This theory is based on the supposition that a difference in elevation of 1,000 feet may be considered the equivalent in its effect on plant and animal life to the normal change of 300 to 500 miles of latitude from the equator at sea level. There are seven major latitudinal life zones from equator to pole; and there are seven corresponding zones in altitude. Very generally, the altitudinal zones, based at the equator on a theoretical mountain of 12,000 feet would be as follows:

Tropical   —sea level to 2,000 feet
Lower Sonoran—2,000 feet to 4,000 feet
Upper Sonoran—4,000 feet to 7,000 feet
Transition   —7,000 feet to 8,000 feet
Candian   —8,000 feet to 9,000 feet
Hudsonian   —9,000 feet to 11,000 feet
Arctic   —Above 11,000 feet

Five of these life zones occur from the glacial beginnings of the Gila River to its confluence with the Colorado. From the Mogollon Mountains in New Mexico to Yuma at the river's mouth they are: Hudsonian, Canadian, Transition, Upper Sonoran, and Lower Sonoran.

Obviously, then, there will be a great variation in the flora and fauna of the Gila Valley from its icy rivulets of melting snow at 10,000 feet to its hot desert atmosphere at Yuma. Nobody ever saw a grizzly bear in Yuma, but the animal is known to have lived high up in the Hudsonian zone. And, in contrast, nobody ever saw a Gila monster in the Mogollon Mountains, but there are plenty of them in the Lower Sonoran zone between Florence and Yuma.

The variation in flora is equally sharp. High in the Mogollon Mountains of New Mexico, at the icy headwaters of the Gila, is the area set aside by the government as the Gila National Forest. This primitive land of Hudsonian and Canadian life zones has scarcely been touched by man, is one of the most inaccessible regions in the United States, and can be reached only on foot or horseback. Ponderosa pine, Douglas fir, blue spruce, white fir, and aspen are plentiful. This is one of the few places in the United States where the grizzly bear is still found, and along with this forest giant are numerous black and brown bears, deer, mountain lions, and bobcats. This is the continental divide, where the small streams that form the Gila eventually flow southwesterly. Just east of this watershed is the Black Range and from its eastern ridges the land falls away to the Rio Grande Valley and all its waters find their way to the Gulf of Mexico. Here, then, is the great backbone of the continent.

As the Gila, a rushing and turbulent river at this point, flows out of the high country it surges through a number of canyons, dropping into the Transition life zone where the vegetation is largely piñon pine, juniper, and some oak and birch. At Cliff, New Mexico, the elevation is about 4,800 feet above sea level. This hamlet of 150 people is the first settlement on the Gila as the river pours downstream from its mountain sources.

Between Cliff in New Mexico and Duncan in Arizona, a distance of approximately fifty-five miles as the river goes, the elevation drops to 3,700 feet. It has passed through the Upper Sonoran life zone. And at Safford, Arizona, the elevation is 2,950 feet and the life zone from there to the river's junction with the Colorado is Lower Sonoran.

Between the town of Duncan at 3,700 feet and the village of Geronimo at 2,700 feet the river flows through a rich valley that was settled by Mormon pioneers in 1879. They were not the first settlers, however, since ranchers had entered the valley in 1871; but it was the Mormons who developed the agricultural possibilities, in the face of great hardships, and made the fertile loam of the Gila bottom lands produce oats, barley, corn, and wheat. One of the towns in this valley is Solomonsville, and three miles from this community are the ruins of Chichilticalli (only a few reddish mounds left), the Indian town that was such an important base and landmark for the Spanish conquistadores in 1540.

From here to its mouth the Gila supports the flora and fauna most popularly associated with its reputation; willow, ocotillo, palo verde, mesquite, greasewood, ironwood, cottonwood, sagebrush, and cactus—with this flora of the great desert plain gradually dominating the landscape. And the animal life consists of coyotes, foxes, badgers, squirrels, wildcats, mule deer, antelopes, skunks, rabbits, gophers, bats, rats, and mice—almost all of which are nocturnal.

Thus it is obvious that the Gila, breaking sharply from the higher life zones, is a Lower Sonoran river for at least four-fifths of its length. And the outstanding floral elements of its lower watershed are the above-listed trees and shrubs and an infinite variety of cactus.

It would take a long book in itself to discuss the cactus (cacti is the proper plural) of Arizona. For an excellent introduction to the flora and fauna of the Lower Sonoran life zone there is no better book to begin with than *Desert Parade* by William H. Carr. But there are certain varieties that are often identified with the Gila Valley, and one is the striking and beautiful organ-pipe cactus that grows to a height of twenty feet or more. So prevalent

is this species at one point that the government has set aside the
Organ Pipe Cactus National Monument on the Mexican border
due south from the copper town of Ajo. It well repays an out-
of-the-way visit, for there is nothing else like it on the face
of the earth.

The one outstanding cactus so indelibly associated with Arizona is, of course, the giant saguaro (pronounced sah-war-oh with
the accent on the "war" and often spelled sahuaro). This stunning specimen prevails throughout the lower Gila. It sometimes
grows more than fifty feet high and weighs as much as ten tons.
It has indeed become Arizona's trademark and colophon. Of these
thousands of cacti, there are no two alike, and the easiest way
for the Gila visitor to see them at close hand is to go to the
Saguaro National Monument near Tucson. The fruit of this cactus
is a favorite food of the Papago Indians. It is a rich, red,
seedy, and pulpy mass, not at all unpleasant at the first taste.
Small woodpeckers and smaller owls like to drill holes in the
saguaro. If you examine this cactus closely don't be surprised to
see a pair of black eyes staring out at you from a small round
hole. And respect the privacy of the owner's home.

Among the other hundreds of varieties of Gila Valley cacti
that are cherished by cactus aficionados are the famous barrel
cactus (desert victims crazed with thirst can cut the top and mix
the pulpy interior into a liquid, but by the time the victim is
in this state he is usually unable to think clearly, much less operate on a cactus), which grow to a height of four to six feet, are
sometimes two feet in diameter, and from which is made cactus
candy; the pincushion, about the size of an artichoke with surprisingly sharp spines and delicate pink and lavender flowers; the
cholla (with numerous subspecies), one of the meanest sticklers
in any desert and quite as dangerous to an automobile tire as
running over a board containing fifty nails all with sharp points

up; the beaver tail with its attractive pink and purple blossoms (touch one and you won't get the tiny spines out of your hand for a week); the prickly pear, with even more subspecies than the cholla, and perhaps best known for the Engelmann type about three feet high and inclined to spread itself over eight to twenty feet of ground, with paddlelike branches with needle-sharp spines one to three inches long (again—admire but don't touch); the night-blooming cereus, with its lush fragrant white flowers, a thing of beauty on any moonlight desert night in May or June; and a host of others that seem endless—the old man, the rainbow, the strawberry, the nigger head, the bull's tongue, the teddy bear, and the deerhorn. You will never learn them all, but a desert prowl in the lower Gila Valley will introduce you to many.

A desert plant that is not a cactus but is as well known as any and is often mistaken for one is the agave. It is also known as mescal, amole, maguey, and lechugilla. The most common name is the century plant, given to it by the popular fallacy that it blooms only once in every hundred years. A healthy young agave will bloom within ten years. It is trunkless, with thick succulent leaves with a sharp barb at each leaf tip. It grows with surprising rapidity, sometimes to thirty feet, and when the main stalk has produced a cream-colored flower it just as suddenly dies. From the agave are made pulque, mescal, and tequila, all three intoxicating beverages and greatly favored by Mexicans and Indians.

Other trees and shrubs common in the Gila basin are the yucca, hackberry, sycamore, cat's-claw, jojoba, tamarisk (not indigenous, but imported for its shade value), desert broom, burro weed, and brittle bush.

Among desert flowers, which can be gorgeously beautiful and will often carpet miles of desert following winter and spring rains (if any) are the yellow daisy, the poppy, sand verbena, primrose, desert mallow, marigold, mariposa lily, pentstemon, wild hyacinth, devil's-claw, datura, small rock ferns, and Canterbury bells.

Where there are trees, bushes, shrubs, cactus, and flowers there are sure to be birds. Again, a large volume could be written on the ornithology of the Gila Valley, and about all that is prac-ticable here is to list some of these creatures and let the reader seek further for himself. A desert is not popularly thought of as a natural aviary, yet it is virtually just that, and some of the crea-tures listed here are among the most attractive birds in North America. As you descend the Gila Valley, although you will surely never observe them all at once, you may see such a variety as: wild turkeys, vultures (sharp-eyed scavengers who can sail for minutes without a wing flap, and sometimes have a wingspread of six feet); hawks of numerous types; Gambel's quail (good eating; hard catching); doves of several types, notably mourning, white-winged, and Inca; a plover popularly known as the killdeer because its call sounds something like "kill-dee"; owls of many types; the road runner, which would rather run than fly and eats snakes and lizards and doesn't seem to know that it is a bird; flickers, woodpeckers, larks, martins, flycatchers, swallows, ravens, verdins, hummingbirds, and cactus wrens. Then there is Say's phoebe of the flycatcher family; mockingbirds, thrashers, shrikes, orioles, cowbirds, cardinals, sparrows, sandpipers, finches, and finally the little-known pyrrhuloxia, which has no popular name, nests in mesquite bushes, and rarely, if ever, seems to need water. These are not all the birds of the Lower Sonoran zone by any margin, but they serve to show the variety of ornithology in what at first blush might be taken for a lifeless desert.

If it can be said that there are many birds in the desert, then it can be said to be teeming with insects. And with insects and reptiles we come to the shunned type of life most generally associated with the Lower Sonoran zone. The Gila country has its share of both and some of its insects and many of its reptiles are especially terrifying to those who know next to nothing about them.

Since the bad man and the bad bug and the bad snake are always more interesting than the good of their respective families, the more frightening denizens of the Gila Valley demand discussion more than the safe, sound, and commonplace. Although some of the creatures taken for granted as poisonous are not always so, as, for instance, an insect that scares almost everyone, the great hairy tarantula.

This arachnid is a fearful object, and apart from his horrific appearance and great size, and sudden startling movements, he is more harmless than a kitten and makes a more trustworthy pet. Sometimes called "bird spider," this frightening creature (a spider is not literally an insect, since insects have six legs and spiders have eight) has the reputation of seizing and killing birds. What he really feeds upon are grasshoppers, locusts, crickets, and other pestiferous insects. A tarantula is nearsighted and cannot risk a stealthy approach toward his prey. When within a foot or more he has to leap at it to assure capture. This has given him the reputation of leaping at human beings—something he never does. In the Gila Valley the large males, sometimes six inches in diameter, are often seen crossing a highway. Most motorists run over them if they can, and that is too bad. The tarantula, while he can bite—or sting—with the ability to raise a small welt comparable to that of a bumblebee, is harmless to man and never attacks unless fighting desperately for his life. Since he preys solely upon crop-destroying insects, he is beneficial to man and, instead of being stupidly exterminated, should be carefully protected. But his shocking appearance is all against him. Nevertheless, the Lower Sonoran life zone is tarantula heaven, and he will doubtless survive all of man's efforts to be rid of him.

The next bloodcurdling creature is the giant desert centipede,

which attains a length of six to eight inches and may have anywhere from forty legs to a hundred and twenty. He usually
walks slowly, but can move at great speed when frightened, and
always runs away. But like any other creature, the centipede will
defend himself when trapped and his bite can be painful and
serious but never fatal—unless the victim is so paralyzed with
fear that he suffers more from shock than from the wound itself.
The theory that to be crawled on by a centipede is enough to
poison an arm or leg has been disproved. His feet carry no poison; it is in his jaws only. The worst feature of the Gila Valley
centipede is his revolting appearance. But if he sees you first,
he'll run; so man must be equally revolting to him.

Next comes one of the really poisonous and dangerous creatures—the scorpion. But even in this case there are many types in
the Gila Valley, three quite common, and only one of the three is
deadly. He doesn't bite—he stings. And one sting is enough. If
ever you find a scorpion on your person, don't slap it or knock
it off with your hand—*shake* it off—and then examine it. Probably it will be the large, ugly, hairy type, menacing and revolting.
If so, he is harmless. He can sting, of course, but you won't die.
A second type, about half the size of the former, is sometimes
known as the striped-tail scorpion. You are more deadly to him
than he is to you. But this second type is all too easy to confuse
with the slender, yellow, whip-tailed scorpion. This creature has
been the cause of forty deaths in Arizona in the past ten years.
He is only about two inches long, and often his victims are children. If you think you have been stung by this killer, whose scientific name is *Centruroides sculpturatus,* get to a physician as soon
as you can. It seems hardly necessary to explain that a scorpion's
poison is located in the needle-sharp end of his tail. He will
always clasp his victim with his pincers and lash the tail forward,
over his head, with lightning speed. For emergency treatment.

place a tourniquet between the wound and the heart, and an ice pack on the wound. Then get the patient to a hospital as soon as possible. A number of Arizona hospitals keep a supply of scorpion antivenom on hand at all times. Never use drugs or alcohol internally. Whisky never cured a snakebite or a scorpion sting, American folklore notwithstanding.

The next "sweet creature" is nationally known and is not limited to the Gila Valley. That is the black widow spider. Probably the public is sufficiently well aware of the black widow to make any detailed discussion unnecessary. But she lives in the Gila Valley, and in almost any other valley in America, and she should be killed on sight. If bitten, the emergency treatment usually recommended is much the same as that for a scorpion sting. Since the venom of the black widow affects the nervous system almost instantly, medical treatment should be sought as soon as possible. Opinions differ, but it is often assumed that the bite of the black widow is more dangerous than that of a rattlesnake.

And if these creatures haven't scared you out of the Gila Valley, there are other types of spiders apart from the tarantula and the black widow; and there are ants, termites, grasshoppers, locusts, hornets, wasps, bees, beetles, June bugs, kissing bugs, and various ticks. But all these latter denizens of the chaparral and the desert are harmless. Your chances of death from an insect would not be one in ten million.

And then we come to snakes.

Here, again, the public is unduly alarmed. Of the more than fifty species, and countless subspecies, of reptiles in the Gila Valley, only the rattlesnake and the coral snake are dangerous. All other snakes are harmless, highly beneficial to man in their extermination of rodents, and should *never* be stupidly and ruthlessly killed. It may sound incredible, but it is better for your health to live in an area where there are snakes than in an area where there are none. Education in herpetology is sorely needed. Snakes are more helpful to man than insects, and more people are bitten by dogs every day than are bitten by snakes every year.

The diamond-back rattlesnake, probably the best known and most feared reptile in North America, may be found anywhere from the Mogollon Mountains down the Gila Valley to Yuma. But if you are ever bitten by him you can charge it up to your own carelessness. Mr. Diamond-back will never attack you; he will try to avoid you; he will even rattle to warn you of his presence; and to prepare for battle he has to coil first and strike later. But once he has decided to make a contest of it, he is not fooling; and if you want to see it through, hit him hard and hit him quickly right back of his head. And if you miss and he strikes . . .

Another important factor for desert dwellers, when it comes to dangerous reptiles, is the fact that virtually every case of snake-bite occurs below the knee or on the hand or wrist. Boots or puttees are a good safeguard. Even baggy and floppy trousers are a help if you decide to pick a fight with a snake, for in his lunge he may bite the trouser leg rather than your leg. And the plain fact is that most people who are bitten by a rattler or a coral snake deserve it. No rattler or coral attacks first. If a rattler could reason he would say, "Man really is something of a damned fool after all. I give him every warning possible, and what thanks do I get—he wants to kill me."

There is one type of desert rattler, however, who will strike without warning. This is known as the sidewinder, technically *Crotalus cerastes*. He is "mean even for a rattlesnake," as one desert character described him. He is sometimes called the horned rattlesnake, but sidewinder is more common because of his peculiar looping movement in locomotion. He doesn't crawl; he throws himself forward leaving a series of J-like tracks in the sand where his body lands and then loops forward again.

The Sonoran coral snake in the Gila Valley is even more shy and seemingly timid than the rattler. This is a beautifully marked reptile with sharply contrasting bands of red, black, and cream which encircle the body. It is seldom more than two feet in length, rarely seen, and so docile that amateurs have handled it without knowing what it was (mistaking it for the harmless Arizona king or coral king, which it resembles) and have never been bitten. But if sufficiently annoyed this snake will be provoked into striking, and when it does it is definitely poisonous. You have to pick a fight with a rattler, or even step on a sidewinder, but to be bitten by a Sonoran coral you almost have to write the snake a letter. Nevertheless, this coral is related to the cobra family, and his venom is deadly.

There are many beautiful and harmless snakes throughout the Gila watershed, and of the fifty major species only two, rattler and coral, are poisonous. Thus the index of danger is decidedly small. Yet there are men and women (mostly women) who are terrified by the sight of any reptile. Why this silly condition should exist goes into psychological reasons beyond the scope of this book. But it still does remain incredible that there are people who can see such handsome and harmless reptiles as the red racer and the blue racer; the friendly bull snake, which will make a devoted pet and keep any house, farm, estate, or shack free of rodents of all kinds; the Arizona king snake, a beautiful specimen averaging three feet in length—and still scream and howl and try to kill the creature in their hysterical ignorance.

Before leaving the subject of Gila Valley reptiles there are two statements that should be made: one is to correct the erroneous idea that the number of rattles on a rattler are indicative of its age, which they are not; and the other is to make it plain that no snake ever carries disease-bearing parasites (or parasites of any kind), which rats and mice certainly do, and which may also be carried by your pet dog or cat.

The animal, creature, object—call it what you will, although it is a lizard—that is most identified with the Gila Valley is the Gila monster.

Many things have been said about the Gila monster and most of them are erroneous and some are ridiculous. But one thing is true—it is poisonous. In fact it is the only poisonous lizard in the United States. And like all other creatures carrying venom, it must be irritated, prodded, and goaded into becoming a menace. The Gila monster, under normal conditions, is a slow-witted, dull, sluggish lizard that much prefers to be let alone. It is beautiful or not, depending upon your taste. The average monster is about a foot and a half long, and the largest is almost two feet. They are usually black with a beaded type of hide or skin with pink or reddish beads projected on the shiny black background.

The poison is secreted by glands in the lower jaw. It affects the nervous system of the victim immediately but is rarely fatal, although deaths have been reported in instances when the poison caused a paralysis of the heart. So revolting is this creature to most people that an apocrypha of fable has grown up about it. Even its breath has been reported as poisonous, and this is not true. Another fallacious theory is the notion that it has no anal opening and is therefore "a walking septic tank." How this idea got abroad is impossible to say, but it is totally wrong. The lizard is found throughout the Lower Sonoran life zone of the Gila River, and is especially numerous in the vicinity of the junction of the Salt River with the Gila. It does not leap at human beings, and unless irritated, will sit stupidly in the sun for hours without making a motion. It can move rapidly, however, when so minded, and it does hiss at an enemy and will spring upon its prey. Its food consists of mice, rats, and insects. It has a rather fat tail in comparison with most lizards, and this tail serves as a storehouse for food. The female lays eggs in the desert sand and no sooner are they deposited than she waddles away, leaving the warmth of the sand to bring on the hatching. Mother love is conspicuous by its absence. Unpleasant as this animal may be, it is a scavenger of sorts and probably has done more good than harm to mankind. But of all the living things in the Gila Valley, this horrendous creature is the most loathsome to the general public.

Few people realize that the Gila monster is a saurian whose ancestors go back to the days of dinosaurs. The great diplodocus or brontosaurus or allosaurus of two hundred million years ago has simply evolved through the aeons, and the Gila monster is 1950's contribution to the saurian chain of life. To the Gila Valley he is unique. And if you meet one of his kind, don't pick him up. He's poison.

There are numerous other lizards in Arizona and all are harmless—the banded gecko and the chuckwalla being among the best known, along with the so-called "horned toad," which is a lizard and not a toad at all. About the only animal left unmentioned so far is the common desert tortoise, slow moving, harmless, shy, and an inveterate sleeper.

And so, in summing up, in spite of the amazing variety of life in the Gila country from that rarity, the grizzly bear, to the shunned Gila monster, there are few creatures really dangerous to man. The Gila Valley is not a haven for all the horrors that creep and crawl. Pay your just respects to the rattlesnake, the coral snake, the sidewinder, scorpions and black widows, and the Gila monster—but always remember that your chances of meeting death are a thousand times greater due to automobiles than they are to the few live things in Arizona that are poisonous.

25

WHERE WERE YOU ON FEBRUARY 14, 1912?

Arizona became the forty-eighth state of the Union when
a few strokes of a pen held by President William Howard Taft
on St. Valentine's Day, February 14, 1912, ended the existence
of the last territory within the continental United States. It was a
time for celebration throughout the Gila Valley.

"Where were you that day?" one Salt River rancher was
heard to ask another on Van Buren Street in Phoenix a few
days later.

"Irrigatin'," said his friend. "What were you doin'?"

"Irrigatin'," said the first rancher.

"Well, let's celebrate," suggested the second rancher.

"Oh, I was irrigatin' myself at Billy Thompson's bar," explained the first rancher.

"Well, I was irrigatin' myself at Daly's saloon," said the second rancher.

"Well, let's celebrate anyway," said the first rancher.

"Don't know why not," agreed the second.

And presumably they did.

There was good reason for celebration on the part of the
people of the Gila Valley. Arizona had come of age. And
while it was a big state in area (only four states are larger—
Texas, California, Montana, and New Mexico) it was still the
baby state of the Union and had a smaller population than any
other. Another anomaly was the fact that while it had fewer people than any other state, people had been living in the Gila Val-

357

ley before there were people in any of the other forty-seven states. These points were argued and discussed in Brewery Gulch and Tombstone, in Phoenix, Prescott, Tucson, and Yuma—but were of no interest whatsoever outside of Arizona. Indeed, most Americans today if asked "What was the forty-eighth state to join the Union?" would have to think twice before answering, if they could answer at all.

And, as always, most of the pioneering work that had been done to create the state of Arizona had been a labor of love. Only a few of the state's early territorial pioneers lived to see the day. Arizona became a territory in 1863, ten years after the Gadsden Purchase. It remained a territory for forty-nine years.

The people who made first the territory possible and eventually the state were a colorful and varied lot: contrast Pete Kitchen, Indian fighter, with the spurious "Lord" Duppa, namer of Phoenix; or opportunist L. J. F. Jaeger with idealist Charles D. Poston; or contrast Sylvester Mowry, officer, gentleman, and metallurgist who loved Arizona so much that he claimed to have been born in the area although he was not, with Estevan Ochoa of pure Spanish blood, gentleman, merchant, and altruist, who bought all the books for Tucson's first school when he learned that poor children had no available texts, and who concealed this charity as long as he could; or contrast territorial Governor Anson P. K. Safford, another stanch advocate of education, who did wonders to organize and build Arizona, with John B. ("Pie") Allen, a down-East Yankee from Maine who, when broke in Tucson after an unsuccessful mining venture, remembered the pies his mother used to bake, and laid the foundation for a future fortune by baking dried-apple pies and selling them for a dollar each, and who eventually served two terms as mayor of Tucson, and whose tombstone states "a man without an enemy."

So they were a varied and colorful lot, the Gila Valley pioneers, and the stories of many belong in a book of Arizona personalities: Mark Aldrich, Solomon Warner, Peter R. Brady, Elias Pennington, Richard Ewell, Fritz Contzen, and King S. Woolsey can only be mentioned, and there are many, many others. But for the pioneer-minded Arizonan there is Frank C. Lockwood's excellent book *Life in Old Tucson*, which will be richly rewarding.

A story which is highly questionable as to its veracity goes like this: at a public meeting to celebrate territorial status in Tucson, the speaker (some say it was Peter R. Brady and others attribute it to Fritz Contzen) addressing the populace in 1863 began with "Fellow citizens, the most glorious territory has just been born." Before he could follow this with verbal qualifications a voice from the crowd called, "What's glorious about it?" The speaker was surprised. He considered carefully for a few moments, staring concentratedly over the heads of his silent and intent audience. Then he lowered his gaze, smiled, and said, "Fellow citizens, the goddamnedest territory has just been born," and the crowd roared and cheered and the rest of his speech was anticlimactic and of no importance.

But that (if true) was in 1863; in 1912 when statehood was achieved the attitude, in spite of individual celebrants, was sober, serious, and dignified.

The people of the Gila Valley had been striving for statehood as early as 1892. A bill providing for the admission of Arizona was defeated by the United States Senate in that year.

Ten years later, in 1902, a senatorial committee took a quick look at New Mexico and Arizona (three days only) and recommended a new state to be created from both territories. New Mexico had the greater population and did not object to this impractical proposal, but Arizonans did. Then, in 1910, Congress passed what was called the Enabling Act, which authorized

Arizona and New Mexico to draw up state constitutions, and if acceptable, the area would become states of the union.

New Mexico moved more rapidly and with little or no friction became the forty-seventh state on January 6, 1912. Thus the people of the upper Gila were residents of a state, but all the people of the lower river were residents of a territory. The state constitution as framed by Arizona met with some difficulties in Washington because of a clause providing for the recall of judges. President Taft refused to let Arizona become a state until this clause was expunged. Arizonans begrudgingly agreed, and on February 14, 1912, the forty-eighth state came into existence, and is sometimes called the Valentine State for that reason. As soon as this had been achieved the first state election was held and the right to recall judges was promptly returned to the constitution. George W. P. Hunt, a former Missourian, was elected the first governor of the state of Arizona and held this office by re-election for a total of fourteen years.

From the chaotic days of the Gadsden Purchase, through territorial status, and up to and inclusive of statehood, mining and stock raising were the basis of the economy of the Gila watershed, and the miner and the cowboy became Arizona types.

First with the Spaniards, and later used advantageously by the Americans, an animal not indigenous to the Gila Valley gradually became of great importance. It is the burro. He is sometimes unflatteringly called a jackass, which he is not, and sometimes an "Arizona nightingale" because of his insistent bray. He is a long-eared, tough, wiry, lazy, stubborn, unpredictable little beast, sometimes called a donkey by Easterners, capable of bearing great loads with docile humor, living on almost anything he can chew (even desert weeds or bark from cottonwood trees), and going for long periods of time without water. If it hadn't been for the dependable burro the mineralogical development of the

Gila Valley would have been considerably delayed, for this Anda-
lusian animal adapted himself very well to the physical conditions
and hardships of the American Southwest. Every prospector had
a horse or a mule, but soon learned that the usually patient but
occasionally willful burro was a better beast for his purposes. Burros multiplied rapidly and today some have run wild in the desert
country of the lower Gila. One "jack" will be the lord and
master of ten or even twenty "jennies" and they roam the desert
at will. But the domestic burro is still a valuable beast in the
Gila watershed. He can carry wood and food and water, and in
spite of his periodic and intractable obstinacy, he makes an
agreeable pet for children. He has come to be identified with
the country.

And this "born of the burro" industry, mineralogy, has
been greater through the years than the aggregate income from all
other sources. It has produced four billion dollars' worth of metals
since 1860. Nearly 87 per cent of this has been copper. Gold
and silver account for about 6 per cent each, and the balance is
made up of lead, zinc, mica, manganese, tungsten, and a scattering of other metals, the most promising of which may turn out
to be uranium.

The industry that followed mining and became as essential
to the economy of the Gila Valley as its predecessor was stock
raising. And with the cattle ranch came the great American figure
popular in "horse operas" from generation unto generation, with
possibly Hopalong Cassidy as the quintessential example—the
cowboy.

The magazine story, novel, stage, screen, radio, television
cowboy will apparently go on forever. He is always and instinctively a gentleman, homespun in his humor but chivalrous with
the fair sex, honest as the day is long, and with a heart as big as
all outdoors; owns a favorite horse called always Silver or Paint

or Pinto, or Old Pal or some similarly endearing term; is a capable drinker but never a drunkard; is able to hold his own in a stampede, a poker game, or quick gunplay; is smart enough to save the ranch for the beautiful and wealthy eastern girl whom he addresses as "ma'am" and removes his hat when he speaks to her; can spot a Mexican rustler, a lurking Indian, or a city slicker in one second flat; is always tall in the saddle, believes that justice always triumphs, lazily rolls cigarettes and scorns "tailor made" smokes; wears "chaps" to dinner, and above all else in the fiction field, be he in print, movie, radio, or television, *never* seems to do any work.

The real cowboy gets up at dawn and works until sunset or later and earns from $60 to $100 a month. There are about eighty-five hundred ranches in Arizona and possibly over a million cattle; and the average size of a ranch is about fifty thousand acres. So there will always be a demand for the cowboy. In desert heat or mountain snowstorm he works all day long at anything from milking cows (which most cowboys detest) to checking water holes, repairing fences, rounding up cattle, branding cattle, shoeing horses, feeding dogies, mending harness, building corrals, repairing windmills, and keeping a weather eye on his particular range. Most cowboys own their own saddles and horses. A good "western" saddle will weigh thirty to forty pounds and may cost as much as $150 to $250. His next prized personal possessions are his high-heeled boots, which may set him back as much as $40. The high heels prevent his feet from slipping out of the stirrups. "Chaps" (from chaparral) of various types protect his thighs from brush scratches. Spurs, contrary to popular opinion, are used sparingly, but a rope is at hand always.

The life of a cowhand is no sinecure, and rarely does a cowboy get rich. His usual ambition is to be a ranch owner. The very least he can start with as a rancher, and make a bare living, are two hundred head of cattle; and depending upon the type of range he will need anywhere from fifty acres to two thousand to run such a herd. And simply to fence in his property can cost as much as $500 a mile. Most cowboys never acquire the capital to become ranchers, and often gamble away their earnings and move on—"pulling up stakes"—from one ranch to another. It is always something of a mystery as to what happens to them when they get old. Rarely is there to be found an elderly, senile, or crotchety cowboy. One answer to this was, "They just dry up and blow away," and it seems to be as good an answer as any for those who are "headed for the last roundup."

In 1939 the price of steers was only 7 and 8 cents a pound; a recent high was 37 cents a pound. This is "on the hoof." Ranching is therefore a big business and a sixty-million dollar industry in Arizona. From the days when cattle roamed a fenceless wilderness and "anything with four feet and horns" was considered a cow by the Spanish vaquero, there have been such developments as controlled range lands, scientific breeding, and the importation of the white-faced Hereford, overseen by the Arizona State Livestock Sanitary Board. So the cowboy is indispensable and will always be seen in the Gila Valley.

The late Tom Mix, who made so many "westerns" in the days of silent movies, was an early and popular prototype of the folklore cowboy. He was killed in an automobile accident not far from the town of Florence on the Gila. His memory, forever associated with the cowboy, has been preserved in the Tom Mix Wash and the Tom Mix monument.

Apart from the mining and cattle business, Arizona developed a third great industry, agriculture. Farming in the Gila Valley began back in the days of the Hohokam people. Their canals, check dams, and diversion ditches were well engineered. It remained for the Mormon farmers, who came down from Utah in the 1860's, to develop the first modern irrigation system. But it remained for the builders of the Roosevelt Dam on the Salt River (named for T.R., not F.D.R.) and the Coolidge Dam on the Gila to develop Arizona's water economy to the point where every available gallon is put to use. It is because of these two great dams—and the later additions such as the Horse Mesa, Mormon Flat, Stewart Mountain, Granite Reef, and Joint Head, all controlling the water below the Roosevelt toward Phoenix into a chain of lakes—that the lower Gila River is dry. A more recent addition is the Bartlett Dam on the Verde River completed in 1939. These engineering feats prevent floods, and not only control the water but make it possible for Arizona to grow crops that go in huge shipments to out-of-state markets. Also this water runs hydro-electric plants which distribute power to Phoenix and the entire Salt River Valley. Land along the Salt River where this stream joins the Gila was once worth $1 an acre; but with water control and desert reclamation, land now sells from $300 to $1,500 an acre. And the crops produced are alfalfa, cotton, wheat, berries, potatoes, lettuce, dates, melons, citrus fruits, and sugar beets.

In view of the long history of the Gila watershed, this boom in agriculture is recent. The Roosevelt Dam, Arizona's first storage basin, was completed in 1910. It was the federal government's first great project of this type. A visit to the dam is at once a scenic attraction and an exposure to the Apache country. For the statistically minded, the dam is 284 feet high, 184 feet thick at its base, and 16 feet thick at the top. The water backed up by this obstacle to nature makes a lake 23 miles long and inundates almost 18,000 acres.

The Coolidge Dam on the Gila was completed in 1929, and was the first multiple-dome dam in America, and presumably in the world. Again, for the fact seeker, the Coolidge is 259 feet high, cost $10,000,000, and was delayed by Washington politics and Apache Indian protests. The Apaches claimed that the dam (on their reservation) would make a lake out of land that had been given to them in perpetuity by the federal government. It did exactly that, it created a lake 26 miles long. And the Apaches couldn't stop it. In fact, a lot of their younger men shrugged their shoulders, accepted the inevitable, and became workers on the project. What annoyed the tribal elders was the fact that the lake would inundate an old tribal burying ground. Or at least, that is what they said, although often Apaches burned bodies instead of interring them. So the government erected a monumental slab where the Apache dead presumably lay, at the cost of almost $12,000, and in time the waters impounded by the dam completely covered it. It is incredible that $12,000 could be spent so ridiculously, and had that sum been provided for Apache education it would have been put to a practical purpose. But the commemorating cenotaph is there—under several hundred feet of water!

No matter how the Gila and its tributaries are disciplined by dams, the Gila will roll when it will roll, and no power of man will stop it. In 1941 the river overflowed its banks at the town of Duncan (well above the various controlling dams) and put the entire community under four feet of water. In 1949 the Gila went on a rampage again. State highway 75 was washed out; ranches and farms were flooded; houses near the river in Duncan and Safford had to be evacuated; a wooden highway bridge east of Duncan went over like a child's toy and came to the raging surface in pieces the size of matchsticks; a Red Cross disaster unit was rushed to the area; and to make it worse the rains poured down. But no lives were lost; and since that date, January 15, 1949, the Gila has been peaceful. But the warning of old residents is always to be heeded: "When she rolls, she rolls, and it's a good time to be somewhere else."

But without the Gila, civilization in most of Arizona would be impossible. It has been a long battle between man and this unpredictable river of the Southwest. Man, with his skill and his science, is winning—apparently.

Dam construction, irrigation projects, and soil conservation, promoted on a large scale since 1910, have made agriculture the Gila watershed's third great industry. Moreover, agriculture employs about 15 per cent of the state's population. The Arizona miner and the Arizona cowboy have had to move over to make a place for the Arizona farmer, who will be even more important if he can get more water.

Although the Gila Valley's economy is predicated upon mineral, animal, and vegetable, a fourth source of income has been developed with astonishing rapidity. Back as recently as 1940 it was estimated that mining, for example, would add more than $70,000,000 to Arizona's income for the year. Agriculture was less than $15,000,000 behind. But since then, rushing forward and passing mining, agriculture, and stock raising, for an all-time high of over $110,000,000 for 1949, was an industry that the casual visitor never suspects. This industry is himself.

Arizona's greatest boon in recent years has been the tourist. Agriculture is practical only where water can be run to the land; mining obviously can be done only where there are minerals in paying quantities; cattle have a broad range, but even this industry must follow recognized grazing rights on specified areas. But the tourist can cover the entire Gila watershed, and he does. In the Gila Valley he is called, without any intention of odium—a dude.

The town of Wickenburg likes to lay claim to the founding

of the dude ranch. People come to Arizona for many reasons, but mainly they fall into three classes: business seekers, health seekers, and pleasure seekers. A Wickenburg rancher asked himself, why not provide for these visitors accommodations that would be typical of the West and simultaneously supply the visitors' wants? As a result, just outside of Wickenburg on the Gila's tributary, the Hassayampa, the first dude ranch was opened.

The idea caught on at once and a vacation industry was born. Today, all over the West, the dude ranch has become an institution. In the Gila Valley, from the desert at Yuma to the Mogollon Mountains in New Mexico, there are all kinds of ranches for all types and for all pocketbooks. Their popularity grows with the years, and a lucrative business has resulted from the Easterner who wants to "go western." What was formerly the tough gold town of Wickenburg now is a clean and pleasant little city whose citizens cheerfully work greenbacks from the pockets of willing tourists.

Most of Arizona's visitors in 1950 came not for business or for health, but for fun. And they enjoyed sybaritic luxury at the Arizona Biltmore or at Jokake Inn near Phoenix; or some of them may have roughed it in a shack in the ghost town of Sweetwater near the Mexican border; or a number of others may have brought trailers or sleeping bags and camped wherever sunset found them. A vacation in the Gila watershed may be prohibitively costly or ridiculously cheap.

Some dude ranches have their own airplane landing fields, golf courses, and swimming pools—and one even has a polo field. Others are real cattle ranches where life is simple, the food wholesome, and dungarees, levis, and flannel shirts are de rigueur. At these less expensive ranches the dude makes a far closer contact with what he is seeking—those magic and somewhat arcane words "the wild West." But the old West is gone, and blended with the familiar hallmarks—drawling and shy cowboys, corrals and hitching posts, chuck wagons and rodeos—are station wagons, jeeps, tractors, airplanes, and television. Thus the modern Gila Valley offers all kinds of ranches for all kinds of dudes, and many of these dudes have liked Arizona sufficiently to become permanent citizens.

Another source of swelling the population was World War II. One million troops were stationed in Arizona. Many of these men had never been in the Southwest before, and they liked it so much that for every civilian who left Arizona to enter the army, two discharged servicemen came back to settle.

A number of these young men took advantage of the government's offer to assist in their education, with the result that there was a sudden increase in the student body of the University of Arizona. This institution is in Tucson and it has some odd antecedents and a colorful history.

Tucson, it will be recalled, was not permitted to be the capital of the newly formed territory in 1863 because of pro-Southern sympathies. But Tucson was certainly the logical choice, and many citizens complained about it. In time the territorial legislature threw the city a bone in the form of the projected territorial University. All Tucson had to do was to donate forty acres of land and the University of Arizona would be hers forever. Tucson pouted and said to hell with it—the capital or nothing.

Almost two years went by and the time allotted for the city to give the forty acres of land was about to expire. Some citizens realized that the town was cutting off its nose to spite its face. A last-minute appeal was made to the town's leading gamblers. They put up the money for forty acres of desert land a mile out of town and the University of Arizona was born. It opened the doors of its single building in 1890, with colleges of agriculture, mines, and engineering. But it had no students.

It couldn't have because there wasn't a single high school in the entire territory.

The situation of a university and a faculty without a student body was long in reaching a balanced pedagogic state. Even as late as 1900 the graduating class numbered only ten students. But as the territory grew in population, newly established high schools began to feed students to the university. New colleges and buildings were added, but it was 1917 before the University of Arizona felt itself academically justified in granting degrees. Since then, with scholastic standards established, the university has grown rapidly and is today one of the finest institutions of higher learning in the Southwest. To the original colleges have been added Fine Arts, Liberal Arts, Law, Education, Music, Business, Military Science, Home Economics, Public Administration, a graduate school, and an extension division. It has a library of more than 110,000 volumes, 12,000 federal documents, and thousands of bulletins and reports. Today the faculty numbers over 300 and the student body is around 5,000, and education in the Gila watershed has come of age.

So it is a long way back to the days of John Spring who was Tucson's first public school teacher in 1871 and who not only taught the "three R's" but washed and combed his pupils and even repaired their clothes. Still, there are some gains yet to be made. Further development of a University of Arizona Press, for example, would fill a much-needed niche in the state's constantly growing interest in its own history and literature.

On the other hand, a state-sponsored magazine of pictures and text, carrying no advertising, called *Arizona Highways* and edited by Raymond Carlson, himself a native Arizonan, has been established and developed until it is possibly the best regional publication in America. Only recently has Arizona had the time to look back at her past, and she has found historical and literary treasure.

The future of the Gila country has great possibilities indeed. The larger cities—Phoenix and Tucson—are developing rapidly, and the whole watershed has no ceiling on its possibilities. Being a kind of crossroads of the Southwest from Spanish times onward, and in the direct line of march of the westward movement, it is impossible for an expanding America to by-pass it. The Gila will always be a natural avenue to the West, even if you fly over it. In spite of the variety of minor cultural groups—Mexicans, Indians, Slavs, Mormons—the people of the Gila country are an integrated lot. They represent, in a sense, a new West. This youngster state is happy and healthy and its future looks bright. Its rapid and recent growth is no longer of the gold-rush or boom-town type, but is a steady and solid evolution. All the old industries continue to function, and surprising new ones crop up, as, for example, the new crafts developed out of cactus. It has been found that cactus wood can be used for making furniture. The result has been a series of knickknacks from small cigarette boxes to chairs and chests of drawers. And many a cholla trunk has been made into a lampstand, and many a tourist has carted one back east. So the cactus, considered by many as only a nuisance, now contributes to the state's economy.

Politically the people of the Gila Valley are primarily Democratic, and that goes for both states of Arizona and New Mexico. But Gila Valley voters can swing either way, and Arizona has, now and then, elected a Republican governor. Since achieving statehood in 1912, Arizonans have participated in ten presidential elections. They voted for Wilson in 1912 and 1916, went Republican for Harding, Coolidge, and Hoover up to 1928, and then Democratic again, overwhelmingly, for Franklin D. Roosevelt from 1932 to 1944. And in 1948 Harry S. Truman carried the state.

As the Gila Valley develops, more demands are being made upon it. Its next fifty years can mean almost anything, and the

THE CRITICS ARE HEARD FROM

basic and all-determining factor is water. More means of desert reclamation must be found. Among other problems there remain Indian education; transient Mexicans and Negroes, who will take
temporary harvesting jobs at low pay and thereby bring on union-
labor resentment; and tax problems that will always arise. But right
now the people of the Gila country have no major worries. They
are progressing and they have the confidence of youth in spite of
the fact that the valley is one of the oldest cradles of civilization
in North America.

This anomaly of being at once so very young on the surface
and so very old beneath the surface sometimes leads visiting authors and analysts into some remarkable errors. John Gunther, in
his unquestionably excellent *Inside U.S.A.*, states that "the first
white child born in Tucson still lives there. He is Harry Arizona
Drachman and he is custodian of the local Masonic lodge." One
wonders who had fun spoofing a visiting author. For the city of
Tucson was founded in 1776 and the first white child was born
there that year. If alive, he would be one hundred and seventy-
five years old. Some custodian! But the Tucson Chamber of
Commerce doesn't resent this at all. It merely points out that the
superb climate is so beneficial that "the first white child born in
Tucson" will probably *never* die, and further states, with undeniable veracity, that the number of people who have come to the
Gila Valley "to die" and are still living is legion.

Nevertheless, the Gila country is always a land of anomalies
and sharp contrasts. Where the Apaches stalked the Oatman family, for example, is today only a short distance off a transcontinental highway which now sprouts such roadside attractions as
"Hunt's Tank and Tummy Place" (filling station for your car
and restaurant for you), and the "Wee Blue Inn," something of
an all-time remarkable name for a motel. And not far from the
town of Mammoth on the Gila's tributary called the San Pedro,

the mail between two small communities—namely, Copper Creek and Sombrero Butte—was carried by pony express all the way up to 1945.

This town of Mammoth on the San Pedro is sleeping today in Arizona's daily sun, but years ago it was as tough as Tombstone or Brewery Gulch. It was formerly a mining town but now hopes that stock raising and farming will bring on a renascence. In the 1880's it had its period of wild oats and, like Tombstone, likes to boast in its old age of its devilment. Its favorite story is that of a gambler who was murdered and the body left in the main street. Instead of removing the remains, other gamblers and miners placed tin cans on the body and had a shooting contest. Those who lost paid for drinks while those who won reset the cans on the dead man's chest for the next round.

Just north of Mammoth, about halfway between this adobe semighost town and the Gila, is the confluence of Aravaipa Creek with the San Pedro. This is a part of the Gila watershed that is seldom visited by tourists, and in a sense that is desirable. On the other hand, for a genuine appraisal of the country as it looked fifty or seventy-five or a hundred years ago, the San Pedro Valley has changed very little. And Aravaipa Creek and its upper canyons look exactly today as they did in the days of Esteban de Dorantes in 1539 and Coronado in 1540. Here is a corner of the Gila watershed that is little known, even to Arizonans. But if you go, prepare to hike. The San Pedro Valley is remote, but the Aravaipa is pristine.

For a punctuating story on the Gila, probably a fitting finale is the San Pedro Torpedo. Where the San Pedro River meets the Gila stands the town of Winkelman today, named for Pete Winkelman, a pioneer stockman. It is a colorful part of the Gila Valley and well worth a visit. If you come over the tricky mountain road from Globe, you will see some beautiful country and have a stunning view of the rushing Gila River far below, and you will want to pause in Winkelman. This town has made popular, at least locally, a drink called the San Pedro Torpedo, and its ingredients are tequila, gin, rum, whisky, vodka, lemon juice, and Coca-Cola. After giving that serious thought you will be certain to order anything from a glass of beer to a glass of milk. But the caliber of the men, and presumably the women, of Winkelman who consume the San Pedro Torpedo is somewhat fascinating, and you wonder just how many "torpedoes" the average habitué can imbibe.

"I suppose nobody can take too many of them?" you suggest cautiously to the bartender.

"That's right," he agrees. "I've never seen anybody take more'n three—and walk."

"The ingredients are rather strong stuff," you concur.

"Hell, no—that stuff won't hurt you. What gets 'em down is the water in it. That comes straight out of the Gila!"

Acknowledgments

It has been said that no one person writes a book. Therefore I want to express my appreciation for the advice and assistance of:

ROBERT BAGNELL, JAMES G. BENNETT, ERSKINE CALD-WELL, JUNE CALDWELL, ROSS CALVIN, RAYMOND CARLSON, MARIE D. CORLE, DAN DAVIS, L. A. EASTBURN, FRANCES B. EBLEN, AUGUST FRUGÉ, NORMAN GABEL, JOHN GEORGE, ARNOLD GILLATT, WALLACE HEBBERD, MARGARET C. IR-WIN, W. B. LANG, FRANK LIGHT, MRS. FRANK C. LOCKWOOD, EDNA MARTIN PARRATT, TED PATRICK, ROSS SANTEE, JACK GAGE STARK, BARRY STORM.

And to the following institutions:

ARIZONA HIGHWAYS MAGAZINE, ARIZONA STATE COLLEGE, AUTOMOBILE CLUB OF SOUTHERN CALIFORNIA, CAL-IFORNIA HISTORICAL SOCIETY, CASA GRANDE NATIONAL MONUMENT, DAWSON'S BOOK SHOP, HOLIDAY MAGAZINE, THE MACMILLAN COMPANY, SANTA BARBARA MUSEUM OF NATURAL HISTORY, UNIVERSITY OF CALIFORNIA PRESS, U.S. BUREAU OF RECLAMATION, YUMA COUNTY CHAMBER OF COMMERCE.

EDWIN CORLE

Bibliography

ALDRICH, LORENZO D.: *A Journal of the Overland Route to California & the Gold Mines*. Dawson's Book Shop, Los Angeles, 1950.

ARNOLD, ELLIOTT: *Blood Brother*. Duell, Sloan & Pearce, New York, 1947.

BANCROFT, HUBERT HOWE: *History of Arizona and New Mexico*. The History Co., San Francisco, 1889.

BARNES, WILL C.: *Arizona Place Names*. University of Arizona Bulletin, Vol. VI, No. 1, Tucson, 1935.

BARROWS, HARLAN H., AND ELIOT BLACKWELDER: *Elements of Geology*. American Book Co., New York, 1911.

BARTLETT, JOHN RUSSELL: *Personal Narrative*. Appleton & Co., New York, 1854.

BISHOP, WILLIAM HENRY: *Old Mexico and Her Lost Provinces*. Harper & Bros., New York, 1883.

BLACKWELDER, ELIOT, AND HARLAN H. BARROWS: *Elements of Geology*. American Book Co., New York, 1911.

BOLTON, HERBERT E.: *Anza's California Expeditions*. 4 Vols. University of California Press, Berkeley, 1930.

——: *Coronado*. Whittlesey House, New York, and the University of New Mexico Press, Albuquerque, 1949.

——: *Font's Complete Diary*. University of California Press, Berkeley, 1931.

——: *Outpost of Empire*. Alfred A. Knopf, New York, 1931.

————: *The Padre on Horseback*. Sonora Press, San Francisco, 1932.

BOURKE, JOHN G.: *On the Border with Crook*. Charles Scribner's Sons, New York, 1892.

BROWN, DEE, AND MARTIN F. SCHMITT: *Fighting Indians of the West*. Charles Scribner's Sons, New York, 1948.

BROWN, JAMES CABELL: *Calabazas: Amusing Recollections of an Arizona "City."* Valleau & Paterson, San Francisco, 1892.

BROWNE, J. ROSS: *Adventures in the Apache Country*. Harper & Bros., New York, 1869.

BRYAN, KIRK: *The Papago Country*. Water Supply Paper 499. Government Printing Office, Washington, D.C., 1925.

BURNS, WALTER NOBLE: *Tombstone*. Doubleday, Doran & Co., New York, 1929.

CALVIN, ROSS: *River of the Sun*. University of New Mexico Press, Albuquerque, 1946.

CARR, HARRY: *The West Is Still Wild*. Houghton Mifflin Co., Boston, 1932.

CARR, WILLIAM: *Desert Parade*. Viking Press, New York, 1947.

CASTANEDA, PEDRO DE: *The Journey of Francisco Vazquez de Coronado*. Grabhorn Press, San Francisco, 1933.

CHISHOLM, JOE: *Brewery Gulch*. Naylor Co., San Antonio, Texas, 1949.

CLELAND, ROBERT GLASS: *This Reckless Breed of Men*. Alfred A. Knopf, New York, 1950.

CLUM, WOODWORTH: *Apache Agent*. Houghton Mifflin Co., Boston, 1936.

COLBERT, EDWIN H.: *The Dinosaur Book*. American Museum of Natural History, New York, 1945.

COLBERT, DONALD, PAUL S. MARTIN, AND GEORGE I. QUIMBY: *Indians Before Columbus*. University of Chicago Press, Chicago, 1947.

COLLIER, JOHN: *Patterns and Ceremonials of the Indians of the Southwest*. E. P. Dutton & Co., New York, 1949.

COMFORT, WILL LEVINGTON: *Apache*. E. P. Dutton & Co., New York, 1931.

CONKLIN, E.: *Picturesque Arizona*. The Mining Record, New York, 1878.

CORLE, EDWIN: *Desert Country*. Duell, Sloan & Pearce, New York, 1941.

———: *Listen, Bright Angel*. Duell, Sloan & Pearce, New York, 1946.

———: *The Royal Highway*. Bobbs-Merrill Company, Inc., Indianapolis, Ind., 1949.

COOKE, P. ST. GEORGE: *The Conquest of New Mexico and California*. G. P. Putnam's Sons, New York, 1878.

COUES, ELLIOTT: *On the Trail of a Spanish Pioneer*. 2 Vols. Francis P. Harper, New York, 1900.

COY, OWEN COCHRAN: *The Great Trek*. Powell Publishing Co., Los Angeles, 1931.

COZZINS, SAMUEL WOODWORTH: *Three Years in Arizona and New Mexico, the Ancient Cibola*. Lee & Shepard, Boston, 1876.

CREMONY, JOHN C.: *Life Among the Apaches*. A. Roman & Co., San Francisco, 1868.

CROOK, GEORGE: *Autobiography*. University of Oklahoma Press, Norman, 1946. Edited by Martin F. Schmitt.

CRUSE, THOMAS: *Apache Days and After*. Caxton Printers, Caldwell, Idaho, 1941.

CUNNINGHAM-GRAHAM, R. D.: *The Horses of the Conquest*. University of Oklahoma Press, Norman, 1949.

CURTIN, L. S. M.: *By the Prophet of the Earth*. San Vicente Foundation, Santa Fe, N. M., 1949.

DALE, EDWARD EVERETT: *Indians of the Southwest*. University of Oklahoma Press, Norman, 1949.

DARTON, N. H.: *Guide Book of the Western United States, Part F*. Government Printing Office, Washington, D.C., 1933.

DAVIS, BRITTON: *The Truth about Geronimo.* Yale University Press, New Haven, 1929.

DeVOTO, BERNARD: *The Year of Decision*—1846. Little, Brown & Co., Boston, 1943.

DIXON, WINIFRED HAWKRIDGE: *Westward Hoboes.* Charles Scribner's Sons, New York, 1921.

DOBIE, J. FRANK: *Apache Gold and Yaqui Silver.* Little, Brown & Co., Boston, 1939.

DODGE, NATT N.: *Poisonous Dwellers of the Desert.* Southwestern Monuments Association, Santa Fe, N. M., 1948.

DUNBAR, CARL O., AND CHARLES SCHUCHERT: *Outlines of Historical Geology.* John Wiley & Sons, New York, 1947.

ECCLESTON, ROBERT: *Overland to California on the Southwestern Trail.* University of California Press, Berkeley and Los Angeles, 1950.

EDITORS OF LOOK IN COLLABORATION WITH PAUL HORGAN: *The Southwest.* Houghton Mifflin Co., Boston, 1947.

ELMORE, FRANCES: *The Casa Grande National Monument.* Southwestern Monuments Association, Coolidge, Ariz.

EMORY, W. H.: *Notes of a Military Reconnoissance from Fort Leavenworth in Missouri to San Diego in California:* U.S. Senate, Executive Document No. 7, 30th Congress. Issued 1848.

FARISH, THOMAS EDWIN: *History of Arizona.* 4 Vols. Filmer Bros., Phoenix, Ariz., 1915.

FEDERAL WRITERS' PROJECT: *Arizona.* Hasting House, New York, 1940.

FEDERAL WRITERS' PROJECT: *California.* Hastings House, New York, 1939.

FERGUSSON, ERNA: *Our Southwest.* Alfred A. Knopf, New York, 1940.

FORREST, EARL R.: *Missions and Pueblos of the Old Southwest.* Arthur H. Clark, Cleveland, 1929.

GLADWIN, HAROLD STIRLING: *Excavations at Snaketown*, Vol. IV. Gila Pueblo, Globe, Ariz., 1948.

GOLDER, FRANK ALFRED: *The March of the Mormon Battalion.* Century Company, New York, 1928.

GRIFFIN, JOHN S.: *A Doctor Comes to California.* California Historical Society, San Francisco, 1943.

GUNTHER, JOHN: *Inside U.S.A.* Harper & Bros., New York, 1947.

HALLENBECK, CLEVE: *Spanish Missions of the Old Southwest.* Doubleday, Page & Co., New York, 1926.

————: *The Journey of Fray Marcos.* University Press in Dallas, Dallas, Texas, 1949.

HALSETH, ODD S.: *Arizona's 1500 Years of Irrigation History.* Pueblo Grande, Phoenix, Ariz., 1947.

————: *Prehistory of the Southwest.* Pueblo Grande, Phoenix, Ariz., 1949.

HENRY, ROBERT SELPH: *The Story of the Mexican War.* Bobbs-Merrill Co., Inc., Indianapolis, Ind., 1950.

HERSCH, VIRGINIA: *The Seven Cities of Gold.* Duell, Sloan & Pearce, New York, 1946.

HEWETT, EDGAR L.: *Ancient Life in the American Southwest.* Bobbs-Merrill Co., Inc., Indianapolis, Ind., 1930.

HIGGINS, ETHEL BAILEY: *Our Native Cacti.* A. T. De la Mare Co., New York, 1931.

HODGE, FREDERICK WEBB: *Handbook of American Indians North of Mexico.* 2 Vols. Government Printing Office, Washington, D.C., 1907.

————: *History of Hawikuh.* Southwest Museum, Los Angeles, 1937.

HODGE, HIRAM C.: *Arizona as it is.* Hurd & Houghton, Boston, 1877.

HOUGH, WALTER: *Antiquities of the Upper Gila and Salt River Valleys in Arizona and New Mexico.* Bureau of American Ethnology, Bulletin 35, Washington, D.C., 1907.

————: *Culture of the Ancient Pueblos of the Upper Gila River Region, New Mexico and Arizona.* U.S. National Museum, Bulletin 87, Washington, D.C., 1914.

JAMES, GEORGE WHARTON: *What the White Race may Learn from the Indian.* Forbes & Co., Chicago, 1908.

————: *Arizona the Wonderland.* Page Co., Boston, 1917.

KIDDER, ALFRED VINCENT: *Southwestern Archaeology.* Yale University Press, New Haven, 1924.

KINO, EUSEBIO FRANCISCO: *Historical Memoir of Primera Alta.* University of California Press, Berkeley and Los Angeles, 1948.

KLUCKHOHN, CLYDE: *Mirror for Man.* Whittlesey House, New York, 1949.

KNECHTEL, MAXWELL, M.: *Geology and Ground Water Resources of the Valley of the Gila River.* Government Printing Office, Washington, D.C., 1938.

LADIES UNION MISSION SCHOOL: *Among the Pimas.* Albany, N. Y., 1893.

LANG, WALTER B.: *The First Overland Mail.* Butterfield Trail. Privately printed, 1940.

LESLEY, LEWIS BURT: *Uncle Sam's Camels.* Harvard University Press. Cambridge, 1929.

LOCKWOOD, FRANK C.: *Life in Old Tucson.* Tucson Civic Committee, Tucson, 1943.

LOCKWOOD, FRANK C.: *Pioneer Days in Arizona.* The Macmillan Co., New York, 1932.

————: *The Apache Indians.* Macmillan Co., New York, 1938.

LUMHULTZ, CARL: *New Trails in Mexico.* Charles Scribner's Sons, New York, 1912.

LUMMIS, CHARLES F.: *Mesa Canon and Pueblo.* Century Co., New York, 1925.

————: *The Spanish Pioneers.* A. C. McClurg & Co., Chicago, 1893.

LYMAN, GEORGE D.: *John Marsh, Pioneer*. Charles Scribner's Sons, New York, 1933.

MACDOUGAL, DANIEL TREMBLY: *Botanical Features of North American Deserts*. Carnegie Institutions, Washington, D.C., 1908.

MADARIAGA, SALVADOR: *The Fall of the Spanish American Empire*. Hollis & Carter, London, 1947.

MADARIAGA, SALVADOR: *The Rise of the Spanish American Empire*. Hollis & Carter, London, 1947.

MARTIN, PAUL S., DONALD COLLIER, AND GEORGE I. QUIMBY: *Indians Before Columbus*. University of Chicago Press, Chicago, 1947.

MAZZANOVICH, ANTON: *Trailing Geronimo*. Privately printed, 1926.

MCCLINTOCK, JAMES HARVEY: *Arizona, Prehistoric, Aboriginal, Pioneer, Modern*. 3 Vols. S. J. Clarke, Chicago, 1916.

MCGREGOR, JOHN C.: *Southwestern Archaeology*. John Wiley & Sons, New York, 1941.

MCNICKLE, D'ARCY: *They Came Here First*. J. B. Lippincott & Co., Philadelphia, 1949.

MORRIS, ANN AXTELL: *Digging in the Southwest*. Doubleday, Doran & Co., New York, 1941.

MOWRY, SYLVESTER: *Arizona and Sonora*. Harper & Bros., New York, 1864.

NASH, OTHNIEL CHARLES: *The Dinosaurs of North America*. U.S. Geological Survey, Washington, D.C., 1896.

NEW MEXICO WRITERS' PROJECT. *New Mexico*. Hastings House, New York, 1940.

PALMER, ROSE A.: *The North American Indians*. Smithsonian Institution, Washington, D.C., 1910.

PATTIE, JAMES O.: *Personal Narrative*. Lakeside Press, Chicago, 1930.

PAXSON, FREDERIC L.: *History of the American Frontier*. Houghton Mifflin Co., Boston, 1924.

Pfefferkorn, Ignaz: *Sonora, a Description of the Province.* Translated by Theodore E. Treutlein. University of New Mexico Press, Albuquerque, 1949.

Pike, Zebulon M.: *Southwestern Expedition.* Lakeside Press, Chicago, 1925.

Poston, Charles D.: *Apache-Land.* A. L. Bancroft & Co., San Francisco, 1878.

Powers, Stephen, *Afoot and Alone: A Walk from Sea to Sea.* Columbian Book Co., Hartford, Conn., 1892.

Prince, L. Bradford: *Historical Sketches of New Mexico.* Ramsey, Millett & Hudson, Kansas City, Mo., 1883.

Pumpelly, Raphael: *Across America and Asia.* Leypoldt & Holt, New York, 1870.

Quimby, George I., Donald Collier, and Paul S. Martin: *Indians Before Columbus.* University of Chicago Press, Chicago, 1947.

Rice, William B.: *The Los Angeles Star.* University of California Press, Berkeley and Los Angeles, 1947.

Richards, G. L., Jr., and L. W. Richards: *Geologic History at a Glance.* Stanford University Press, Palo Alto, 1934.

Richards, L. W., and G. L. Richards, Jr.: *Geologic History at a Glance.* Stanford University Press, Palo Alto, 1934.

Roberts, Frank H. H.: *Archaeology in the Southwest.* American Antiquity, Vol. 3, 1937.

Sabin, Edwin L.: *General Crook and the Fighting Apaches.* J. B. Lippincott Co., Philadelphia, 1918.

———: *Kit Carson Days.* 2 Vols. The Press of the Pioneers, New York, 1935.

Sanford, Trent E.: *The Architecture of the Southwest.* W. W. Norton & Co., New York, 1950.

Santee, Ross: *Apache Land.* Charles Scribner's Sons, New York, 1947.

———: *Cowboy.* Cosmopolitan Book Corp., New York, 1928.

SCHMITT, MARTIN F. AND DEE BROWN: *Fighting Indians of the West*. Charles Scribner's Sons, New York, 1948.

SCHROEDER, ALBERT H.: *Cultural Implications of Ball Courts in Arizona*. Southwestern Journal of Anthropology, Vol. 5, 1949.

————: *Prehistoric Canals in the Salt River Valley, Arizona*. American Antiquity, Vol. 8, 1943.

SCHUCHERT, CHARLES, AND CARL O. DUNBAR: *Outlines of Historical Geology*. John Wiley & Sons, New York, 1947.

SISK, HANSON R.: *Fray Marcos de Niza*. Nogales, Ariz., 1939.

SONNICHSEN, C. L.: *Billy King's Tombstone*. Caxton Printers, Caldwell, Idaho, 1946.

SPIER, LESLIE: *Cultural Relations of the Gila River and Lower Colorado Tribes*. Yale University Publications in Anthropology, New Haven, 1936.

STEELE, JAMES W.: *Frontier Army Sketches*. Jansen, McClurg & Co., Chicago, 1883.

STORM, BARRY: *Thunder Gods Gold*. Southwest Publishing Co., Tortilla Flat, Ariz., 1945.

STRATTON, R. B.: *The Captivity of the Oatman Girls*. Printed for the Author, New York, 1858.

SUMMERHAYES, MARTHA: *Vanished Arizona*. J. B. Lippincott Co., Philadelphia, 1908.

SYKES, GODFREY: *A Westerly Trend*. Arizona Pioneers Historical Society, Tucson, 1944.

THOMPSON, STITH: *Tales of the North American Indians*. Harvard University Press, Cambridge, 1929.

THORP, RAYMOND W., AND WELDON D. WOODSON: *Black Widow*. University of North Carolina Press, Chapel Hill, N. C., 1945.

UNDERHILL, RUTH MURRAY: *Singing for Power*. University of California Press, Berkeley, 1938.

————: *The Papago Indians of Arizona and Their Relatives, the Pima*. U.S. Office of Indian Affairs, Washington, D.C., 1940.

UNIVERSITY OF ARIZONA PUBLICATIONS: *Arizona and Its Heritage*. Vol. 7, No. 3, Tucson, 1936.

Van Dyke, John C.: *The Desert*. Charles Scribner's Sons, New York, 1901.

Waters, Frank: *The Colorado*. Rinehart & Co., New York, 1946.

Wellman, Paul I.: *Death in the Desert*. Macmillan Co., New York, 1935.

Woodson, Weldon D., and Raymond W. Thorp: *Black Widow*. University of North Carolina Press, Chapel Hill, N. C., 1945.

Wyllys, Rufus Kay: *Pioneer Padre—the Life and Times of Eusebio Francisco Kino*. Southwest Press, Dallas, Texas, 1935.

————: *Arizona: the History of a Frontier State*. Hobson & Herr, Phoenix, 1950.

NEWSPAPERS

Los Angeles *Times*
Los Angeles *Star*
Nogales (Ariz.) *Herald*
Phoenix (Ariz.) *Republic*
Prescott (Ariz.) *Miner*
Silver City (N. M.) *Daily Press*
Tombstone (Ariz.) *Epitaph*
Tucson (Ariz.) *Star*
Yuma (Ariz.) *Sun*

INDEX

387